THERE'S A NEW SHERIFF IN TOWN

THERE'S A NEW SHERIFF IN TOWN

THE PROJECT MANAGER'S PROVEN GUIDE TO SUCCESSFULLY TAKING OVER ONGOING PROJECTS AND GETTING THE WORK DONE

MARTIN J. FENELON III, SC.D., PMP, CGEIT

For more information, email NewSheriffPM@gmail.com

Library of Congress Control Number: 2022924010

ISBN: 979-8-88759-014-1 (paperback)
ISBN: 979-8-88759-015-8 (ebook)

GET YOUR FREE GIFT!

To get the best experience with this book, I've found readers who download and use the supporting workbook are able to implement faster and take the next steps needed to successfully take over and run their next project.

You can get a copy by visiting:
www.subscribepage.io/24CLmg

DEDICATION

This book was formed over a number of years working with great people on many different teams in a variety of organizations. While led by a Project Manager, projects are only successful through team effort. I have benefitted from having a number of great teammates and mentors over the years who helped me learn the lessons and ideas shared in this book. Although they are too many to name, this book is as much theirs as mine. However, I would especially like to call out my colleagues in the Engagement Assessment Services (EAS) Team at CGI, Inc. Specialists in identifying and aiding challenged projects. They "live the dream" every day.

Most importantly, I want to thank my dear wife Deborah for her encouragement to start this project, her patience as I took time to develop this book, and her unwavering support along the way. Thank you!

CONTENTS

PREFACE

"There is nothing more difficult to take in hand, more perilous to conduct, or more uncertain in its success, than to take the lead in the introduction of a new order of things."

--Niccolo Machiavelli

"Every project is an opportunity to learn, to figure out problems and challenges, to invent and reinvent."

--David Rockwell

"Marty, your project is going well, but I need you to look into this other project."

How many times have you had a similar start to joining a project that was already underway or in trouble? Every project or program manager that I have ever met has had to take over an existing project at least once, and many have spent most of their careers managing projects that they did not start from scratch. Only on rare occasions do Project Managers (PMs) get to initiate a project before the charter has been written, the budget and schedule set, and the team built. Unfortunately, the majority of PM guides, books, articles, and frameworks assume a "greenfield" project start, along with the PM having more control over the triple constraints (scope/quality, budget, and schedule) than they do. This book is aimed at the real-world PM, someone who must rapidly assume leadership of a project that has already begun, possibly with a different PM and sometimes without any PM. Regardless of the delivery methodology, these typical circumstances are unlikely to change anytime soon.

Throughout this book, we'll go through the process of understanding the true status of the project, identifying the challenges and opportunities that attend any project, joining the existing team, and reshaping it as needed through getting on a path leading to a successful outcome. Sometimes a successful outcome for the organization means ending a project and applying the resources elsewhere. We'll explore how to come to that conclusion and assist senior management in terminating projects that need to be terminated.

Key benefits from following the processes and steps in this book include:

- Rapidly identifying key issues and problems in an existing project, if there are any
- Identifying leverage points to turn around troubled projects and teams
- Tactics to keep the project team focused and committed despite changing project dynamics

Although much of the terminology used within seems tied to waterfall, or sequential delivery, the approach and tools apply to *all* project delivery methodologies. Most of the terminology used for project management was developed for waterfall or sequential delivery and continues in use as newer methodologies are introduced. Iterative, Agile, and other delivery methodologies that are run as projects have similar components and challenges that we will address. They may be named differently, and they are likely to overlap other tasks and phases, but the same things will be done through the course of the project.

At different times in this book, we will discuss specific tasks or decisions that apply if the PM, and potentially the project team, are contractors or if they are members of the organization benefitting from the project. I've been fortunate enough in my career to have managed projects on both sides of the table, leading all-employee, mixed vendor-employee, and all-vendor teams. I've also been in the role of a vendor PM managing teams made up entirely of my customers' employees, which can be a difficult challenge, especially when replacing or supervising an employee PM that had difficulties. I hope to share what I've learned in these situations so you can benefit from my experience and the experience of the hundreds of skilled PMs that I have worked with over the years.

I have been very fortunate to have had great PM mentors and coaches throughout my career and to have benefitted from the growing body of research and publications covering project management. This book is my humble attempt to give back to the profession that has given so much to me and to pay forward the lessons learned in over 40 years of leading projects.

CHAPTER 1

WHY IS THIS BOOK NECESSARY?

"I hate it when they say 'don't change horses midstream'...if your horse can't swim and he's way over his head"

James Taylor

We Don't Always Start Fresh

Project Management texts usually assume we're starting at the beginning of a project, with control over scope, schedule, and resources. Frequently, project scope, resources, and schedule are already determined through strategic planning, Project Portfolio Management (PPM), or the project charter process. In other cases, we take on projects that are in progress. This can occur as a normal part of the project lifecycle as a hand-off from a project initiation team to a project delivery team or due to other circumstances. The existing Project Manager (PM) may be moving to a different, higher priority project, assuming other responsibilities within the organization, leaving the organization for other career opportunities, or leaving the project due to the problems that have arisen. A particularly difficult

1

situation is when the existing PM is being supported by a coach or senior PM who assumes responsibility for successfully completing the project while the existing PM continues in a management role of some kind. In all these cases, the new PM is required to assess the current status of the project, update or create a plan leading to a successful conclusion of the project, and execute that plan through project completion.

While leading the project team through the remainder of the project, the PM is expected to follow the organization's methodology, which can range from waterfall to Agile, with plenty of local variations and tools. There are many books, courses, and articles describing these methodologies, tasks, and tools, principally the Project Management Body of Knowledge (PMBOK) from the Project Management Institute (PMI). Familiarity with this PM knowledge and skills is necessary to successfully deliver projects, as modified by the specifics of the organization involved. We're going to focus on the specific tasks, tools, knowledge, and skills that apply in the situation of interest, assuming responsibility for an ongoing project. A basic familiarity with common project management tools and processes is assumed, and experience delivering projects will also be helpful.

The goal of this book is to identify and describe specific things that we can do to improve our chances of successfully completing the ongoing project, regardless of its current state or delivery phase. When determining successful completion, we include deciding to terminate and wrap up those projects that should be terminated by the organization as being successful. Sometimes the best overall outcome for an organization is to terminate a project and apply those resources to other endeavors. So even though the specific project may have failed, it is a success for the organization because an objective decision was made to end the project and free up limited resources that are better used elsewhere.

Throughout the book, there are items enclosed in gray boxes, or highlighted by gray shading, to assist the reader. The first type consists of real-world examples that support topics within the chapter. For example, there is the *Breaking Up Is Hard to Do* story below. There are also tables and lists that support specific topics within a chapter that are noted as such. These are also enclosed in gray boxes to make them easier to find throughout the book. These lists and additional supporting materials can also be found in the Appendix at the end of the book. Helpful Tips are sprinkled throughout the book, shaded in gray, intended to help PMs working through that phase of assuming leadership of the project. Finally, many chapters include exercises to be completed by the reader as they go through this book. They will aid in understanding the ideas being presented and help the reader to prepare to take over projects, now or in the future. Please take the time to complete each exercise as you go through the book; it will assist in understanding the lessons being taught and applying them to your projects.

Breaking Up Is Hard to Do

A senior Program Director (PD) was asked to cover some Executive Steering Committee Meetings (ESC) while the managing VP was on travel. In the first meeting, the PD learned that the project was nine months over the planned three-year schedule, and the client was continuing to demand changes to the original requirements, classifying them as software defects. Realizing that a thorough project review was required, the PD held detailed conversations with the delivery team and Project Manager (PM), which confirmed the difficulties dealing with the client organization and their unwillingness to accept the process changes that the new software would require. Direct interaction with client managers reinforced the organizational change issues and indicated that a successful project outcome was unlikely. After two weeks of review, the PD recommended terminating the project and negotiating an exit with the client. Unwilling to do so, the managing VP kept the project going for an additional 12 months at company expense before the project was terminated due to unresolved contractual disputes. The additional time before termination cost the combined customer/ contractor team an estimated $2 million, not counting the legal costs required to settle the contract dispute.

Assuming management of an ongoing project is a lot more common than many people think. All the PMs that I've met over the years, through work, at conferences, and online, have taken over projects that were already started. One of the largest programs that I managed already had a charter, a budget, a firm deadline, and over 25% of its staff assigned when I was brought in. The program was not in trouble at this stage, but the executive team realized that their organization needed someone with more experience in large program delivery. There were other considerations that led to my assignment as well, which meant there were multiple objectives and boundaries that shaped the program and constrained our flexibility. Ultimately successful, the program literally saved the company from bankruptcy and led to multiple successful programs over the next few years. My experience is not unique. Industry results and surveys also show that the overwhelming majority of PMs have had to assume projects or programs that were already in flight.

Close to 200 project managers responded in 2022 to an online global survey on their experience with joining projects that had already been started. The survey questions are included with Figures 1-1 through 1-5, which also provide graphical views of the responses received. Requests to participate in the survey were posted in a number of online forums for PMs, with results gathered over a three-week period. The results confirmed what I have observed over the decades in different industries and across the globe—PMs are much more likely to take over existing projects than to start with a "clean slate." Let's take a brief look at the survey results.

Roughly 93% of the PMs responding have had to take over a project that was already started at least once in their careers. Clearly, this scenario is much more common than the assumed start from scratch postulated by project management literature. As we'll describe in Chapter 2, there are significant differences and additional challenges when taking over projects that have already started. Despite these circumstances being very common, they are not routine and should not be treated as such. We need to recognize the challenges of joining a project that has already started, along with the typical challenges of managing projects. We'll describe these additional challenges and how to address them in this book.

**Figure 1-1: PMs That Have Taken
Over an Existing Project**

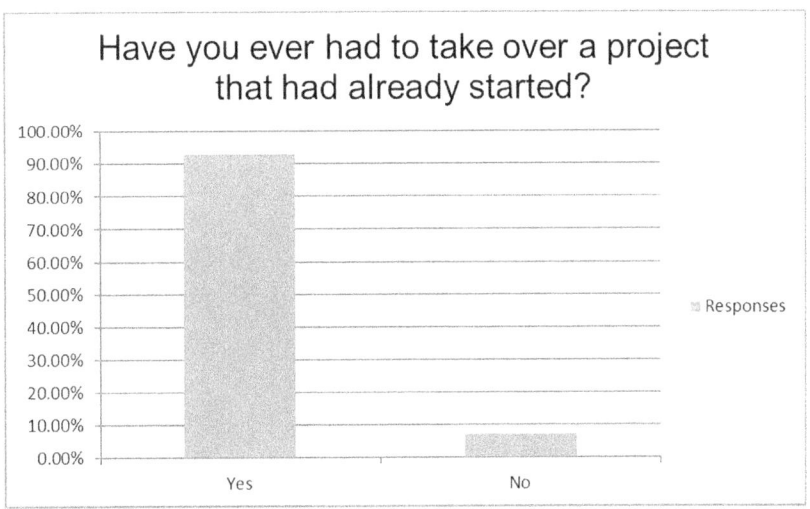

Responses to this question showed that almost all PMs will have to take over an existing project at least once in their careers, but it doesn't show how frequently it may happen during a PM's career. If it happens once in a 40-year career, do we really need to spend time focusing on a "black swan" event? The responses to our second question will surprise you and again demonstrate the need for this book. When asked what percentage of all projects that they had managed were ones started by someone else, only 6% responded that they had never taken over a project that was already started, while another *6% indicated that they had never started a project from scratch*! As noted in the chart below, 40% of responding PMs have had roughly 25% of their projects started by someone else, and for 18% of respondents, that ratio was 75% of all the projects they have ever managed. Clearly, taking over an existing project is something that every PM should expect to do in their career. This book will help prepare you for when it happens and guide you along the way when it does.

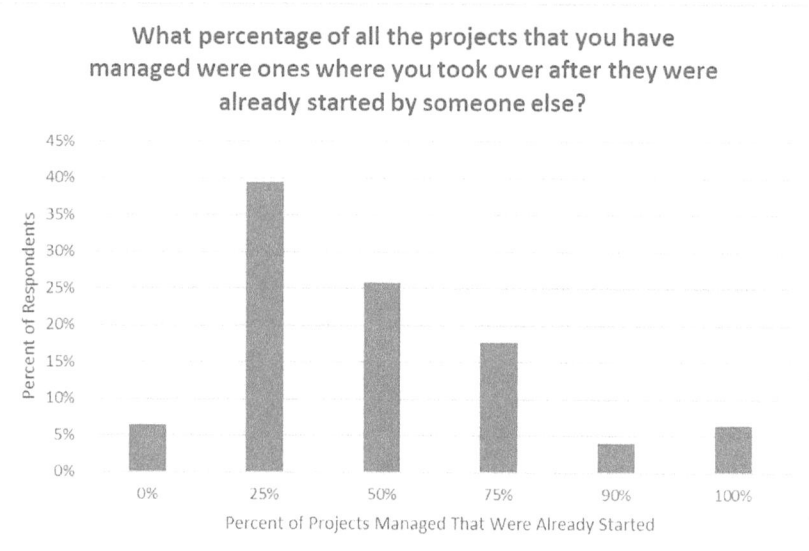

Figure 1-2: Percentage of All PM Managed Projects That Were Already Started

While recognizing that project managers are almost certain to take over an existing project at least once in their careers, we can't focus exclusively on that scenario either. As noted by the survey respondents, 92% have also started projects from scratch at least once in their careers. This is not an either/or situation; PMs should be able to handle both scenarios. Possessing a firm understanding and foundation of basic PM skills is necessary regardless of the scenario. Successful PMs must have the Knowledge, Skills, and Attributes (or Attitudes), or KSAs, coupled with industry experience to be successful. We are going to focus on the KSA most applicable to projects where the PM is joining after it has started to reduce possible missteps and to increase the likelihood of successfully completing the project.

Figure 1-3: PMs That Have Started
a Project From Scratch

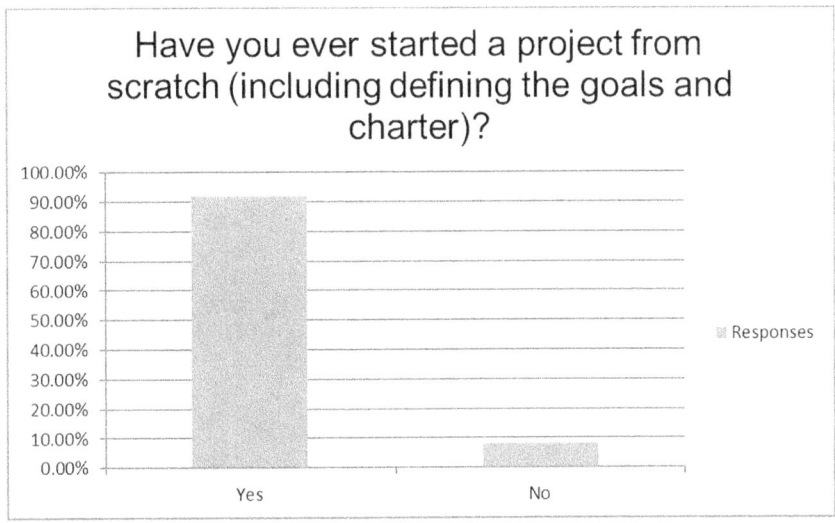

Continuing with the theme of leading a project at the beginning, how common is it to take it across the finish line? If most PMs get to finish the projects that they start, then taking over a project from another PM should be a rare event. While the survey responses showed some good results, there are still some troubling conclusions to be drawn. When asked what percentage of the projects they had started that they were able to lead through completion, only 33% of the PMs indicated that it happened all the time (100%). In fact, 25% of the responding PMs indicated that they were there from start to finish half or less of the time!

Consider the numbers in Figure 1-4 for a moment. *Two-thirds (67%) of all the projects managed by these PMs had a different PM when they finished.* Far from being a rare occurrence, we should assume that most projects *will have a change in leadership* before they finish. How many PMs plan to hand over leadership to another PM? All too often, we assume that we will finish what we start, so if a change in leadership does occur, we are not prepared for it. Whether we are handing off the project to another PM, or if we are the incoming PM, the hand-off will be more challenging and less successful if we are not prepared for it. In addition to covering how to assume leadership of a project, we also address handing it off to others in Chapters 12 and 13. Many of the tools, tips, and tricks we cover throughout this book will improve transitions out of your projects, as well as transitions in. Providing a successful transition as you leave a project is just as important to your professional reputation and career as being able to transition in.

Figure 1-4: Percentage of PM Projects Managed from Beginning to End

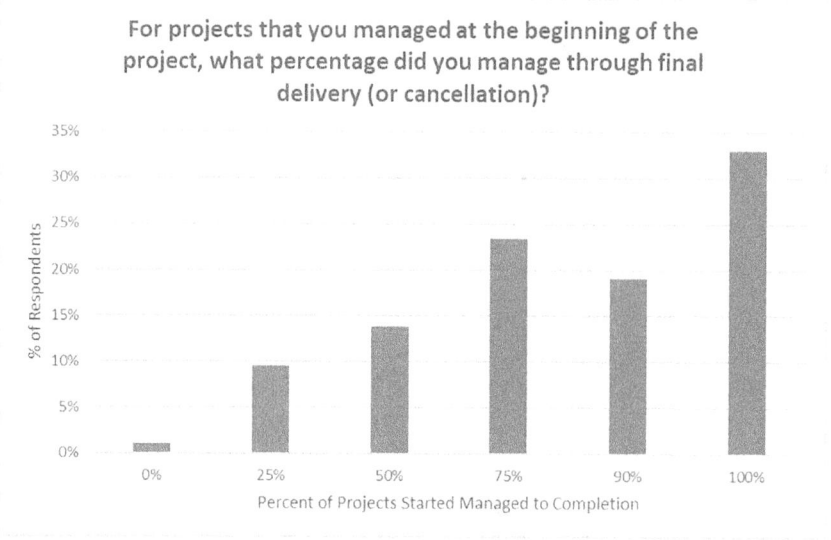

The final question in our survey focused on one of the most difficult issues facing a PM on any project—recommending that their project be stopped. While this may happen with a project that the PM has started, it is more common with projects that have a new PM coming in or that are having a project review done. A fresh look at the facts on the ground at the point of the review or change in leadership often brings critical issues and challenges into focus. Organizations and sponsors need to use that focus, and the advice of the PM, to decide if the project is worth continuing. Recommending that a project you are leading or going to be leading be stopped is difficult psychologically. Essentially it is stating that the project cannot meet its objectives under your leadership under the current conditions.

My wife asserts that all PMs are optimists because we always assume we can successfully complete our projects. Optimism is a necessary attitude for a PM, but it must be balanced by realism. As we will describe in Chapters 5 through 7, there may be critical project issues that lead to a recommendation to stop the project. Our survey results showed that 62% of PMs had faced this situation in their careers. Understanding that such a recommendation may be needed and the facts required to support the stop recommendation will position the PM to guide the organization to the best overall decision. Do not assume that you will never have to bring a stop recommendation forward. Be prepared for it.

Figure 1-5: PMs That Have Recommended Stopping a Project

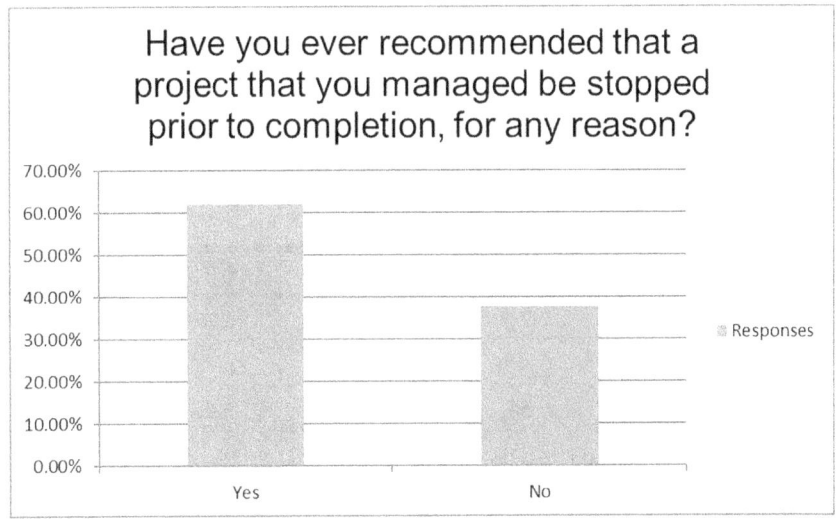

Many organizations refer to the CHAOS Report from the Standish Group when assessing the success rate for software development projects. Although their data collection and analysis methodologies are unclear, numbers from the Standish Group have been referred to for decades. Their latest report (The 2020 CHAOS Report) shows that they assess 31% of software projects as successful, 50% as challenged, and 19% as failed (or canceled)—these numbers have not changed much over the decades that the CHAOS Report has been issued, despite the shift to different methodologies, including greatly increased use of Agile techniques.[1] These numbers show that the need for PMs to rescue challenged or failing projects will continue into the future. However, there are very few resources available for PMs taking over ongoing projects. This book will fill this gap.

Why is assuming management of an ongoing project different than starting a new project? Table 1-1 provides a listing of project characteristics, components, and key management decisions that are still being formulated when a project is initiated but are usually set once a project has started. We typically discuss three key project constraints—Budget, Schedule, and Scope (which includes quality). These should be defined at the initiation of a project, even if there is some remaining flexibility (e.g., budget is plus or minus 20%). There is less flexibility with an ongoing project, and there may be additional challenges due to the project having already started. Let's briefly review some of these issues.

Table 1-1: New Projects Versus Ongoing Projects

COMPONENT	NEW PROJECT	ONGOING PROJECT
Objectives	Loosely Defined	Established
Scope/Requirements	Being Determined	Preliminary or Approved
Quality	Being Negotiated	Defined
Schedule	Being Negotiated	Set
Budget	Rough Order of Magnitude (ROM)	Set
Delivery Method	Candidates identified	Chosen
Technology	May be defined, flexibility will vary	Selected

---

[1] Review Standish Group—CHAOS 2020: Beyond Infinity by Henny Portman, retrieved from https://hennyportman.wordpress.com/2021/01/06/review-standish-group-chaos-2020-beyond-infinity/ on 17 August 2022.

COMPONENT	NEW PROJECT	ONGOING PROJECT
Delivery Team	Being Selected	Created and working
Delivery Location	May be open	Set
Delivery Tools	Being determined based on technology and delivery methodology selected	In Use
Project Plans	Being Drafted	Published and Approved

The Sponsor, Business Owner, or Client (we'll summarize these as the "Customer" for now) has allocated a budget for the project, expecting to get specific benefits by an agreed date. Even under Agile or Flow methodologies, the Customer expects to get certain non-negotiable benefits or features, although there may be flexibility around others. The Customer is paying money out to get benefits that are worth the investment being made. These expectations are set during the initiation of the project, even though they can change during the course of the project. A PM coming into an ongoing project must understand these expectations in their current form and determine if they can still be met. For example, based on work completed to date and the work completion rate, will the agreed scope be delivered on time? If not, this is a problem that must be resolved by the PM.

With a new project just being initiated, there should be more flexibility in determining a reasonable budget and schedule to achieve the desired benefits (scope). Negotiating changes in scope later in the project is likely to be seen as altering the earlier agreement and will necessitate changes to the formal agreements that established the project. This could be a project charter or similar document if the Customer and Delivery Team both belong to the same organization, or they may require contract changes (Change Orders (CO)) if the delivery team is an outside contractor. The extent and impact of the requested changes can lead to contentious discussions and possibly project termination. Managing customer and project team expectations and issues is a PM responsibility, so those expectations are placed on the new PM as soon as they join the project. There may not be a transition or "warm-up" period for the new PM to establish the desired relationships in a way similar to forming a new team.

Other issues may have risen due to the progress made against the planned schedule. Often a new PM is brought in because a project is behind schedule. As we'll describe later, the incoming PM needs to accurately assess progress against the schedule and work with the team to develop a realistic schedule based on current conditions. This is much harder to do when compared to developing a schedule with the Customer and Delivery Team before the project has started. Discussions on scope, quality, deliverables, etc., are more open, and joint agreements are reached more easily. For example, if the delivery date is firm, there may be scope that can be deferred until later.

A common project management example is building a house. If the move-in date for the owners is firmly set, but there are going to be challenges making that date identified by the delivery team, there are options. The outside deck and landscaping could be deferred since they are not required for the house to be certified for occupancy. Once Customer expectations are set, changing them is more difficult, especially if the Customer believes the delivery team was unproductive, which is an easy assumption to make even when it isn't true.

There may also be quality issues that require rework. These could be software defects, selected technology that does not have the desired capabilities, or work that need to be redone. Returning to the house example, what if the concrete used in the foundation was the wrong type? Additional work is needed to tear down the foundation, dispose of the debris, and build a new foundation. The impacts will ripple through the schedule and will impact other teams that were already scheduled to do their work at specific times, such as the plumbers. With software projects, similar problems could be created by poor quality code, software that fails initial testing, or software interfaces that do not work as intended. In addition to spending time to fix these issues, other teams may be impacted. An incoming PM may have to deal with these challenges, along with the related budget and schedule impacts. When a project is just being started, quality targets can be established, along with quality checks and testing along the way to minimize the chance of quality issues occurring and to minimize the impact when they do occur. An incoming PM may have to add these quality checks to the scope, budget, and schedule and negotiate the impacts with the Customer.

As project timelines, budgets, and resources are compressed, there are likely to be more gaps in required plans and documentation. Agile approaches stress deliverables as opposed to documentation, but the end results must also be supported by the right documentation for maintenance, repair, and future upgrades. Many PMs joining projects discover a lack of documentation, from designs to operational instructions and training materials. These gaps hinder project progress and may delay ultimate acceptance by the Customer. Identifying and closing documentation gaps can be especially challenging when joining a team that is already behind and under pressure to catch up.

When a new team is being formed to deliver a project, team members are brought together for the contributions they will make to the team. Ideally, the entire delivery team or at least the sub-team leads participate in defining the scope, schedule, and budget with the customer. This increases the commitment of the team to meeting the objectives of the plan and should result in realistic estimates. As team members work together, they go through the typical team maturity cycle, often referred to as Forming, Storming, Norming, Performing, developed by Bruce Tuckman in the 1960s. Bringing in a new PM, often with other changes to team membership, can push the team back to the Forming stage. Other interpersonal and communication issues are also likely to arise, impacting team dynamics, morale, and productivity. The incoming PM needs to understand these issues and impacts and quickly address them to get the team productive again as quickly as possible. We'll cover this in more detail in Chapter 5.

These are just a few examples of why taking over an ongoing project is very different from starting a new project. The usual Knowledge, Skills, and Attitudes/Attributes (KSA) that a PM needs to have to be successful are not sufficient when taking over an ongoing project. These additional KSAs are not hard, they are not secret, and they can be learned. The problem has been that they have often not been explicit or easy to find since they are not part of typical project delivery methodologies, courses, or books. This book intends to change that.

Through the following chapters, we will describe how to rapidly identify key issues and problems in an existing project. This isn't always easy but is an important step in determining the true status of the project and identifying what needs to be done to keep the project moving towards success or to getting it back on track for a successful conclusion. Although we cover some tips and techniques on how to do this in the early chapters, it is really an ongoing activity. In addition to maintaining or establishing metrics to objectively track progress, identify risks and issues, and report progress, the PM needs to monitor qualitative trends as well. Communication, both within and external to the team, is also vital and must be continued. These communication channels are also important feedback routes that provide the PM with early clues that additional challenges may be developing.

Most PMs joining ongoing projects need assistance in identifying leverage points to turn around troubled projects and project teams or identifying what must be done to keep the project on track. We'll provide a game plan to do so, including specific questions to ask different stakeholders from the Business Owner (Sponsor) through delivery team members. Capturing this information early provides significant benefits that will continue to pay off as the project continues. Sample questions and templates to organize the information gathered are included in the appendices for easy reference. Downloadable versions are available from our website at www.subscribepage.io/24CLmg.

While the new PM is assessing the current state of affairs and developing a revised project plan, it is critical to keep the existing project team focused. A common analogy is changing the tires on a car while still moving down the road and not driving off a cliff in the process. As the picture below shows, it can be done with the right team, but it is always risky business.

We will cover tactics to keep the project team focused and involved while changing project dynamics, including some important organizational management principles that apply in these situations. Situational Leadership approaches usually apply and provide a useful paradigm to follow when assuming leadership of an existing team. A great example of applying situational leadership to an existing team under stressful conditions is the 1948 movie *12 O'Clock High*, starring Gregory Peck. Often used by the U.S. military in courses teaching situational leadership, you can learn useful lessons from the movie, even without going through the formal curriculum. If you take the time to view the movie, imagine General Savage (Gregory Peck) as a PM brought in to get a project back on track. Think about the tactics he uses to assess the current situation, determine a course of action, and ultimately reshape the team to the point that they are routinely successful. Isn't that what you're being called to do when taking over a project?

Before proceeding to the next chapter, take some time to reflect on your experience as a PM. Have you ever taken over an in-flight project? If so, how did it go? If you have not done so yet, how do you think you'll handle it? Have you worked with PMs who have taken over projects that were started by someone else? How did they handle it? Did any of those projects end successfully?

Perhaps you have been asked to step into an ongoing project, or you are already working with a project team that started the project before you were assigned. The goal of this book is to help you benefit from the experience of other successful PMs and learn how to be successful in taking responsibility for completing a project, regardless of its current status. The following chapters describe a proven process that has been used in many organizations by PMs with varying levels of experience. You will adapt the tools and processes that we describe to fit your leadership style and organization's methodologies, but maintaining the core ideas and steps will lead to success.

Let's start on the journey.

CHAPTER 2

CHALLENGES WITH TAKING OVER AN ONGOING PROJECT

**"Life is about challenges and
how we face up to them."**

Martina Navratilova

What's the Buzz? Tell Me What's Happening.

I was called to company headquarters to meet with the VP to whom my boss reported. I knocked on his door and went in. He didn't waste any time getting to the point.

"Marty, I'd like you to check into a project for me. We're contracted to develop a training course with all the supporting materials for a new electronic and software system that the Navy is going to deploy on over 100 ships. The customer just called, and he's concerned about the progress that we're making. We haven't missed a deliverable date yet, but there have been some quality concerns requiring rewrites of key planning deliverables. There is concern that this may lead to significant issues with the course deliverables, and there won't be time to get them corrected. This is a fixed-price contract, so

---

if there is a lot of rework or a schedule extension, we'll have to pay for it."

"Get with the PM and the team and find out what the real story is. Do some of that MBA stuff, and let me know where we stand. If we need to change the PM, it will get added to your plate. I need a report from you by the end of the week. So make it happen."

"Make it Happen" was the company motto, but the assignment put me in a tough spot. The PM was a peer and a good friend. What were the issues causing the customer to be concerned? Were they real? Was the project really challenged, or were these just the symptoms of a demanding customer who was nervous about a highly-visible, multi-million dollar project? I needed to find the real story quickly, without upsetting or slowing down the team. The first step was determining what challenges the team might be facing and if there were clear steps to resolve them.

What's the Challenge?

When joining a project that has already started or when tasked to review an existing project, a PM is faced with a number of challenges. These primarily relate to not having been with the project team from the beginning and, therefore, not having been part of the planning process. As noted in the last chapter, scope, schedule, and budget are probably already set. Many other decisions have also been made, some explicit, some implicit. This leads to the first challenge that the new PM has—what is the true status of the project? We'll describe how to determine the true status of the project in more detail in Chapter 5, along with providing some useful tools. Before going there, we should look at potential challenges that arise because a change in PM is contemplated or occurring. These challenges or issues will be added to those that already exist in the project and will also need to be addressed as part of the takeover and recovery plan.

There are many reasons for another PM taking over a project, and the project itself may not be in trouble; it may truly be in "Green" status. While that is great and makes things easier for the incoming PM, there are still challenges tied to the change in management that must be dealt with. Let's review a few of these.

First, the previous PM may no longer be available. They may have left the organization, be out on extended personal leave, been moved to a different project, and not available for a hand-off, etc. This means the incoming PM is unlikely to have access to all the information that the previous PM had, especially around the reasons why certain decisions were made. For example, why was the delivery broken into three increments? Why are there four Scrum Teams instead of three? While interviewing the Business Owner (BO), Sponsor, Customer, and delivery team should provide some insights, if we can't talk to the previous PM directly, we are unlikely to know why they made the decisions that they did.

Second, at the opposite end of the spectrum, the former PM may still be around, perhaps due to subject matter or technical expertise. Since they are still part of the delivery team, there are likely to be team and political issues with them no longer being in charge. The incoming PM needs to understand the reasons for the change and the decision to keep the former PM on the team. Specific actions will be needed to reduce any team or political fallout from the change and to ensure that the team continues to move forward as a team.

Why Did You Fire Our PM?

We had a team working very closely with a client establishing the requirements for a highway management system. The PM spent a lot of time with the road crews, riding with them in their trucks, bringing donuts to the worksites, etc. The same team tailored an existing software package to meet these requirements. Despite very positive status reports, the initial software delivery was rejected by the client steering committee, as the PM and team had failed to incorporate requirements

> *from other parts of the organization. At the direction of the client, the PM was replaced with a more experienced PM, but the prior PM was kept on the team due to his familiarity with the existing requirements and software.*
>
> *It soon became apparent that the former PM and some team members resented the change, and they were not cooperating with the new PM and architect. Despite a number of team-building sessions and individual counseling, the situation continued to fester. Finally, the Program Director had to fire the original PM and add more team members to get the remaining work done. Despite a very happy client after the final delivery, the overall project was six months late and 35% over budget on a fixed-price contract. The team dynamic and interpersonal issues were so tough for the new PM that he decided to leave the company after the project was completed.*

As noted in the story above, the true status of the project may not be known by the incoming PM. This requires the PM to rapidly assess the current status, identify any issues, and prioritize them for correction while keeping the project running (remember the analogy of changing tires on a moving automobile). If possible, the incoming PM should request help from the Project Management Office (PMO), project recovery team (if one exists), or even another PM to assist during this period. As we'll cover in Chapter 5, there are specific things to check to determine the true status, so getting some support can lighten the load.

Another challenge can arise if the Sponsor, Business Owner, or Customer change at the same time as the PM. Or if one is assessing a project due to a Business Owner change and a project review is requested. There have been cases where a successful Business Owner and PM that work well together are moved to higher priority programs or projects, especially if the current project is going well. This adds to the existing challenge of building a relationship with the new Business Owner and rebuilding the team dynamic. Many Business Owners joining a project want to review prior decisions, change requirements and agreements, and potentially alter the goals of the project, all to mold the project to meet their goals and add their personal stamp onto the project. While this is a natural human reaction, it can be deadly in a project. The incoming PM needs to hold the line and minimize the disruption to the project, often without a full understanding of the rationale behind decisions already made. This is difficult to do, even while promising to look further into issues raised by the Business Owner. Diplomacy and firmness are both needed to avoid unnecessarily impacting the project.

Figure 2-1: Basic Project Organization

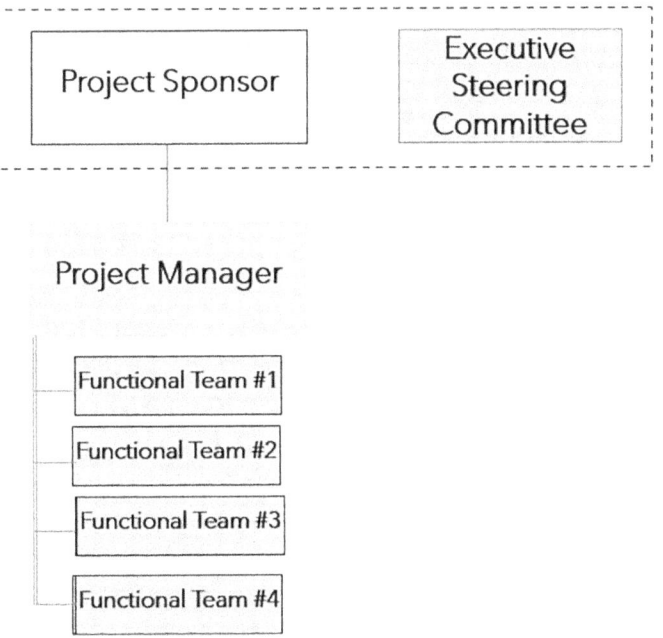

There can also be challenges of a more serious nature. Depending upon the nature of the project, the contract, the customer, or actions already taken within the project, legal or ethical issues may be involved. These can range from a simple dispute over which requirements are in scope to issues where fines or jail time may be involved. These may or may not be related to work that the project team has done or has not done. Obviously, there will be more management attention when these issues arise, and they may be connected to a request for a project review or change in PM. If they are discovered during a project review, especially if one is an incoming PM, clear and open communication with management is required. If appropriate, Human Resources (HR) and Legal Departments should be consulted as well. Nothing good will come from concealing contractual, legal, or ethical issues from your managers and organization.

Ethical Dilemma

We had a subcontract with another company to complete an independent analysis of an engineering contract that a government agency had with a third-party engineering firm. These are known as Independent Verification and Validation (IV&V) contracts. Our PM was also the Principal Investigator (PI) for the team, with several engineers working part-time to assist with specific aspects of the analysis. Little progress had been made, despite the status reports always reporting Green. On Friday, the PM announced that he was resigning immediately since he had not received an unjustified promotion that he had demanded. On Monday, he showed up in the lobby with a manager from the company holding the prime contract, who was his new employer. They demanded a meeting with our VP and indicated that unless we completed the required IV&V reports to the government customer's satisfaction in one week, they would terminate the contract with us and tell the government client that we were in default.

It was clear that the PM who left had done a substandard job, blaming the company, while planning to join the other firm if his demands for a promotion were not met. While his actions were unethical, they created contractual and potential legal issues for us. We pulled an experienced technical PM off

---

another project and added subject matter experts to the team. Working 18-hour days, including the weekend, we were able to complete the work that the departing PM had not done over the prior two months. We insisted that our new PM be in the meeting with the government client to ensure we had truthful feedback.

The end client was happy with the deliverables and stated that they were much improved over anything they had seen in the past two months. The manager from the prime contractor indicated that the improvement was entirely due to his intervention and switching the former PM to his firm so the manager could personally supervise the work. The fact that neither of them had even reviewed the updated deliverables before the meeting was not mentioned. Our PM was faced with an ethical dilemma because of these lies but chose to stay silent instead of creating controversy with the client by revealing the true story. Sometimes dirty players get away with things they shouldn't.

Senior management was kept informed of the ongoing situation, and the decision was made to no longer subcontract with the other firm once the current project was completed. Although the potential for future projects via that route was lost, the company would avoid similar situations in the future. It took a few months to wrap up the existing project, but then a clean break was arranged.

Sometimes a project truly is challenged, perhaps due to inadequate resources, a team that has been over-worked, a team that is missing the experience or technical skills to do the work, or even due to interpersonal issues within the team. These issues may be readily apparent or hidden underneath other symptoms. For example, are repeated failures during software testing due to poor software design, architecture decisions, or poor requirements? Maybe the tests themselves are the problem? Maybe there is poor communication between the different members involved? Are issues arising due to a geographically dispersed team?

These are all possibilities that should be considered. Very rarely is the root cause someone intentionally doing a bad job (despite the "Ethical Dilemma" story). Getting to that root cause can take time, and we'll explore some tactics to follow in Chapter 5.

Most organizations today have some form of matrix management structure. That is, there is more than one person or manager that team members report to. Members of a Scrum Team usually have a member manager that controls their team assignments, salary, performance reviews, and promotions. The member may have another manager for their discipline or technical area, such as Business Analyst or Software Architect. Then there is the Business Owner that owns the project and perhaps a Product Manager who owns the product line or suite of applications that provides service to external clients. Whether a profit or non-profit business, there are financial managers watching budgets and expenditures. So there are many managers involved, along with different goals, agendas, rules, etc.

The PM and Project Team need to deal with all these entities and managers. If they are not aligned, and maintaining alignment is difficult, this can create project challenges. With a new PM coming in, these challenges are likely to be magnified since each dimension of the matrix has its own view of the project and its status. They are also likely to see the opportunity to shift the balance of power or influence over the project since the new PM does not have all the history of agreements that were reached before. This can place the new PM in a difficult position, especially as they are meeting with managers and teams for the first time, getting the lay of the land. The PM must be extremely careful not to be unduly influenced by any one individual or group or to prematurely agree to milestones, tasks, deliverables, etc., until the full picture of the project is in hand.

Another problematic aspect of matrix management, which can also occur with other management structures, is having responsibility for a project without the required authority. There are multiple forms that this may take, and the issue is usually easy to spot. Essentially, the PM is accountable for meeting specific goals without having the authority needed over the resources and decisions needed to meet those goals. A common example in Agile projects is the Business Owner controlling scope, requirements, and priority of requirements, but the PM is responsible for keeping on schedule and meeting the assigned budget. A properly designed organizational structure and methodology can prevent this, but it is rare to find ones that well designed. A PM taking over an ongoing project needs to assess the current arrangements and identify if they will have responsibilities without commensurate authority as soon as possible, so these issues can be raised and resolved before more problems occur.

The final challenges with assuming responsibility for an ongoing project deal with the priority of the project. There may be an assigned priority, but does the reality on the ground reflect that? Do the resources assigned, management attention, and progress reflect the advertised priority of the project or not? Have larger organizational priorities, or perhaps the business environment, changed since the project was created? If so, is the project still worth doing? Should the goals of the project be changed? Who within the organization has decision-making/override authority? Is there a clear appeal path from the PM to that manager? Is the PM change just one step on the path to canceling the project? Or has the priority of the project increased, perhaps due to a business need to get the project completed sooner?

Again, the PM should seek to identify the true priority of the project when being asked to step in (see Chapter 3) and determine if it may make more sense to stop the project entirely or perhaps reshape the project into a new project. It can be very upsetting to join a project team and spend a lot of effort getting the project on track, only to learn that completing the project is no longer a top priority of the organization. In turn, this will create more issues with getting required resources and support, management attention, and keeping team members motivated.

Why does an incoming PM need to ensure that they have the right authority as well as responsibility? To change a common phrase, "You didn't break it, but you own it." Once PM responsibilities are assumed, the incoming PM owns the project outcomes, good or bad. The "half-life" of blaming the former PM is a lot shorter than you may think. It may not even be a day! By accepting the PM role, you accept responsibility for final outcomes, even if the project is already in serious trouble. Documenting the true status of the project upfront is important, as is communicating that status to the Business Owner, Sponsor, and ultimate Customer, as well as to your manager. In those discussions, make sure that your responsibilities are clearly laid out and that you have the authority required to fulfill those responsibilities. If possible, get these spelled out in writing, perhaps in an updated project charter, project plan, or member assignment document. If there is going to be a disconnect between responsibilities and authority, highlight it in the Risks & Issues Log.

> **Tip:** Make sure you have authority that aligns with your responsibilities.

Despite the challenges noted above, in my experience, incoming PMs are able to achieve good results most of the time. The project may not be in trouble, or the issues may be identified and resolved with the right support from the project team and broader organization. There is no need to assume the worst when a change in PM is contemplated or a project review is requested. It can be mentally difficult, but we need to focus on the facts, stay objective, and make sure we have the true picture before taking action. This is challenging when senior management wants answers right away, especially if they think a project is going badly. We'll explore some things to discuss with senior management when we are called upon to review or take over a project in the next chapter.

What's the Buzz? What Happened?

After interviewing the customer, PM, and key leads, along with reviewing the deliverables, the underlying issue was clear. Although the team included the right technical experts who understood the system and how it should be operated, they were struggling to understand the Data Item Descriptions

(DID) that contractually specified the format and content of each deliverable. In addition, the customer had a degree in English, and the writing style of the team members was overly technical and filled with grammatical errors. We added a technical editor experienced with the relevant DIDs to the team. The quality of the deliverables improved, and the customer's concerns were abated. By adjusting the schedule and work effort of the team members drafting the materials, the PM avoided impacting the overall budget or schedule of the project while improving the quality of the deliverables that were in scope. Due to the customer's increased confidence in the team, the company won another contract for similar work before the first project was completed.

Often the key to a challenged project is not replacing the PM or team. That is why we need to understand the challenges and potential solutions first.

As the results of the story show, the true status of a project, and the challenges that may be occurring, are not always apparent on the surface. That is why conducting a thorough project review, as described in Chapter 5, is so important. Before we get to that step, there are a few other matters that need to be handled, including getting the call to take over a project and the initial steps required before conducting the project review. We'll cover those in the next two chapters. We've discussed a number of challenges in taking over an ongoing project and how these are different from starting a new project. One of the key differences is that the ongoing project may already show evidence of problems or have challenges. Table 2-1 lists some common project challenges and possible causes. The challenges that are identified when a new PM is being asked to take over a project are going to impact the initial steps in assuming command and should be discussed with management as part of accepting the assignment. We'll cover this in more detail in the next chapter.

Table 2-1: Potential Challenges Taking Over an Ongoing Project

CHALLENGE	POSSIBLE CAUSES
Behind schedule	Low productivity; scope not limited; external dependencies not being met; resources lacking; unrealistic schedule
Productivity lower than expected	Team missing key skills and/or experience; unsuitable tools; unclear requirements or deadlines; distracted team
Over budget	More expensive resources assigned than planned (people, tools, materials, etc.); low productivity; changing requirements
Under budget	Progress not keeping up with schedule; lower cost members assigned; planned expenditures not being made on time (items not being ordered in time to get them when needed); resources not being assigned when planned and needed—likely leading to schedule issues
Poor quality	Team members lack needed skills; poor requirements; poor architecture; poor design; team members burned out; behind schedule so skimping on testing to catch up
Changing requirements	Unclear objectives; changing priorities, Business Owner changing their mind; additional stakeholders getting involved; changes in business needs
Contractual dispute	Unclear requirements; differences over scope, schedule, budget, goals; client desire to exit contract without penalty; changes in business environment; hostile client; either party seeking to exit an unprofitable agreement
Team understaffed	Project priority too low; resources not available; staff turnover; budget too low for scope of work and schedule

CHALLENGE	POSSIBLE CAUSES
Team over staffed	Productivity higher than expected; project budget being used to cover expenses that should be allocated to another project; project being used to train junior staff; poor planning
Selected technology appears unsuitable	Technology was selected before requirements were clear; architecture set arbitrarily; promised capabilities not actually available in chosen technology; team not experienced enough with technology to use it correctly; client unwilling to select or pay for new technology
Change in sponsor	Project priority changed; sponsor not wanting to be connected to a failing project; sponsor may have other priorities that are more important to them; sponsor may have left the organization; senior management may believe sponsor was causing the issues with project performance
Dependencies on external teams not being met	Unrealistic schedules; external team not connected to project team; project team not communicating dependencies and impact of unmet targets to external team
Previous PM left project or company	Responsibility without authority; better opportunities on other projects or at other companies; issues with project team or company; disputes with Business Owner or Sponsor
Team not willing to change processes; uncooperative with new PM	Previous PM remains on project, despite new PM being appointed; lack of training in new processes and tools; poor communication of need to change approach for ultimate success
Sabotage by others	Disagreement with project objectives; competing priorities; hidden stakeholder(s) influencing team and/or project support
End users or customers not happy with project outputs	Lack of Organizational Change Management (OCM); disagreement over requirements; hidden stakeholders; incomplete requirements

CHALLENGE	POSSIBLE CAUSES
Loss of resources	Changing organization priorities; team members being burned out or no longer in agreement with project goals or processes; internal team issues; perception that project is failing and desire to avoid blame
Loss of Priority	Business goals change; change in status of Sponsor; external business environment changes; newer projects are more visible and "hot"
Competing projects taking resources from this project	Other project has higher priority; potentially overlapping requirements; overlapping resource needs
Unsuitable methodology	Wrong methodology chosen for designated scope, budget, and schedule; Agile chosen before organization is ready to do Agile; interdependencies with other projects and teams not handled well by methodology; methodology unsuitable for the type of project or technology
Lack of alignment on project processes and objectives	Global team not aligned on project vision, which can be increased by team dynamic issues, cultural differences, and being spread across multiple time zones

As you can see in the table, many challenges (symptoms) can result from similar causes and be related to multiple issues. So it is important to avoid jumping to conclusions or developing action plans before getting to the real causes of the challenges. We'll cover how to do this in Chapter 5.

Exercise: Before going to Chapter 3, take some time to think about similar situations you have been in or may encounter in the future. List potential problems taking over a project after it has started.

CHAPTER 3

GETTING THE CALL TO ACTION

"When placed in command, take charge."
Norman Schwarzkopf, General, US Army

Toy Story

My VP popped into my cubicle on a sunny morning in March. She brought coffee, which was never a good sign.

Her voice was cheery, and she smiled as the payment for my coffee came due. "Marty, we've got a 'Toys' project initiated by the president of the Personal Lines Division that seems to be off course. I'm moving it into your portfolio now, and I want you to do a thorough project review. You'll be the Program Director responsible for this project, reporting directly to me. I'm worried about the Project Manager and the team. The scope of the project seems to be growing well beyond the initial $300K budget. You need to get it under control and determine what the real cost and schedule should be. If you need to replace the PM, review it with me first, but you will own that decision."

I was being asked to step into a troubled project and potentially remove a PM that I hadn't even met yet. Not the way I liked to start a morning. That cup of coffee was already a bit too expensive for my taste.

"Any questions for me?"

> *Trying to sound both professional and motivated, I tested a politically acceptable way to turn down the assignment. "Yes. I'm currently busy with three other teams, totaling over 300 members, and I'm starting up a fourth team to keep to the Product Manager's schedule. Can you pass this on to someone else?"*
>
> *She smiled. "No. Just get it done."*
>
> *I had my call to action.*

We usually don't identify projects that we want to take over and then go to senior management to have them assigned to us. Instead, we are identified as a candidate, or sometimes, the only candidate, to assist or take over an ongoing project. As noted in Chapter 2, there may be many reasons for this to occur. The existing PM may no longer be available, the project may be seen as having challenges, we may have unique skills or experience that the project needs, or any of a hundred other reasons. The net result is that we get requested, or told, to get involved with a project, a call to action.

One of the most important characteristics of a PM is a bias towards action. That is, we see a problem or a goal, and we take action to solve the problem or reach the goal. PMs are not passive observers standing by as the world passes by. If a PM sees a car (project) veering off the road (not meeting its objectives), their first instinct is to take over the wheel and get it back on the road. This is a vital attitude for PMs to have and one that we screen for when interviewing prospective PMs. However, there is a dark side to this as well.

My wife always says that PMs must be optimists because they always assume they can successfully complete their projects. That optimism often causes us to believe we can fix projects that are challenged or that we can take over project teams and keep things running smoothly. While being optimistic and positive is great, it also needs to be tempered with a dose of realism. The remainder of this chapter will describe how to get that dose of realism to support a decision to accept the opportunity or to build a case to gracefully decline the assignment. There may not be an option to decline taking over a project, as noted in the "Toy Story," but the information obtained will be very useful going forward, especially in working with the executive team.

The goal at this point is to quickly assess the current situation, focusing on the executive or management level, to help us decide if this is an opportunity that we want to take or if we should steer clear. Even if we cannot decline the opportunity, the information gathered here should help us plan our first steps (see Chapter 4) and should help us determine the extent of executive commitment to the project and the way to improve it. The gathered information will also assist our assuming leadership of the project.

The most critical question is, "Why are we changing the PM now?" As noted earlier, there are many good answers to this question. The PM may have been moved to a more important assignment, transferred to a different position as part of their career growth, or may just be on extended leave (e.g., parental leave for a new baby). If one or more of these is the reason given, there may still be some challenges in taking over the project, but there aren't any warning signs yet.

Another answer to the question of "Why are we changing the PM now?" that may indicate real trouble is when the customer (external client or internal business owner/sponsor) demands a change. This may be due to the customer raising too many issues over the head of the PM or going around the PM to senior management. This can create the impression that the PM is not competent or proactive, even if this is not the case. The management team may have decided to replace the PM just to reduce the "noise" coming from the customer, even if the PM is not at fault. Once the decision is made to replace the PM and a new PM is called in, it is too late to revisit the decision, but the incoming PM should determine the real issue so it can be dealt with upfront. We'll describe some tactics to use in the next few chapters, but the effort starts during the discussions being held at this point. Seek agreement on communication processes and channels with management, and get agreement to keep you, as the new PM, in the loop on all communications regarding the project.

There may also be answers that raise warning flags, such as "We just fired the PM." Or "The PM quit unexpectedly." These usually indicate a project with known issues and probably additional issues that haven't been uncovered yet. This initial discussion may also describe issues that have been noted or management concerns. Another red flag warning is when the customer (internal or external) has demanded a change in the PM. While this may just be a style or personality conflict between the individuals, there are usually deeper issues. For example, if the PM is trying to maintain control over scope, and the customer wants to keep adding requirements or make contractual changes without going through the change order process, the customer may be trying to remove the constraints imposed by the PM by replacing the PM. A revealing comment from the customer is "they are difficult to work with." Translation—"The PM won't do whatever I tell them to do."

Carefully consider the responses you get to the question, "Why are we changing the PM now?" before proceeding. Is this shaping up as a situation where you will be the next PM being replaced, potentially harming your professional reputation and career? Do there appear to be political games being played? If so, do you want to join the game? Again, if you have to take the assignment, the responses to this question should also shape your plans for the project.

The next key question for management, especially the Project Sponsor and Business Owner, is "What does success look like?" If they cannot succinctly describe this, we have to ask, how can the project be successful? Even under Agile or Flow Methodologies, "do good stuff" is never enough guidance. If we are building a house, we need to have a plan that shows what the finished building looks like. If we are implementing a new process, creating a new product, or building a software application, they all have objectives. While these objectives may be modified through the course of the project (being "agile"), at any given point in time, the objective must be clear and understood by all the stakeholders. If your initial discussions cannot establish a clear response to this question, which should be written down and confirmed with key executive stakeholders, this issue must be flagged. Think about this carefully. How can you successfully hit the target if the target itself is not defined? Framing the discussion in this manner with the Project Sponsor and Business Owner usually helps them clarify their goals and can provide a clear objective for the project.

A more difficult question to ask is, "What is the current status of the project?" The true status may not be known, and different stakeholders are likely to hold different views. We'll independently determine the true status in later chapters since that is critical to updating project plans and setting the path forward. At this stage, all we want to determine is what views are held by the key stakeholders. If negative views are expressed, this is an ideal time to lay the foundation for future requests for help or support. Regardless of whether positive or negative views are shared, dig a little deeper into why they feel that way. Are these views based on factual assessments or perhaps opinions tied to feelings or the amount of communication with the PM and project team? For example, "I don't have confidence in the progress reports I'm getting" may just indicate a communications issue, not a delivery issue. Note what you hear to help guide your future steps.

If there seems to be a consensus that the project is challenged or adrift, an immediate follow-up question needs to be asked: "Should this project be terminated?" Getting this option on the table at this point will save a lot of time and effort later and could help you avoid being the PM if it is terminated in the future. Note that we are not *recommending* that the project be terminated, though we may do so later after we've done a thorough review. At this stage, we are reminding the executive team that this is an option they should be considering if they haven't already done so.

The costs already sunk into the project are not recoverable, so they are not reasons to continue to pour resources into an effort that may ultimately fail. If this turns into a longer discussion, stay polite, objective, and professional. Focus on the project objectives (what success looks like) and current progress towards those objectives, not how we got here or the performance of the project team or PM. Objectively, given the current status, is it worth continuing? There may be cases where there are regulatory requirements or business reasons why the end goal of the project must be met by a specific date. While this usually results in plans to rescue a troubled project, it may be better to terminate the current project and start fresh. For example, if the technical solution or methodology chosen is not working out, starting over with different technology or methodology is likely to be more efficient, especially if some of the work already done can be carried over (e.g., the functional requirements).

Assuming the decision is made to continue if the project is not on track, the next question is, "If it is not on track, what caused it to go off track?" Again, we will get into the actual reasons as part of our project review later on. At this point, we want to discover the executive view. In the "Toy Story" example, the VP and executive team believe that scope control is lacking and that the original objectives of the project are being expanded beyond the mandate of the team. This will help us plan the initial steps of our review. While we should not assume that this initial view is 100% true, there are probably some facts that support it.

If we discover that the executive(s) have misunderstood the true situation, we are obligated to go back to them and describe the true situation. Another point to remember is that very few people ever get up in the morning and think, "Today, I'm going to do a bad job at work." So whatever issues may be occurring on the project are probably not due to intentional malice. If we hear views that contradict this, such as "the PM isn't committed to the success of the project" or "the team doesn't care about their results," we need to proceed carefully. While we should verify the commitment of the PM and team to the success of the project, we should not proceed assuming lack of commitment or incompetence are the primary issues.

The remaining questions for the executives are more focused on their commitment to the project and our accepting the opportunity to join as the PM. These should be much easier for them to answer, and they should lay the foundation for the next steps that you will take as you assume leadership of the project team.

More than simple curiosity, we need to learn, "Why was I selected for this project?" Do not look at this as an opportunity to boost your ego. The goal is to learn more about the project and why they are coming to you to take over. Is it just because you are available? Are you a lower-cost alternative to a more experienced and costly PM (if so, watch out!)? Do you have specific skills and experience that they think are needed (this ties back to "what caused it to go off track")? How this question is answered will determine how much time you need to spend on the discussion that follows. For example, throughout my career, I've had a lot of experience with testing, from testing software to destructive testing of hardware. I sometimes joke about wearing a QA Team (quality assurance) baseball hat. There have been many occasions where I've been asked to help a team with quality issues or to take over a team with similar issues. This makes sense from an organizational point of view. It would not make sense to put me into a project struggling with software architecture issues, so I would have to question that type of assignment if offered. Listen to the answer carefully to decide if there is good alignment with your skills, experience, and career goals.

Some of the key knowledge, skills, and attitudes (KSA) that the incoming PM needs to possess go beyond the level normally expected of a PM. While these KSA are beneficial for all PMs to have, they can be critical for a PM taking over a challenged project. Do these align with your KSA, or can you develop them while managing this project? Would assigning a more experienced PM as a coach or mentor help you develop these KSA while managing this project? Try to be objective when asking these questions. If the situation is not a good fit, and there are no ways to improve the fit, work with management to consider other options. The PM KSAs that are more critical when transitioning into a project include:

- Skill at reading organizational and project politics and understanding that they must be dealt with and cannot be ignored
- Honesty in dealing with issues and communicating both within and external to the team
- Ability to separate facts from emotions and opinions to get to the heart of matters
- Willingness to handle the stress that comes from assuming an ongoing project, especially if the project is currently in a Red or Yellow status
- Knowledge and skill with multiple project delivery methodologies to support assessing and modifying the current tools and methodologies as needed

- Ability to identify solutions and convince others to follow those solutions, even when departing from prior methods

Another question for the executives that should be easy to answer is, "What do you need from me to help this project succeed?" Essentially a follow-up to the previous question, we are identifying the knowledge, skills, time, and commitment that they expect us to bring to the project. Internally, we need to ask ourselves if it is a good match for what we can do and what we want to do. Can we commit the time and effort needed? Will this impact other assignments that we have? If so, will those assignments go to someone else? Are we OK with that? Will the assignment require considerable travel or coordination across different time zones, and if so, will that impact our personal life? We usually are not going to make a decision on the opportunity at this point, but we want to gather as many facts as we can in order to make an informed decision. Don't be afraid to ask for some time to consider the options before accepting the opportunity. Most managers will give you that time.

Depending upon the answers received to this point, we may need to know if the intent is for us to carry the project through to completion. Ask, "Do you intend for me to stay as the PM through the end of the project?" If the answer is no, follow up with, "What is the desired project status to trigger my transition out?" These answers are important to have upfront since they will impact your plans for assuming responsibility for the project and how you will be viewed by both management and the delivery team. If the new PM is being brought in to "fix the project," it is likely to make things more challenging. There are likely to be continuing questions about the extent of the PM's authority, the permanence of decisions and policies, and the PM's commitment to project and project team success. It is better to know these potential issues up front and to discuss them with management to get the support you will need from them to address the challenges than to run into them later. Once project plans have been revised (see Chapter 8), revisit the transition issue with management again, and agree on a suitable milestone or project status to trigger the next PM transition. Reach a joint agreement on when and how this will be communicated more broadly to the overall team to ensure that it does not leak out as a rumor and create additional team issues.

The next two questions are perhaps the most important ones for indicating the likelihood of success with the project. First, "What authority will I have over the project team? Over external teams or resources that we need to succeed?" An all-too-common problem with modern organizations and teams is dispersed authority. Although there are many situations where this is beneficial, having responsibility for a successful outcome without having commensurate authority over the resources and teams needed to be successful is not only difficult, it is a recipe for frustration and disappointment. Uncover any potential issues of this kind now, and be prepared to discuss why the organizational arrangements need to be changed. If you see a problem with the responsibility/authority arrangement but cannot fix it or avoid the assignment, note it upfront. Identify the issues, suggest changes to the limitations or boundaries that may cause problems, and seek their agreement to make those changes. If the desired changes cannot be made, stress the need for executive support to make up for the authority that you will not have, which leads to the next important question.

Ask your manager, the Project Sponsor, and the Business Owner, "What will you do to help this project succeed?" If they appear indifferent or show a lack of commitment to project success, this is a clear sign that the project is unlikely to succeed. Be very careful about boarding the Titanic while the captain is eyeing the lifeboat. Although you are likely to come back to the executive team with specific requests and needs as you deliver the project, at this point, you are looking for their commitment and their boundaries on that commitment. For example, in the "Toy Story" scenario, the Project Sponsor was unwilling to budget more than $500K for the entire project. An updated budget forecast of $1.5M had already shaken his commitment. After having these conversations, it is usually a good idea to summarize them in a brief e-mail to each of the key executives, documenting their commitment and support. This is not meant to be a Cover Your Ass (CYA) e-mail trail; the intent is to ensure that both of you are on the same page and that your mutual commitment to project success is clear. As we note under communications in Chapter 10, returning to the management team with your 30/60/90-day plan(s) to get their approval is a good way to keep their commitment and support. As the items in the plan are accomplished, confidence in the PM and team will grow, along with the management team's commitment to the project.

At this point, there may be clear warning signs that the project is in trouble or not. The commitment of key stakeholders should be clear, along with the opportunities and challenges for the incoming PM. You need to make a decision about accepting the opportunity or if you should try to avoid it. So, ask, "Do I have the option to turn down this assignment?" The answer may be yes, in which case you need to decide based on your career goals, your current personal situation, and everything you've learned about the project to this point. Do not be afraid to ask for some time to think about your decision, especially if it is likely to involve travel, long hours, or working weekends. Most managers will provide a day or two to do so. If you decide to accept the opportunity, do so with the firm intention to do your best and to be fully committed to a successful outcome for the organization, the project, and the project team. That success may include a recommendation to terminate the project if it is in the best interests of the organization to do so.

If the answer is that you have to take the assignment, be professional about it. This may be a good opportunity to request specific things you need to be successful—key personnel; increased authority; ability to request scope, schedule, and budget changes later; etc. Explain that you are going to do a thorough project review and discuss the results with the key stakeholders. That discussion may include recommendations for them to consider, including additional support. Set the groundwork for your review and that follow-up meeting, indicating that you cannot promise a successful project outcome before then.

11 Questions to Ask Before Taking Over a Project

1. Why are we changing the PM now?
2. What does success look like?
3. What is the current status of the project?
4. If it is not on track, what caused it to go off track?
5. Why was I selected for this project?
6. What do you need from me to help this project succeed?
7. Do you intend for me to stay as PM through the end of the project? If not, what is the desired project status to trigger my transition out?
8. What authority will I have over the project team?
9. What authority will I have over external teams or resources that we need to succeed?
10. What will you do to help this project succeed?
11. Do I have the option to turn down this assignment?

In movie westerns, the new sheriff always seems to have a plan before they ride into town. This makes a lot of sense since the sheriff may need to take some immediate actions or face some challenges right away. Incoming PMs also need to have a plan on how to proceed with the project and project team, even if that plan gets changed by circumstances on the first day. In the next chapter, we'll describe the first steps you need to take after joining an ongoing project, either as the new PM or to review and assess the project.

Exercise: Think about who the key stakeholders are for projects in your organization. What questions will you ask them if you are being asked to take over an ongoing project? What information do you want to have before accepting or declining the opportunity? Are there any circumstances where you will not take on a project?

41

Toy Story—Results

Just a week spent interviewing the Project Sponsor, PM, Product Owner, and key team members identified the problem. The Product Owner and the Project Sponsor (President of the Personal Lines Division) had both agreed to keep the addition of motorcycles, boats, RVs, jet skis, etc., (the "toys") to the list of items we would insure within a limited project scope and budget. The intent was to broaden the appeal of our traditional home and auto products to potential customers without complicating the work of our agents or significantly altering our existing software systems. Unfortunately, in the course of defining system requirements, the stakeholders being interviewed kept adding to the list of "must-haves." The PM had done a good job of updating the project budget and schedule to account for these, increasing the budget estimate to $1.5 million, with additional growth in sight.

Bringing together my VP with the Product Owner, we reviewed my findings. I emphasized that this was not a PM issue and that she had a good handle on managing the project. The Product Owner and my VP went to the Project Sponsor and got an agreement to kill the project. Based on my recommendation, the PM and her team became the core of the new project that I was spinning up instead of being let go. That much larger project was delivered over a month early and 18% under budget, demonstrating the skill and value of the PM and her team despite the issues in the Toys Project.

The key lesson here is that project issues are not necessarily the fault of the project team, so we need to keep these assessments separate. We can terminate projects that need to be terminated without impacting the reputation or careers of the PM and team.

CHAPTER 4

THERE'S A NEW SHERIFF
IN TOWN—FIRST STEPS

"When you come up against trouble, it's
never half as bad if you face up to it."

John Wayne

In many western movies, the hero rides into town expecting just a routine visit for supplies, a drink, or perhaps to visit an old friend. Instead, they discover a series of problems that eventually lead to the hero becoming responsible for cleaning up the problems. Sometimes the formula is changed a bit, and the hero is already the new sheriff coming to town to clean it up. Regardless, we first see the problems take shape and the sheriff getting more information on the problems and potential solutions before the sheriff takes action. In this chapter, we'll lay out an initial plan of action. In subsequent chapters, we'll cover additional steps in the plan in more detail, along with providing supporting tools and checklists. We'll stick with our new sheriff theme and use some analogies to the old-time westerns as we go.

While it is often tempting to just dive in and make decisions, take action, fire off e-mails, and demonstrate that we are large and in charge, that is exactly the wrong approach to take when joining an ongoing project team as the new PM. Before meeting with the customer and team, you need to have an initial plan of attack. This plan does not need to be detailed, and it will undoubtedly change, but you still need to have a plan. We'll start by mapping out the phases that you will need to go through, then elaborate on each phase. As noted, subsequent chapters will cover the remaining phases in more detail and provide additional tools to be used in that phase.

So, what are the phases?

The first steps deal with confirming your mandate, assembling the preliminary information that is available, planning the following phases in a rough outline, and negotiating the time to execute your plan. Whether you were given a choice on taking the assignment or not, there will be pressure to hurry up and make a difference and to demonstrate that the project is on the right path and problems have been solved, thereby letting senior management focus their attention elsewhere. This can be a continuing challenge, and it can be the most difficult one to overcome. That also makes it an important one to address up front and to set the right tone at the very beginning with the key stakeholders, including your management, the Sponsor, Business Owner, and the delivery team.

How do we set the right tone? First, always be calm and professional in your interactions with others. Quiet confidence in your ability to handle whatever problems are encountered is key while not coming across as arrogant or overly sure of yourself. Ask thoughtful questions, listen to the responses, and work with the people involved to identify problems and potential solutions. Avoid making snap judgments. Just as the people of the town expect the ace gunslinging sheriff to have the experience and capabilities to take care of the bad guys, you have been brought in to solve problems. While being careful not to make promises or commitments too early, you can express confidence in your ability to work with the team and get things sorted out.

We've Never Done This Before

My VP Dean and I were meeting with a prospective client from a large, international insurance company. Just like every other organization on the planet, they needed to ensure all their IT systems were ready for the Year 2000 date change. They needed to execute a large number of projects to investigate potential issues, resolve those issues through software and hardware changes, verify that the solutions worked, and put them into production while not interrupting their current business operations. Add in the complication of having a single end date that could not be missed to the constraints, and the pressure on this executive was immense. She had just been tasked with assembling a large Quality Assurance Team from scratch, with no methodology for testing so many large, complex systems in such a short time. She had met with a number of consulting firms but had not found any of them to meet her needs.

All this information came out after we asked her what her challenges were. Before describing what our firm was offering, I described being in a similar situation before. Although it was in a different industry, and the challenge did not include an immovable end date, there were a lot of similarities to her situation. After briefly describing the steps we took for that client, we discussed what she had already done and asked about her plans. Within 15 minutes, we had identified some key steps that she had missed and the types of skills needed on the team to execute her revised plan.

As the end of the meeting time approached, she turned to Dean and asked if I could stay with her and further detail the plan while he worked up a contract for the members we would bring to the joint team. Not expecting to get to this stage so fast, Dean asked her if he should draw up a short planning contract or something longer. She replied that she wanted an initial contract for the first project, including establishing the QA methodology, training plan, organizational change management, and supplying QA leads to pair one-on-one with her leads.

"We've never done this before, but it's clear that you and Marty have. I'm buying your experience so we don't lose time learning things you already know. I'm confident that this is going to be money well spent."

The first step to success had been taken.

The next phase involves getting the lay of the land. What is the true situation? This requires research and investigation, looking for specific information that we'll cover in the next chapter. Just as with medical triage situations, you're going to find some issues that need a rapid response (the Ugly). These are issues that will cause further problems if not addressed quickly, even if all we can do at this point is limit the damage to the team or overall project. For example, there may be a troublesome individual on the team impacting performance and morale. They need to be counseled to change their behavior and, if the expectations are not met, removed from the team. There will be other issues that allow us time to analyze them in more detail and address them in the near term (the Bad). For example, issues with a supporting tool or process that will need to be modified or replaced. There will also be plenty of things that do not need to be changed, at least not at the present time (the Good). Identifying the Good, the Bad, and the Ugly allows us to refine our plan, adjust priorities, and determine if additional resources or support are required.

Now that we have an updated plan with priorities, we can focus on gathering a posse to help us clean up the town—share what we've found with the stakeholders and delivery team, clear up any misunderstandings or issues with what we've found, and establish good communications throughout the team. We should have an updated stakeholder map at this point, which forms the basis of an updated (or new) communication plan. Verify the communication plan with the involved parties to ensure that their communication needs are being met. Work with the delivery team to update the project plans, including any steps required to resolve the Ugly and Bad issues that have been identified. We need them to be committed to the plan, so they must be part of developing and refining the plan.

At this point, we can focus on cleaning up the town. While our initial efforts should be on stabilizing the situation, so things do not get worse, these steps should also contribute to getting the project running smoothly in the future. As we proceed through the actions we've mapped out with the key stakeholders and delivery team, adjust expectations, revisit assumptions, and update plans. An old military saying is that no plan survives contact with the enemy. We can rephrase that for projects to "no plan survives contact with reality." So, expect more challenges to arise, and be ready to revise plans frequently.

As plans change, we need to keep everyone informed and potentially reset expectations. There will likely arise new issues from inside or outside the project that will require triage and will impact schedules, budgets, and scope. It is important not to overreact to these challenges, especially ones that seemingly come out of nowhere from outside the project. As we'll describe later, identify and manage some slack in the schedule and reserve in the budget, and have change management processes in place to address potential scope changes. Expecting these things to occur and having plans to deal with them not only makes them easier to handle but also reduces the impact on the team.

The final phase is to keep the herd secure. Too often, we get distracted when things start to go well, and the immediate crisis is past. Continue to execute the revised plan, keeping the team moving to the finish line together. Use appropriate metrics to track progress and update plans. Build quality checks into the plans and continue to monitor quality performance. As the team gets closer to completing the project, there will be other tasks. Lay the groundwork for properly handing the results of the project off to the customer or maintenance team. For example, if building a house, how will all the warranty, operating instructions, and maintenance requirements be passed to owners? With a software project, how will it be handed off to the maintenance team? There are also requirements for the project team completing the project, such as gathering lessons learned, preparing members for their new assignments, etc. In some circumstances, you are going to be replaced. Are you ready to hand off the project to another PM? In many organizations, there are PMs identified as problem solvers, the gunslingers needed to clean up challenged projects and get them out of trouble and running smoothly. Once that happens, there may be a desire to bring in a caretaker sheriff to keep things running smoothly while the gunslinger moves to the next town (project) in trouble. Are the plans, processes, and information set up in a manner that the project can continue to function without you at the helm?

Now that we've outlined the phases that we will go through when taking over the project, let's go into more detail on the first steps.

A sheriff needs a badge to be official. Meet with your manager and the Sponsor to confirm your role, responsibility, and the authority that you have been given. If the responsibilities are not complemented by the required authority, now is the time to discuss the issue and get it resolved. Depending upon organizational norms, and if there is a client-contractor relationship, there may be formal paperwork involved. If so, it is helpful to have the full scope of your authority and responsibilities spelled out. In the absence of formal documentation, a simple e-mail to the appropriate parties will do. The Sponsor, Business Owner, your manager, and potentially other key stakeholders should all be aligned on your role. Write out your understanding of the project objectives and scope, your responsibilities, and the authority that you need to have to meet the objectives and responsibilities being assigned. Putting them in writing is a good way to identify any miscommunication and to ensure that all the parties involved have the same understanding. Get this resolved now to avoid more challenging issues later.

Next, if it has not been made clear before, confirm what happened to the old sheriff. This needs to be clear, so you know exactly the situation you are getting into. There may have been some ambiguity in earlier discussions. Are you there to advise the current PM? Assess the situation and report to management? If you are replacing the existing PM, has the PM and team been informed of the change? As noted below, you may be placed in a very uncomfortable situation if you don't know the true picture.

Loaded for Bear

Hired to take over a business process reengineering (BPR) team at a large consulting firm, I was waiting for the elevator in the lobby early Monday morning when a well-dressed young man approached me.

"You must be Marty, coming in to take over the BPR Team today."

"Yes, that's right. Who are you?"

"I'm Bruce, the former manager who was demoted so you could come in and take over. I heard that you like to show up for work early. We need to talk before you go upstairs."

Suddenly feeling very uncomfortable, I motioned Bruce aside and asked for an explanation. In two minutes, we established that while I was told he had requested changing his status back to being an analyst because he wanted to do more hands-on work, that was not the case. He had been pushing back on his managing VP, who kept reducing the cost and schedule estimates coming out of the team, responding to pressure from the primary client to keep their costs down. This had resulted in several projects going over schedule and budget, and Bruce was being blamed for it. He and the team were told at 4 p.m. Friday that I was coming in to "clean things up" Monday morning. His next words were chilling.

"The entire team is in a conference room waiting for you. They're loaded for bear and ready to resign en masse if things don't go right. I just wanted to let you know. Good luck!"

We took the next elevator up to the 6th floor, my palms sweating. Thoughts of this being a fun opportunity were dashed beyond repair.

Examine any information that you have on the project at this point to broaden your understanding of the situation. As noted in the "Loaded for Bear" story, you may not have the full story or accurate facts. At this stage, you need to investigate status and assess the information available, but don't make snap judgments. Seek objective information such as PMO audit results if they are available, project metrics, contracts, Statements of Work (SOW), etc. Although you're going to do a more in-depth review soon, at this point, you need to have a plan for who to talk to first, what you should focus on, and any Ugly issues that have to be rapidly addressed.

Bear in a Trap

Realizing that the first priority was keeping the team together, my initial plans for the first day were scrapped. I asked Bruce to let the team know that I looked forward to meeting them but that I needed a few minutes to find my desk and drop off my coat before joining them. Seeking a way out of the trap I was in, all I could think of was preventing the team from resigning in the next hour.

I entered a conference room with over a dozen people in it. If looks could kill, I would have been dead a dozen times over.

"Good morning, everyone. I was hoping to have some time to learn a bit more about the team and your projects before meeting all of you, but this works too. I met Bruce on the way up, and I learned that I don't have a true picture of the current situation. I'd like to meet with each of you individually today to learn about your projects and anything that I can do to help you with those projects. Until then, can we go through some quick introductions since I'd like to know more about the people I'm going to work with? I'll go first."

After I spoke, Bruce stood up.

"I'm impressed with Marty's BPR experience and his willingness to meet with us before making any decisions. I'm looking forward to meeting with him today and helping him get oriented on the true status of our projects. It's only fair that we give him a chance to get to know us. As you know, I've been leading this team for the past 18 months..."

> *The tension in the room dropped noticeably. If Bruce was willing to give me a chance, so would they. I knew that I had an ally in Bruce and that I already owed him a lot.*

Based on the information you have, decide on your take-over plan. Identify first steps and things that you think need immediate attention. Do some brainstorming, and think about projects you've managed in the past. Jot down some ideas and flesh them out as you go. If you have an experienced colleague, review your plan with them and incorporate their feedback. In short, do the kind of planning you always do for projects, but focus on your plan to assume leadership of the project. Understand that your plan may have to change suddenly, as noted in the "Loaded for Bear" story. It is much better to have a plan in mind, even if it has to change, than to go in with no plan at all. Some managers will want you to discuss your plan with them, helping them gain confidence that you are on the right path.

The plan that you've mapped out may need some time to work. Is there a need for a detailed review before making any changes to the existing plans and schedules? Is the team dispersed geographically so meeting with them will take time? Determine how much time you think you will need to get an accurate assessment of the project and delivery team. Meet with your manager and key stakeholders to get the time to execute your plan, especially if it may affect the delivery of project deliverables. It may take a few weeks before the budget and schedule for a large project can be updated. Set that expectation upfront. Try to avoid scenarios where you have to delay announced target dates for get-well plans, revised schedules, official hand-overs from the outgoing PM, etc. Missing early dates and expectations will undermine confidence in your ability to take over and may result in unwanted micro-management by senior management. For example, in the "Loaded for Bear" situation, I met with my new VP that morning to let her know what had occurred and that I needed a few days to settle the team down before meeting with clients. To make it easier for her to agree to the delays, I noted that the team discussions would also provide the information needed to have productive client meetings.

At this point, it is also important to keep the delivery team committed to the project, especially those members who already seem highly committed. These members are likely critical to the morale and commitment of the larger team, so we need to obtain their support. Unfortunately, they may also be the ones most impacted by the change in PM or the perception that the project is in trouble. Try to quickly identify these key members and meet with them to gauge their feelings, provide reassurance as needed, and get them on your side.

As noted in the "Loaded for Bear" story, this may be challenging. In that case, support from the prior manager was critical, and the team held together through the transition. The initial client meetings were also challenging, but the team noted that the new manager pushed back on the clients and reached agreements that made sense for both the client and the BPR teams. A number of "Red" issues were closed, and pressure on the team eased. This led to a greater commitment by the team, and an acceptable steady state was reached in a few weeks. Don't be afraid to ask members for their trust, support, and commitment for a period long enough for you to show that you deserve it. Most team members will give you that benefit.

We've Never Done This Before—Results

Working closely with an organizational change management firm that was familiar with the culture of the insurance company proved to be a critical success factor. With their help, we were able to tailor our existing tools and methodology in ways that facilitated adoption by the QA team that was formed. Despite a number of challenges that arose, the first project covering 13.5 million lines of code was delivered four weeks early, with zero defects and with estimated labor savings of $250K. The VP and her leads were immediately awarded bonuses, and the team was rapidly expanded as more projects were brought in. The tools and methodology were also provided to other

---

divisions within the company, as they were proving to be more successful than some other approaches that had been tried.

The keys for this success were laid in the first few days of our work with the customer organization. As the days turned into weeks, their leads and then their entire team could see that the joint plan was going off on time, the processes worked, and the tools were effective. The confidence and professionalism of the QA Team calmed the Business Owners and took the pressure off the broader IT Team. Having a plan, and having confidence in that plan, were key contributors to an overall successful outcome.

On 1 January 2000, there were no date-related errors in any system in the organization.

In the next chapter, we'll describe steps to take to learn more details about the project and its current status and provide some tools and checklists to help you do so. Projects are completed by people, so we'll briefly describe some typical team member concerns and emotions when new leadership comes in and how to deal with them. Having a new PM means the team membership has changed, so the team will return to an earlier stage of maturity and performance, which also needs to be addressed. Taking action to support the members and team is an important step in gaining their confidence and trust, which in turn will assist with reviewing artifacts (Chapter 6) and developing updated project plans (Chapter 7). As noted in the "We've Never Done This Before" story, addressing the organizational change and human aspects are just as important as solving the technical and process issues.

Exercise: *Think about taking over an ongoing project. What will your first step be?*

CHAPTER 5

GETTING THE LAY OF THE LAND

"Discovery consists not in seeking *new lands*, but in seeing with *new eyes*."

Marcel Proust

Don't Spook the Herd

The Chief Technology Officer (CTO) and Software Development Manager of a small start-up company showed up at my door Friday morning and asked to talk. As they came into my office, Ashish, the CTO, shut the door. This was a true "dot-com" company, with very few offices with doors and a very open culture. So, I immediately sensed that something unusual was up. Dave, the Software Development Manager, started. "You know that my team has been working 18-hour days and most weekends to get the 3.1 release done on time, right?"

"Yes, and members of my Professional Services Team with the right skills have been helping out. We're also developing the training and installation materials and working with sales and marketing to generate their materials. Do you need more help from my team?"

"No, we think we need your help. CJ tells us that you have a heavy background in QA."

"Guys, I've been trying to hang up that QA baseball hat for a while now. CJ knows what she's doing, and she's got the QA Team. What do you need from me?"

Ashish took over. *"We need someone to do an independent evaluation of the QA Team from the leader through tools and processes. Come back to CJ and to us with any recommendations, including changing out team members. Software testing results have been irregular, the turn-around times seem slow, and there is increasing tension between the QA and development teams. We need an objective assessment, and you're here."*

"How soon do you need the results?"

"End of day today would be good, but we can give you the weekend. We can't let this situation get worse." Ashish flashed his winning smile, providing the illusion that I had a choice in the matter.

"You're the boss. Do CJ and the QA Team know what's coming?"

"CJ does, but you'll need to work out communications with her team. You were a consultant; you should be good at that." More salesmanship from Ashish.

"OK, but I'm also going to interview the key stakeholders and participants in the process, which include you two and members of your development team. I'll provide a list of everyone I need to speak with and the documentation that I need."

"Don't get too formal; we don't want to spook the herd. Just do what you need to do to get us an answer first thing Monday morning or earlier." Ashish and Dave were no longer smiling. They hadn't understood the effort it would take to do this right, but it needed to be done.

Initial Steps—Interviews

Don't spook the herd is a good thought to keep in mind as you start researching the team and current status to determine the lay of the land. Whether you are coming in as the new PM or doing a project review, team members are likely to have concerns about what will happen to them, if their performance is being evaluated, and even if the project will be canceled. Regardless of the background information you may have at this point, no one benefits from members getting anxious.

One approach is to have a brief kick-off meeting with the team. The purpose is to introduce the new PM or the member(s) conducting the project review. Ideally, the next management level up, or even higher, should start the meeting. This should be the Sponsor, Business Owner, or another executive that made the decision to bring in the new PM. The goal is to clearly and unemotionally describe the change being made and perhaps a key reason or two behind the change. This is not the time to get into a debate or to question the decisions that have been made but to ensure that the key stakeholders and team members have the same information about the change (or the review). During the meeting, the new PM should describe the initial plan, which can be as simple as "keep doing what you are doing for now." Note that the PM is going to meet with key stakeholders and members individually in small groups, providing the meeting schedule is available at this point. Emphasize that the intent is to determine how things are going from their point of view and to gather their suggestions on how to improve project performance.

Why meet with members one-on-one? First, we want them to feel comfortable and safe so that we can have an honest discussion. Second, we are going to have different questions for each stakeholder and team, tailored to their responsibilities and connection to the project (see the Appendix and online resources for sample tailored questionnaires). Third, we want to ensure we get multiple points of view. There always tend to be some people in group meetings who speak more than others. The loudest voice may not be the most informed voice, and we need to ensure that we get information from the introverts as well as the extroverts. This can be especially crucial with technical people who tend to be more introverted and reticent than people in sales and marketing, for example. Finally, there may be cultural issues with global teams where members only feel free to present their views in a one-on-one setting. Providing this opportunity demonstrates that they are valued members of the team, and their inputs are desired. Meeting like this can also help overcome language issues that may occur, especially for members who may not be comfortable in the primary language being used by the project team.

Key stakeholders and team members should be interviewed about the project, their roles, any issues that they see, concerns they may have, and suggestions for improvements. Key members to interview are shown in Table 5-1 in recommended progression order.

Table 5-1: Project Members to Interview (In Recommended Order)

- Sponsor
- Business Owner
- Manager Owning Project Delivery
- Project Management Office (PMO) liaison for the project
- Agile/Scrum Coach (if applicable)
- Current PM (if available, even if they have moved to another project or organization)
- Scrum Master (if applicable)
- Finance/Budget Manager
- Customer/Client Team Managers (if applicable), including Contract or Procurement Manager for the project
- Project Team Members, starting with team leads
- Customer/Client Team Members on the Project Team (if applicable)

Why start at the top? It is usually best to start at the top since that is often where the need or desire to change PMs originates. They should also be committed to the success of the project, and we need to know what their definition of success (or definition of done) is since it will frame discussions with other stakeholders and team members. There is also a danger in starting at this level. Be careful not to prejudge members based on information gathered at this level and these early stages. There are likely to be assumptions and opinions that do not have a factual basis, and there may be politics in play. Note any issues or concerns about members or teams for further review, but do not make judgments or promise actions at this point. Make sure you meet with the parties involved and have factual information first.

With large teams, you won't be able to meet with each member, and that's OK. Focus on the managers and leads that you will work with directly. If you are concerned that there may be more to the story than you are getting from the leads, meet with a sample of the next level down and determine if there really is a disconnect between the messages that you are hearing. Before meeting with members, let them know if there are documents or specific data that you want to discuss so they can be prepared. At this stage, there may not be time to go into detailed reviews of schedules, budgets, invoices, quality reports, etc. If this is the case, set the groundwork to review them later with the appropriate team or individuals.

Some of the key questions that we need to ask at this point are listed below. These are just a starting point. Questions specific to the project, current situation, and the role of the member being interviewed should be developed beforehand. A good practice is to write the questions out ahead of the interview to be used as an interview guide and to aid in keeping the discussion on track. It can also be formatted to support taking notes. Telling the person being interviewed that you are going to take notes to help you remember what was discussed is a common courtesy and should reduce their anxiety. Ideally, you should be able to keep individual responses confidential, and if so, tell that to the members being interviewed. Don't violate this promise without going back to the member involved first, or you will lose credibility and create a trust issue that will endure long after this stage of the transition.

During meetings and interviews, be sure to include a mix of question types. An open-ended question encourages someone to talk since there isn't a simple yes/no type of answer. One can usually get more information from an open-ended question, which is why the list below has so many of them. Some people may not respond well to open-ended questions, especially if they are not comfortable with the person asking the questions. In this case, a closed question, which has a single answer, may be best to start with. While closed questions do not encourage further explanation, they do provide clear answers that may provide the opportunity to explore further with open-ended questions.

For example:

"Do you think the project will be completed on time?"

"No."

Following that with "Why do you think the project will not be completed on time?" encourages the person to explain. With open-ended questions, people will often mention things that you wouldn't have thought to ask about with closed questions. Closed questions come from your existing knowledge and may limit the discussion within the paradigm that you have already formed in your mind, while open-ended questions can explore areas that you don't necessarily know about or haven't considered.

**Table 5-2: Key Questions to Ask to Assess
the Current Project Situation**

1   Please describe your role in the project.
2   What is the current status of the project?
3   What does success look like?
4   Why is it important that this project be successful?
5   If it is not on track, what caused it to go off track?
6   What should be done to keep it on track or get
    it back on track (the Silver Bullet question)?
7   Do you have the resources you need?
8   What is the right mix of resources to get back on track?

---

9   Is there someone we should get for the team
      to improve our chance of success?
10   What can you do to help this project succeed?
11   What do you need from me to help this project succeed?
12   Do you have any other concerns about this project?
13   Will you work with me to help this project succeed?
14   Do you have any questions for me?

Financial Situation *(Discuss with members handling finances.)*
15   Are there financial challenges? If so, is a joint
      approach possible (when dealing with a contract)?
16   Is there a problem (i.e., accounts receivable, invoices
      being refused or delayed, unfunded changes)?
17   Will the customer and/or supplier commit to
      sharing the cost of changes in dispute?
18   Will all parties put "skin in the game"?
19   What is each executive stakeholder willing
      to commit to fixing the project?

Exercise: What other questions should you ask?

As the discussions continue with different members, look for similar issues or suggestions that come up. These may include project processes or actions to start, stop, or continue to do to get and keep the project on a successful track. While it is too early to make any decisions or commitments on what you will do, note these suggestions for further consideration as part of the replanning effort. As noted in Chapter 7, some may need more urgent action than others, but be wary of making any promises to stakeholders before you have a complete picture. Each stakeholder has their own point of view and biases, which also need to be considered as we place their comments in context.

The goal at this point is to quickly assess the true status of the project. Expand your understanding of the project and current status regarding scope, schedule, budget, and quality, as well as gauge the morale of the team. Although there is likely to be disagreement over the true status of the project overall, key deliverables, or progress on some items, a picture should start to emerge. As the picture evolves, initial transition plans may need to change, but be cautious about taking any action before completing the initial round of interviews. Schedule follow-up interviews, document reviews, and working groups as indicated by the information being uncovered during the interviews. Finally, do not forget that these interviews are also a great chance to build relationships with the people and teams that you are going to work with. Do not turn these into grilling sessions or come across as judgmental or critical. There isn't enough information at this point to draw these conclusions.

These interviews may reveal the need to take quick action on some issues. For example, can a delivery date be met? Does the team need critical resources that have not been available? Are there contractual, legal, or HR issues that demand immediate action? Be careful before taking action. Determine who else may need to be involved in making key decisions and get them involved. Make sure the Sponsor, Business Owner, and other key stakeholders are consulted and get their support before taking action.

Another danger is being pressured to make commitments to key stakeholders or even team members. For example, promising to meet key delivery dates, staying within a specified budget target, stop requiring the team to work on the weekend, etc. It is OK to indicate that you understand the desired goal and indicate that you need to look into it further and gather more information before making any promises. Human nature means that when we discuss a problem or concern with someone, we expect them to solve the problem. As the incoming PM, we need to avoid leaving that impression. Be clear that you are documenting the issue or concern, that you will investigate it further to see what can be done, but that you cannot promise to resolve it at this point in time.

During these discussions, be alert for signs that the true objectives of the project may not be understood throughout the team. Large, complex projects tend to develop their own motivations and objectives that may no longer correspond with the original goals of the project or match the needs of the end-users or other stakeholders. Listen carefully to the answers to the questions "What does success look like?" and "Why is it important that this project be successful?" Do the answers align with what is in the project charter? Do they match the answers from the project Sponsor and Business Owner? If not, this issue needs to be addressed quickly. As we learned in the "Toy Story" example, projects can inadvertently drift away from their intended objectives and scope, essentially taking on a life of their own. In these cases, the true objectives may need to be recommunicated to the team or have the objectives updated to match current sponsor and stakeholder goals, or end the project and start a new project at the business case step.

There may also be cases where the current goals are no longer achievable, as shown in the "Toy Story" example. If the project is not going to be terminated, work needs to be done with the Sponsor, Business Owner, and Executive Steering committee (ESC) to adjust the goals to something that is achievable within the boundaries defined for the project. Teams are disheartened when they see the project goals as unrealistic, and this frustration makes it even harder to achieve good results. On the other hand, adjusting the team goals to something that can realistically be achieved can remotivate the team and provide the energy needed to successfully complete the revised project.

As we are gathering information on the project, we need to be alert to biases that can influence what others are telling us and the conclusions that we draw from what we hear and read. Biases are natural; they provide shortcuts to understanding what is going on and what actions we should take. Biases can also lead us down the wrong path, so we need to be sensitive to their presence and continually ask ourselves at this point in the process—are these real facts, or are they projections based on biases? Some of the biases that we may fall prey to while scoping out a project we are taking over can include:

- *Confirmation Bias* – The tendency to seek out, believe, and give more weight to evidence that confirms opinions that we already hold, such as the prior schedule was poorly thought out. Repeatedly ask yourself if there is other information that can lead to different conclusions and if you have examined all the relevant evidence.

- *Spillover Bias* – Allowing positive or negative impressions from one area to influence another area. For example, weighing the information from a friendly interviewee more heavily than information from a less friendly individual. Are you checking the information from friendly or authoritative sources the same way you are checking information from other sources?

- *Stereotyping* – Assuming that certain traits and abilities belong to specific groups (e.g., all QA members are going to have negative opinions about product quality, or they are going to want to do more testing).

- *Availability Bias* – Giving more weight to the information that is easily available instead of looking for objective data that may be more difficult to obtain. We'll address this in more detail in the next chapter and when we discuss metrics.

- *Recent Event Bias* – Focusing on the events that have happened most recently rather than putting them in the context of the entire project. For example, emphasizing a failed test event instead of assessing the overall quality of the application. If an application passed prior system tests but failed a performance test, is the entire design bad?

- *Group Think* – The tendency to go with the majority opinion or to conform to expected results instead of relying upon facts to develop independent opinions and options. This can be particularly challenging when new to a project and receiving consistent opinions from executives—do the facts support those opinions?

- *My Group Bias* – It is easier to believe and support the opinions and views of members of our own group. For example, if the departing PM says that the ESC is difficult to work with, we are likely to hold that view when planning and conducting ESC meetings. This is difficult to overcome but continuing to seek facts and form our own opinions is a way to counteract this bias.

- *Loss Aversion* – There is a tendency to avoid risk and future losses by continuing the current situation (e.g., continuing a project rather than acknowledging the need to terminate it). This often appears as a reluctance to adjust scope or schedule with a challenged project and pushing the team to hit the original delivery date. During interviews, this often shows up as "we can still meet the deadline if …" This can be a very difficult bias for the incoming PM to address with key executives.

At this point, there is a clear divergence between scenarios where a new PM is taking over an ongoing project and where a manager or team is reviewing a project that may be challenged to determine its true status. While the new PM is clearly expected to take charge and get the project completed to meet specific goals, the review team is more focused on determining the true status of the project and if it is on track to be successful. The results of the review may or may not result in a change in the project manager or changes to project plans.

Although the steps described, the questions to ask, and the documents to be reviewed are very similar, there will be a different atmosphere and tone with a project review. In particular, it is likely for the project team to be more reticent with the review team, so the true information may be more difficult to determine. In addition, the review team rarely has the power to modify project objectives and plans, though that may change later. The review team is making recommendations, not decisions on changes. There are some additional considerations required during a project review as well, including assessing the current and future performance of the existing PM and if the project should be continued.

The Tale of Slim & Jim

It seems that the cattle drive had finally reached its destination and cowboys Slim and Jim headed into town with their pay, looking for a good time. Well, they had that good time and became separated. Jim realized he'd had too much to drink and headed back to the campsite to sleep it off. As Jim walked down the trail through a cactus patch, he heard a commotion. Knowing that bandits often robbed drunken cowboys, Jim pulled his six-shooter and called out, "Show yourself, or I'll shoot!"

"Jim, is that you?" came the unsteady reply.

"Slim, is that you?" responded Jim, relieved that it wasn't a bandit.

"Yes, it's me," called Slim as he emerged from behind a cactus, the moonlight showing that he was wearing nothing except his red long johns.

"Slim, what are you doing in a cactus patch after midnight, wearing your long johns?" queried Jim, his puzzlement coming through clearly.

"Well, Jim, I don't rightly recollect, but I do recollect thinking it was a good idea at the time."

Just as Slim found himself in a spot of bother, many people and teams make reasonable, thoughtful decisions as they go that don't work out over time. They may even be the best decisions available at the time, but things can change and often do. So, later on, with better information and perhaps with hindsight, those decisions are questioned and may need to be changed. This doesn't mean that the people responsible for making the decisions were wrong or foolish. It just means that different decisions need to be made now based on the current circumstances.

As project managers, we have a tendency to focus on things that are easy to predict, measure, and adjust, such as schedules, budgets, requirements, and resources. At this stage, it is very important to remember the people aspect of the team that we are joining. Regardless of the current state of the project, there is an existing team that has gone through at least some of the stages of team building. Bringing in a new "sheriff" changes the existing team dynamics, which adds stress to the team. This stress may be minor and not impact team performance, or it could be significant, perhaps bringing the stress level of an already overworked and under pressure team to an unsustainable level.

We need to assess the situation as we conduct our initial interviews and investigation, looking for signs of stress or dissatisfaction as we go. Sometimes it is better to simply ask team leads and members how they feel. Listen carefully and with empathy. There is often management pressure to get projects back on track, meet deadlines that were previously set, or fulfill commitments to key stakeholders and customers. Resisting this pressure is difficult, but if the team is broken, even more time will be lost. Many project management textbooks assume that everyone is professional and that they will always do what is required to make the project successful. While members want to do a good job and be successful, they also have to believe that positive outcomes are possible and that there are benefits to them. Member motivation cannot be ignored! We'll briefly cover two management models that apply in these situations that can help you understand what is going on and that you can use to explain to management why time spent focusing on team dynamics and member motivation is not just a good idea; it is a necessity.

Project Organization Models

Projects can use many different organizational models depending upon the goals of the project, the industry, the alignment of the performing organization, the selected delivery methodology, and many other factors. The responsibilities and authority of the PM will vary along with the organization model, though it is important to emphasize that PM authority should be aligned with the PM's responsibilities. As noted in Chapter 3, ensuring the alignment of PM responsibilities and authority should be done as early as possible, with any issues identified for resolution as part of the PM taking over the project. While we will not go into project organizations in detail, we have presented a few different models below, along with very brief descriptions of the key strengths and weaknesses of each model. Please refer to the Project Management Body of Knowledge (PMBOK) from the Project Management Institute (PMI) and similar books for more detailed descriptions of project organizations. At this stage, the incoming PM should focus on understanding the model that is in place and determining if any organizational changes are going to be needed to better align the organization with the characteristics of the project.

As shown earlier, the simplest project organization may be created for a specific project and dissolved upon completion. In this case, the project sponsor decides to establish a project to accomplish a specific goal—build a house, create a phone app, create a new consumer product, etc. The triple constraints are established, preferably after a PM is assigned, but usually, the initial charter or business case is developed to a certain level before the desired PM capabilities are established, and a PM is found. There are many variations of this simple organization, with the position names and descriptions varying with the delivery methodology, the industry, and organizational preferences. However, the basic responsibilities are consistent with what we describe throughout this book. The project sponsor provides the budget for the project, approves the charter, and is the one expecting to get specific benefits from the completed project. The project sponsor is usually supported by an Executive Steering Committee (ESC) composed of senior managers or representatives from impacted stakeholders. In this simple organization, the PM reports directly to the project sponsor, though there are usually intermediaries in most organizations.

Figure 5-1: Basic Project Organization

Some of the more complex project organizations involve one or more vendor teams delivering to a customer organization. A possible project organization is shown in Figure 5-2, which includes a number of the roles that we cover in this book. A key success factor for this organization is maintaining relationships at each level of delivery. For example, the vendor account manager is probably the one who negotiated the contract with the project sponsor in the customer organization. Although they should both be part of the ESC, maintaining direct communications throughout the project is important to maintain alignment and to quickly communicate any issues or concerns that arise. Similarly, the customer business owner will work with the vendor project director, providing a more detailed level of oversight and coordination over the project.

Figure 5-2: Possible Vendor Project Organization

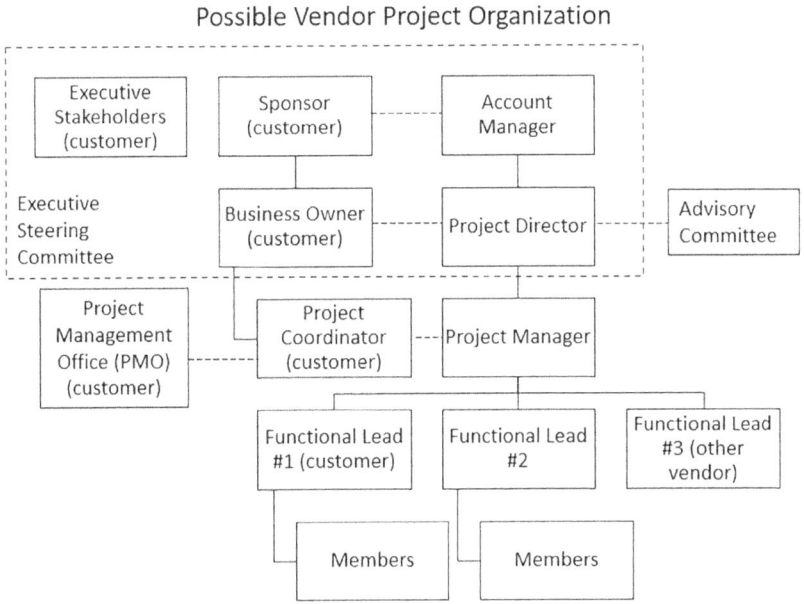

Note that there is only one PM. Although many customers will set up a PM in parallel with the vendor PM that is responsible for the success of the project (or vice-versa), we recommend against this. There should be only one PM with commensurate authority and responsibility. The PM is supported by the project coordinator, as well as the functional leads and team members. The customer PMO will usually work via the project coordinator, who is more familiar with the customer's methodology, budgeting, reporting, and other processes. This should keep the project aligned with these processes while reducing the effort for the PM to learn the details of these processes. If the project is bringing in new technology or equipment to the customer organization, it is usually beneficial to establish a technical advisory committee to assist with technical decisions and issues that may arise. If the PM or other members of the delivery team need additional training, coaching, or support, this can also be arranged with the advisory committee.

The Executive Steering Committee (ESC) shown in Figure 5-2 is a good example of how they can be set up for long-term success. In addition to the expected members (Sponsor, Business Owner, Account Manager, and Project Director), other impacted key executives from the customer organization are included. For example, if the project was implementing a new insurance claims system, the Sponsor is likely to be the CIO, but the VP of Claims and the VP of Agent Management will be very involved in how the system is implemented and how it will impact their organizations and stakeholders. Including them in the ESC keeps them informed and involved, along with providing them a formal role in making key decisions. The ESC can also call in members of the advisory team or PMO as desired. Note that the PM and Project Coordinator are not part of the ESC, though they should be at all regular ESC status meetings. Usually, they do not get a "vote" on decisions that go to the ESC level, and the ESC may decide to discuss some sensitive matters without the PM or project coordinator being present.

As noted earlier, many organizations are set up in a "matrix" where delivery team members are assigned to a manager other than the PM. The most common form is shown in Figure 5-3. People are assigned to a manager aligned with their primary function, such as software developers. That manager is responsible for the hiring, development, management, and promotion of their members, with the manager usually having many years of experience in that function. In this way, each group has common KSAs and forms a community of interest around their key function. Senior members can mentor junior members, and standard expectations can be established for each skill or salary level. As projects are created, the PM works with these functional or "resource" managers to obtain the right members for the delivery team. This can sometimes be a problem when resource managers assign someone that is available to the project, not the person with the right skill set. Remember, availability is *not* a skillset!

Figure 5-3: Projects in a Matrix Organization

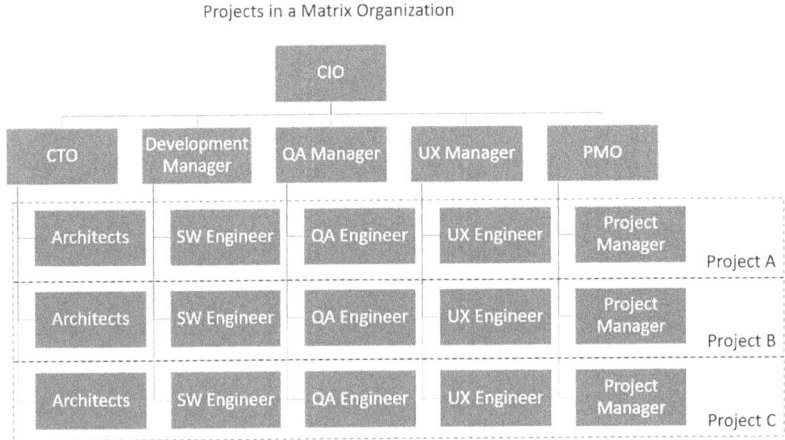

Projects in a Matrix Organization

Another issue that can arise with matrix organizations is the limited ability of the PM to reward or promote team members. The functional manager controls pay, bonuses, educational opportunities, project assignments, and salary. Although the PM should have an input into performance reviews and treatment of their team members, they usually do not. This makes it more challenging for the PM to motivate and reward members and can negatively affect member commitment to the team. Matrix organizations also make it more likely that team assignments will change, which also impacts project progress and performance. Some organizations have multiple-dimension matrices, which can further erode project team loyalty and performance.

I worked at a company that had a nine-dimensional matrix organization. No exaggeration, managers from nine different organizations within the company could impact my team, my budget, and the other resources needed to deliver the project. Only by carefully drawing out the project organization chart and including the managers that controlled different aspects of the project was I able to create a stakeholder map and communication plan that allowed us to move forward with confidence. With luck, you will not run into anything as bizarre, but be sure to carefully identify the organization and managers that exist around the project to ensure you understand the challenges that you may face.

This was a very cursory review of some different project management organizations. As noted earlier, please refer to the PMBOK and other management books for more information on different organizational approaches, along with their strengths and weaknesses. If you are joining a project within your own organization, assessing the project structure and suitability to meet the project objectives may be easy. If you are new to the organization, or if a unique structure has been set up just for this project, assessing its suitability for the project will be more difficult. Do not hesitate to seek help to understand the organization, along with the roles and responsibilities of key stakeholders. Ideally, there should be organizational charts, communication plans, and a stakeholder plan to provide all the needed information. If so, try to confirm their contents as you go, as everything changes with time. If these items do not exist, work with your team and management to build them as you go. As noted in Chapters 8 through 10, this information is vital to effectively updating and executing your plans.

If you note potential issues with the current structure, bring your concerns and improvement suggestions to the ESC and see what accommodations can be made. In some cases, there may be opportunities to put special rules in place for your project. For example, for a "save the company" project, the CIO mandated that no member of the project team could be given an additional assignment or removed from the project without their approval. This dramatically reduced the staffing churn that had occurred in the first six weeks of the project. This mandate was in response to a specific issue raised in the Risks and Issues Log and discussed in a project review with the CIO and PMO. Raising the issue objectively, with supporting facts, made getting the desired result much easier. This is much easier to do when the PM has a good understanding of both the project team and broader organization, as well as the benefits and drawbacks of different organization models. There is a large body of literature covering the management of organizations and organizational behavior available, as well as the material available in the PMBOK and PM textbooks. Getting familiar with this information is worth the time invested by any PM.

Stages of Team Development

Bruce Tuckman was an American Psychological Researcher in the field of group dynamics and organizational behavior. In 1965, his research and observations led him to propose that there are four stages of team development: Forming, Storming, Norming, and Performing. A fifth stage, Adjourning, was added later (1977),[2] which we'll cover in Chapter 12. At this point, we need to focus on the first four stages. Essentially, whether they are conscious of it or not, groups of people working together for a common purpose (teams) develop relationships and assume roles within the team that they are comfortable with and which leads to a feeling that the team is working effectively towards the common purpose. It is possible for teams to become stuck at a development stage that is not productive or to return to a less productive stage when the team is subject to stress or changes. It is also possible for a team leader to facilitate moving the team to a higher development stage that is better at accomplishing the purpose of the team.

The first stage is FORMING, which is the process of putting the team together, with members learning about each other and seeking to determine their roles within the team. Team members may feel ambiguous about the team and their membership in it. Some may avoid conflict due to a need to be accepted by the team. Team members may look for a team leader to emerge and provide direction and guidance. This leader may not be the manager assigned to lead the team by the organization. The members need to develop a common understanding of team goals and begin to release personal or organizational goals that may be in conflict with the team objective. Having the team formally define goals, create ground rules for the team, and define standards of behavior can help a team move through this phase more rapidly.

As team members get more comfortable with each other, they begin to voice their opinions and feel it is safe to disagree, which we call the STORMING stage. There may be shifts in roles and power within the team. Some members may have communication or work styles that

---

[2]   Stephen P. Robbins and Mary Coulter, *Management*, 11th ed., Pearson, New York, 2012 (pp. 346–348); Don Hellriegel and John W. Slocum, Jr., *Organizational Behavior*, 11th ed., Thomson-Southwestern, Mason, OH, 2007 (pp. 269–272).

conflict with others, and this can lead to disagreements and arguments. Members may react to these disagreements in different ways. If there is a strong leader who has been accepted at this stage, they can help members work through these disagreements by establishing ways to handle conflicts and update team behavior guidelines. There may be personality clashes and trust issues that need to be resolved. The key is to have the team work through these issues so that members trust each other and feel that future issues can be resolved fairly in a manner that keeps the team working together.

By resolving disagreements and establishing revised norms for the group, the team is more tightly bonded. This, in turn, leads to more focus on the tasks assigned to the group and an established way of completing those tasks. The NORMING stage is where team members are comfortable with each other, working arrangements are understood, either implicitly or explicitly, and there is little disruption within the team. Members have roles within the team that they accept, and other members implicitly recognize those roles. For example, Suzy is good about keeping meetings running on time, while Tom takes good notes and distributes minutes after the meetings. There is a risk that teams may fail to progress beyond this stage, perhaps due to a fear of conflict or a loss of focus on the external goals assigned to the team.

Now the team enters the most beneficial stage from a project perspective—PERFORMING. The team focuses on the common goals of the team, which should be the same as project goals. Members are knowledgeable, working relationships are established and optimized, and members can work together or separately as needed to accomplish team tasks. The team can make decisions on its own and can handle task changes or issues internally. Very little external management is required. This is the target stage for teams, but some teams never get here. Leadership intervention and support may be required, and this may push a team back to the Storming stage so they can ultimately progress to Performing at the level desired by the broader organization.

We noted earlier that changing the Project Manager is altering the team. This will move the team back to the Forming Stage and is likely to impact team performance, at least in the short term. By recognizing this and working with the team to go through the Storming and Norming Phases quickly to return to the Performing Phase, we can minimize the negative impacts of the change. There are a number of team-building exercises, guides, and programs that can assist with this if you need more support in this area.

Don't Ignore Emotions

When the composition of a project team changes, and when projects are seen to be challenged, team members are affected emotionally and psychologically. In addition to the impacts on team unity and performance, which we just covered, individual impacts also occur. A useful model to help understand and deal with the emotions that team members and potentially external stakeholders are going through is Abraham Maslow's Hierarchy of Needs.[3] First postulated in 1943 and updated over the years, we can divide human needs into five groups or levels. These are typically shown as a pyramid with these five levels, as shown below.

---

[3] Stephen P. Robbins and Timothy A. Judge, *Organizational Behavior*, 15th ed., Pearson, New York, 2003 (pp. 203–204); Stephen P. Robbins and Mary Coulter, *Management*, 11th ed., Pearson, New York, 2012 (pp. 431–432); Don Hellriegel and John W. Slocum, Jr., *Organizational Behavior*, 11th ed., Thomson-Southwestern, Mason, OH, 2007 (pp. 123–125); Rodney C. Vandeveer and Michael L. Menefee, *Human Behavior in Organizations*, Pearson-Prentice Hall, Upper Saddle River, NJ, 2006 (pp. 43–44).

Figure 5-4: Maslow's Hierarchy of Needs

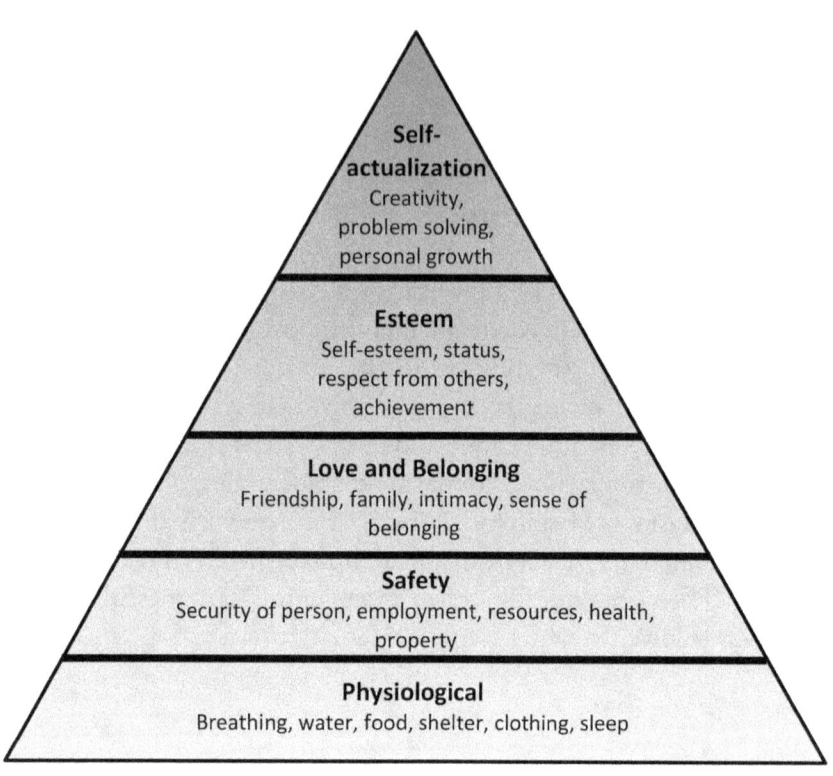

Human beings start at the bottom level. If these physiological needs are not met, it will be difficult, if not impossible, for them to focus on other needs. For example, if someone is starving, their primary need is food, so they are motivated and focused on getting food. They are willing to compromise a higher-level need in order to satisfy their current primary need, for example, going on a hunt for food, even though that may be unsafe. As each need is met, and this may mean partially met (satisfied, not fulfilled, or maximized), humans focus on the next level. From a project team view, peak performance is at the top, Self-Actualization. Ideally, we would like to have all project team members healthy, happy, and performing at this top level where they are most productive.

When there is a change to team structure, including bringing in a new Project Manager, or if there is sudden management involvement due to perceived project issues, members are likely to go back down to lower levels of the pyramid. If the prior PM was dismissed from the organization, that is likely to push team members to the Safety level, as they become worried about their own employment and future prospects within the organization. These feelings must be recognized and addressed. Rapidly bringing members back up the pyramid to a level where they can focus on performing on the project and not on their own job security is critical. There are a number of approaches that can be taken, both at the individual and team levels. Members should be given an opportunity to discuss their concerns in the one-on-one interviews being conducted at this stage, and it may be beneficial to address project team and job security issues at an early team meeting. Working with an experienced Organizational Change Management (OCM) or Human Resources (HR) professional should help in developing an appropriate plan to bring team members back up to the top of the pyramid of needs.

If the project has been challenged, especially if the prior PM was removed for project or personal performance reasons, communicating that there is going to be a blame-free restart should reassure team members. Don't make promises that you can't keep, so make sure to discuss the team morale impacts with management first. Using Maslow's model often helps with this discussion and can help management understand the psychological impacts of the current situation. Get a commitment to let the PM control project personnel assignments, if possible, then meet with the members. Often, there will be a few key members who are the most impacted by the departure of the previous PM or other project members. Putting them at ease first should calm the concerns of the rest of the team and provide the time needed to meet with the others. In most cases, it is better to limit or eliminate contact between the delivery team and the departing PM. We do not want to stretch out the departure and extend the period of time that it weighs on the minds of the team. If the departing PM has a negative attitude about their replacement, we need to limit this being communicated to the team. Most PMs are professionals, so having a frank one-on-one discussion about your concerns or any issues regarding their communications with the team usually solves these issues.

Unfortunately, there are going to be situations where the incoming PM will always be seen as the enemy, especially if the prior PM is fired or if the new PM is from outside the organization. This will make things more difficult for the incoming PM and will likely make the activities described in Chapters 6 and 7 harder to accomplish. While difficult, the challenges will have to be navigated, even if the atmosphere is unpleasant. Continue to be fair and professional, and the situation should improve with time. While the PM needs to lead the project team and needs their support in getting the project done, being their friend is not a requirement for project success. Do the best that you can under the circumstances, and move on when the project is completed or handed off to another PM once it is stable. Surprisingly, the third PM is often more readily accepted than the PM that replaced the one who started the project.

> **Exercise:** Have you ever had a new manager assigned mid-project—how did you feel? What helped or would have helped you accept the new manager?

Don't Spook the Herd—Results

Keeping with the informal culture of the organization, CJ and I met with her team to explain that we were doing a review to see if we could streamline processes and if we needed any additional QA tools. CJ sat in on the interviews with her team members since this was a learning opportunity for her as well. Although she had plenty of software testing experience, she had always worked within a defined methodology and tool set.

As expected, there was a combination of small issues leading to the delays. A few configuration changes to the test suite, more discipline in test planning and reporting, and holding daily test meetings with a defined agenda solved most of the problems. Discussions with the Development Team focused on seeing test results as helpful information they needed, not a criticism of their work. This had been an issue because many of the developers were right out of college and had never had their code tested by other people before. We set up training sessions to improve the skills of members on both teams and to communicate the revised QA methodology. Within three weeks, things were running smoothly, and what my PM tracking the project had forecast as a six-week schedule slip was reduced to just two weeks. The biggest benefit was improved cooperation and communication between the QA and Development Teams. A wall had come down, and they were working very closely together, greatly speeding things up.

Not all projects will have challenges and solutions as apparent as in the story above. Some will give the appearance of running smoothly, while others will have multiple overlapping challenges. Diagnosing the true status of the project and adjusting plans to address those challenges and get the project to a successful conclusion will take additional time and effort. Now that we've covered the initial plans for taking over a project and project team, we need to identify the information that we need to obtain quickly and use in updating project plans and commitments to reflect current circumstances and capabilities. We'll go over this in Chapter 6.

CHAPTER 6

CONDUCTING UNBIASED RESEARCH

> **"Do your own research. Enlighten yourself. It's better to know than to assume."**
>
> Scottie Waves

In addition to interviewing project team members and key stakeholders, the incoming PM also needs to review other project information, usually contained in artifacts and deliverables. In this chapter, we will briefly review some of the key documents to be reviewed, what to look for, and how they support the replanning step covered in Chapter 7. The number and type of planning documents will vary widely based on the industry, type of project, project methodology, current phase of the project, etc., so this list is not going to be overly detailed or exhaustive. The incoming PM or project review team should be familiar enough with the industry, organization, and methodology to know what items to look for and how to interpret them. Referring to organization methodology or delivery materials, potentially including training materials as needed may also be required. As mentioned before, we assume that the incoming PM (or reviewers) are experienced in the PM role in their industry. If this is not the case, then include time in the plans for this phase for the PM to obtain additional expertise from others and to learn more about the specific aspects of the industry, organization, delivery methodology, and project. Do not be afraid to ask questions and do some research. No one is expected to know everything, especially if new to the organization.

Can We Meet the Deadline?

Our company had taken on a large, complicated project to implement a new insurance platform that would comply with new market opportunities and regulations that were coming into effect in less than two years. The changes would significantly impact the insurance business, from policy types and pricing to services offered and how supporting organizations would operate. The customer was also merging two large existing organizations into a new entity focused on the future insurance market. Three months into the project, our team was struggling and indicated their status as yellow. A project review team was formed to meet with the joint delivery team to determine what the issues were, make recommendations to resolve these issues, and provide an assessment of the joint team's ability to meet the current deadline. Results were to be reported to both management teams (customer and contractor).

The review team was given a week to complete the review and provide a draft report, with a final report due within 10 days. This was only possible because the contractor's delivery team was following an established methodology that had been tailored for the specifics of the contract, and the review team had an established project review process. This made notifying the delivery team of the review, requesting artifacts, and setting up interviews much easier since there were existing tools and templates to use for the review and to compare the artifacts against. In addition, the review team made sure to include insurance industry experts that were familiar with the upcoming regulatory changes. Regardless of these preparations, accurately assessing the true status of an ongoing project under these circumstances would be challenging.

Any sheriff that is new to a town knows that they need to learn the territory. The time and effort that this will take are going to vary with the situation. If the incoming PM is already part of the organization and is familiar with the industry, delivery methodology, and organization itself, things will go easier and faster. If the PM is coming from outside the delivery organization and has to learn about the industry, business processes, delivery methodology, etc., it will take longer to learn the territory. The number, availability, format, state of completion, and accuracy of the artifacts also significantly impact the time and effort needed to understand the true status of the project. As we go through a number of key artifacts that should be reviewed and assessed, there are some overarching considerations, which are covered in the next section.

As you go through the review, look for key leverage points. These are places where some quick work can provide beneficial results disproportionate to the effort required, hence "leverage." For example, posting a consolidated schedule with key milestones and team assignments where everyone can see it may improve coordination across teams and completing tasks on time. Celebrating accomplishments with a small ceremony may improve team morale and demonstrate that the project is making progress. Properly conducted Sprint Retrospectives may significantly reduce quality issues. There may be key artifacts that can have a broad impact if they are updated and distributed. The team may have a few hidden stars who can improve team performance if given the opportunity. Or there may be members who are slowing progress or holding the team back. Consider the changes needed, and be prepared to make some changes that can improve team performance and accelerate the project.

General Questions to Consider When Reviewing Artifacts

Are all the artifacts that should be available at this stage of the project actually available? If the project is proceeding on schedule, the artifacts required by the delivery methodology should be available and in an appropriate state of completion. For example, if in the Design Phase of a waterfall project, the Project Charter, Project Plan, Business Requirements, Functional Requirements, and Non-Functional Requirements should all be complete. If key artifacts are not available, are still in draft form, or have been intentionally skipped, these are all warning signs.

Are the artifacts complete? Are there a lot of TBDs? Incomplete artifacts, which include artifacts with items and facts shown as "To Be Determined" (TBD), can indicate challenges in making decisions and getting stakeholder agreement, as well as indicating schedule issues. There can be several different causes for these issues in artifacts, so identifying the root cause and determining if it can be fixed needs to be done as early as possible in the review process. For example, in the "Can We Meet the Deadline?" project, the two customer organizations had very different views of what the future business process should be. An inability to resolve these differences led to many requirements, screen layouts, and workflows having TBDs. These made it difficult for the team to not only complete the requirements phase but also impacted other phases such as design and test planning.

Are the artifacts approved? An artifact that is complete but has not been approved by the required stakeholder or Business Owner is also a problem. Research is needed to determine why it has not been approved. It may be a sign of an overloaded Business Owner or stakeholders unable to agree on decisions that need to be made. There may also be deeper political or contractual issues going on. The most dangerous situation is where a client or customer withholds final approval so they can continue to make changes without having to go through the change management process and potentially pay for changes. When reviewing approved artifacts, check to see if they have been updated to reflect currently approved changes. Changes are likely to occur as a project proceeds, regardless of the methodology being used. If proper change management procedures are being followed, approved changes should impact at least some of the artifacts that have already been approved. This should be reflected in the change log within the artifact. Yes, this does apply to Agile methodologies as well, since supporting documentation should be done as part of each sprint and should be updated with subsequent sprints. There should also be overarching artifacts that will change as the Agile project proceeds.

Regardless of the industry, technology, or methodology involved, do the artifacts show that the delivery team is following the methodology and templates applicable to this project? If not, why not? Were these deviations approved by the correct stakeholders? Do the artifacts provide evidence that the delivery team understands the methodology and associated artifacts that they are using? The answers to these questions should either build confidence in the current team or indicate issues that will need to be addressed in recovery plans. The answers can also lead to additional conversations with delivery team members and stakeholders about the appropriateness of the methodology and templates for the project. Perhaps a different methodology would be better suited to the project.

Are the artifacts accurate? Do the artifacts properly reflect the objectives and requirements of the project? Do they appear to be internally consistent? For example, are there conflicting requirements within the Business Requirements document? Are they consistent with other artifacts? For example, do the Functional Requirements tie back to the Business Requirements? Can each Functional Requirement be easily traced back to a Business Requirement? Do the User Stories support the Epics? Are there test cases for the Epics and User Stories that support the Definition of Done? Inconsistencies within and between artifacts not only confuse the delivery team but can also lead to delivery issues, defects, and problems with stakeholder acceptance. With large or dispersed teams, there may also be communication and coordination issues that need to be addressed with conflicting artifacts.

There are cases where project artifacts are complete, consistent, and approved by key stakeholders, and yet they are unrealistic. When reviewing artifacts, particularly schedules, staffing plans, and budgets, look for lack of realism. Use professional judgment and experience to determine if estimates look too optimistic. Try to find applicable metrics related to the artifacts in question and see if the metrics support the current projections in the artifact. For example, if the Burn Down Chart shows a Scrum Team consistently failing to meet their planned progress, is that reflected in the schedule? Is scope being reduced to meet a set release date, or is scope being added to an already over-burdened team? Have early test results shown quality issues? If so, have the schedule, staffing plans, and budgets been adjusted to reflect the likelihood that subsequent testing efforts are likely to increase?

Are the artifacts being used properly by the right members, both internal and external to the project team? For example, are the test cases being developed based on the approved user stories, requirements, and design decisions that have been made? If the end users are creating User Acceptance Test plans and cases, do they have access to and are they using the same materials as the delivery team members? Do the members using the artifacts understand how they fit together and how to use them to complete their tasks? Is there good communication between the members on the artifacts, especially when questions or contradictions arise?

Finally, the most important question for the incoming PM (or project reviewer) is will the artifacts need to be updated to get the project completed with the current or revised plan? If so, has that time and effort been included in the schedule? If not, what is a reasonable estimate of the time and effort needed to make the updates? Can that time and effort be worked into the schedule and budget? Are there any artifact issues that require slowing or stopping work within the project to get them corrected? For example, if the functional requirements appear to be accurate and complete, but the associated artifacts don't comply with the template, and there are some traceability issues, can the project continue while these are addressed?

Keep these questions in mind as you review each of the artifacts. There are also things to check that are specific to certain key artifacts, which are described below. These questions are also consolidated into artifact review checklists in the Appendix. The list of key documents is not exhaustive, and they are likely to have different names within different methodologies. However, reviewing these artifacts should provide an accurate view of project status, challenges, issues, and areas that should be addressed as part of the recovery plan.

Key Artifacts to Review

It is important to start at the beginning and to understand the background leading up to the project, its original and current objectives, and the desired benefits from the project. There are many different names for project origination documents. We'll refer to them collectively as the Project Charter. The Project Charter should describe the key stakeholders, including the Sponsor, Business Owner, Executive Steering Committee, and so on. Verify that these role assignments are current. The charter should also include the project objective (definition of done), along with its constraints (scope, schedule, budget, quality). Compare the information in the charter with the information gathered during your initial interviews. Is it consistent? Is it current? Does the charter need to be updated, or do project plans and the project team need to be brought into compliance with the charter? It is often beneficial to briefly review the charter with the Sponsor and Business Owner after your initial review is complete to confirm that all of you have the same vision of what success looks like, given the current status of the project.

The project requirements and specifications should flow from the project charter and definition of done. Confirm this through a thorough review, and determine if there are any discrepancies. Do the requirements fulfill the agreed-upon scope of the project charter or expand it? Are there requirements, business processes, or stakeholder needs missing from the requirements (remember the "Why Did You Fire Our PM?" story)? Traceability from top-level artifacts to lower-level ones covering requirements and specifications should be present, although the exact nature and format can vary widely with the methodology being used.

If lower-level requirements cannot ultimately be traced back to the charter, should they be included in the agreed-upon scope or go through the change request process before being included? Often what appears to be a schedule or quality issue is really due to a lack of scope control and requirements being changed to include things not covered by the charter. While reviewing requirements and specifications, look at the test strategy, test plans, and a sample of test cases. They should relate back to the charter and requirements as well, ideally with clear traceability. Identify any discrepancies since they should be addressed while addressing requirement discrepancies.

Logically, the next level is the design documents developed to meet the charter and requirements. The nature of the project and the methodology will determine the format and extent of the design documents. When building a house, these are likely to be blueprints, and even these come in different forms. There are the renderings that show what the complete house will look like, construction blueprints used by the carpenters, plumbers, and electricians for their respective trades, Bills of Materials (BoM), etc. In addition, there are building codes and safety standards that must be complied with, and there may be specific instructions for key components, such as a geothermal heating and cooling system. Software projects can have architectural specifications, coding standards, high-level and detailed design documents, etc. The degree of formality and rigor of these documents will vary with the delivery methodology being used.

Do the artifacts provide the information needed by the delivery team? Are they under configuration control (no evidence of unauthorized changes)? Are the design documents being followed? Are key regulatory and security requirements included? Do the design documents meet the needs of the overall project? The intent is not for the PM to second guess the technical experts but to identify questions to ask the experts if there seems to be a misalignment. It may help to bring in technical experts from outside the delivery team to benefit from their expert judgment. This is recommended for project reviews of technical projects, from software development through highway construction. The PM is usually not expected to be a technical expert, so bring in the expertise that you need.

Now that the project goals, scope, requirements, and design are understood, the latest Schedule, Resource Plan, and Budget should be reviewed to see if they support the project goals. Do the artifacts and plans for each area reflect what you have learned so far? Are they consistent with each other? Do they go to appropriate levels of detail for the methodology being used and the scope of the project? Are they realistic? Does the schedule clearly show any slack or management reserve time? Does the resource plan reflect current and future project staffing in agreement with what you have learned so far? Are members with the right skills assigned to the team, or are there gaps (Note: Availability is not a skillset—would you have a plumber do the wiring in a house just because they were more available or cheaper than an electrician?)?

Are there any upcoming disruptions to the resource schedule that are known? This could range from a planned factory shutdown to key members taking family leave or extended vacations. If extra resources have been added to the team, does the budget reflect this? Have budget expenditures aligned with the budget plan and the work schedule? Is it costing more than expected to get specific milestones completed? Are required materials, equipment, software, outside services, etc., coming in at or below budget? There may have been significant increases in prices for these items since the original budget was developed. Have they been reflected in the budget plan? Does the budget target need to be increased? If the project is significantly under budget, can this be turned back to the organization, or have expenses just been delayed? Completing these reviews at this point may not be as in-depth as will be needed during replanning and may have to be done in a compressed period of time. The key is to develop an overall impression of how solid the artifacts are and what issues are found or are likely to occur in the future. This will inform the actions that you have to take over the next few days and weeks.

With an understanding of the overall project, looking at recent Status Reports will be more informative and productive. What picture is presented by the status reports? Is it Red, Yellow, or Green overall? Do the text, milestone completion data, and reported metrics provide the same story, or are they in conflict? Review the last three or four reports to see if there are any trends. If the reports seem to just be the same information, report after report, are they accurate? Perhaps the prior PM was just going through the motions, and the reports can't be trusted. Are there other reports that can be reviewed, such as software development metrics, Burn Down Charts, Kanban Charts, quality reports, test status reports, etc.? Do these reports match the project level status reports? Is there a consistent picture presented across the different reports? If there are executive-level reports, minutes from Executive Steering Committee (ESC) meetings, and so on, do they agree with the lower-level reports?

There should be consistency across the reports and reporting levels, and the reports should match the metrics. Although you will not have time to go through a lot of these in detail at this time, spend enough time to assess the true status of the project and identify the top issues that need to be addressed. You may also identify the need to change what is being reported and how it is prepared, including changing or adding to the metrics being collected and reported, report formats, etc. If you believe there is a significant difference between what has been reported and the true status of the project, let the key executives know. Even if more investigation is needed to develop a picture of the true status, the executives need to know that you are working on it and that there will be adjustments made to the project and project plans to reflect the actual status.

Carefully review the Risks and Issues Log. It should include closed risks and issues as well as those currently being tracked and acted upon. While the current risks and issues are important and will probably require attention from the new PM, the historical record provides a view of how the project team thinks. Were they diligent about identifying and tracking risks and issues? Were the current issues identified as risks before they became issues? Are risks and issues assigned to an owner, and is there evidence that the owners took action to avoid or mitigate risks? This information not only provides insight into how the project team and ESC think, but it also shows if there was a bias toward action and effort spent to mitigate risks before they become issues. Does it appear that the team was just going through the motions of handling risks and issues? Was there a lack of understanding of which risks to identify and which ones to prioritize? Can you identify risks and issues that are not in the log that should be?

The Change Log also provides an indication of the thoroughness and diligence of the team. Regardless of the delivery methodology or type of project, there will be changes in directions as the project proceeds. These should be tracked in the Change Log and the associated documentation and artifacts updated to reflect approved changes. Not all changes will have a cost or schedule impact, and not all change requests will be approved. Regardless, it is important that all change requests and approved changes be tracked to resolution. In Agile methodologies, this can include updates to epics, user stories, and definition of done, if they were approved and the original definition of ready met. Changes done during development, such as font color, minor graphical changes, etc., are to be expected, but significant changes, such as adding more screens, deleting reports, etc., should be noted in the change log. This is to provide traceability of the management decisions made that resulted in these changes and to support changing the associated artifacts to reflect the as-built state of the ultimate deliverables. Regardless of methodology, changes that impact the scope, schedule, cost, or quality of the project should be tracked. If they are not, this is another warning flag and an issue that will have to be addressed by the incoming PM.

If available, PMO reports should also be reviewed, preferably the last few that were done. Sometimes it is better to form an independent opinion of project status before diving into PMO reports. The accuracy of PMO reports may be impacted by internal politics, the degree of visibility the PMO Team has into the project, the purpose of the PMO, etc. Especially if coming from outside the delivery organization, try to meet with the PMO Lead to get an understanding of their charter and operations. Some PMOs simply consolidate reports without adding any intelligence to them. Other PMOs may be the enforcers of organizational norms and methodologies. Ideally, the PMO will also be charged with coaching and supporting the PMs and project teams to reach successful project outcomes.

The mission and tasking of the PMO are likely to color the tone of their reports and should be remembered when reading them. Taken with a grain of salt, the PMO reports can still be very useful and can provide an independent view of the project. A critical question at this point is, do the artifacts reviewed provide the same picture of the project as the PMO reports? Do they describe similar trends in project performance? If the project artifacts are indicating overall Yellow or Red status, but the PMO reports show it as Green, where is the disconnect? If management has not been getting a true indication of project status from the reports at their level, the incoming PM will have to address this. This can be a difficult conversation to have, especially if the true status is worse than has been reported. Be ready to justify your assessment with artifacts and data and to discuss the issues that you find with the PMO reports, if there are any. Reforming the PMO or changing its mandate is NOT your responsibility, so do not venture into that type of discussion, especially at this stage of assuming project leadership. Save those ideas and conversations for another day. Focus on communicating the true project status following your assessment.

Exercise: Are there any other key documents you should review?

Results of the Artifact Review

You've largely completed your reviews, and a picture of the true project status and any underlying issues is forming. What are some additional steps that should be taken during this phase of taking over a project? We'll cover these briefly in the remainder of the chapter. It is important to note that many of these are not "one and done" activities. Instead, they will need to be continuously reviewed and updated. As noted above, when completing regularly scheduled status reports, updating key metrics, etc., that is also a good time to step back and identify other artifacts and items that should be reviewed and updated. Develop the habit of doing so, at least bi-weekly, as the project continues. Do not turn completing status reports into a "check the box" activity. Take the time to seriously consider what was planned for the period, what was actually accomplished, and how that impacts plans for the upcoming period. Identify actions that need to be completed as well as those completed. Think about the metrics and other data that you have on the project. Does it answer the questions that you and the ESC have about progress, quality, costs, and completing on time? If not, what metrics may be used to provide that information?

As you go through team interviews and review artifacts, make sure that you update the Risks & Issues Log with key items that come up. It may make sense to create a personal copy where you can record your candid observations and concerns before bringing them to team reviews of risks and issues where the formal log is updated and actions assigned to address the items in the log. There are many different templates for Risk & Issues Logs (or Risk Registers). There is a template in the Appendix that includes the minimum information needed to track and address risks and issues during a project. It is important to remember that risks and issues are not just negative things that can impact a project; there may be positive things as well. As noted in Chapter 8—Revise the Plan, gather the team together, including the Sponsor and Business Owner, to formally review and update the Risk & Issues Log together as part of revising key project management artifacts.

Not All Risks Are Bad

Updating an existing auto insurance suite of applications for a third wave of states was going well. Lessons Learned from the first two waves had been incorporated, and artifacts from those waves were being updated for the new states instead of being written from scratch. The Software Development Manager noted that software development was trending well ahead of schedule and unit testing was going well. There was a risk that they would be ready to move into the Systems Integration Test (SIT) environment three weeks early. Great news, but the Infrastructure Manager said they couldn't be ready to handle the accelerated schedule, even if the QA Team was ready to start testing. The risk had quickly become an issue!

Fortunately, everyone involved recognized the benefits to the organization of accelerating the schedule by three weeks. With senior management approval, we temporarily added staff to the QA Team to complete their test planning early and accelerated the reconditioning of infrastructure equipment to allow the key components in the SIT environment to be ready three weeks early. Other components would be added to the environment in time to support testing interfaces and so on. Other teams also had to accelerate their schedules to meet the new release date.

The project was ultimately delivered four weeks ahead of the original schedule, saving over $130K in labor costs and providing an additional $12 million in premiums that year. When was the last time you heard of software being released ahead of the originally promised date?

Checklists can be useful tools when used correctly. If the organization has a Project Audit Checklist that supports the methodology and tools in place, consider using it as a guide while doing your review. The checklist should indicate the artifacts that should be available at the current stage of the project and identify other items to review. There is a generic Project Audit Checklist in the Appendix and available for download. Over time, tailor the checklist based on your experience and the types of projects that you encounter. At this stage of review, be cautious about sharing your findings and comments, as some may need to be confirmed through additional research. Compare and discuss results with the Project Management Office (PMO) Team if they have done a project review or have been tracking the project in their systems. It may turn out that some artifacts or data that you could not find are actually available, and the PMO Team may have insights that help you with your assessment. This can be especially helpful if you are new to the organization or new to working with this part of the organization. Stay objective; do not make a lot of assumptions.

While we need to avoid jumping to conclusions at this point, we probably have a good idea of what the root causes of a challenged project are. This supports planning to confirm the root causes with appropriate data, if needed, and planning on how to address them. It is critical to remember that someone intentionally doing a bad job is hardly ever the answer. I have never met anyone who came to work in the morning with the idea, "I'm going to screw things up today!" There may be misunderstandings, confusion, incorrect processes or tools, or a lack of knowledge or skills—all things that we can identify and correct. Look for these underlying issues before assuming that politics or bad intentions are the cause of problems. That said, there will be cases where organizational politics or interpersonal issues are present. These will also need to be handled in a professional manner, potentially with the support of HR or the Sponsor.

We also want to identify key influencers within the team, so we can use them as leverage points. How many times have we seen a trusty deputy help the new sheriff identify problems in the town, point out townspeople that will help the sheriff, and guide the sheriff around the town? Identifying a few key players, ideally the leads, and getting them on your side will be very helpful. Do not be afraid to approach them individually and ask for their support. As you go through the artifacts and research the current status of the project, meeting with potential key influencers will be needed and should provide an opportunity to identify them and directly ask for their support. Some of the key influencers may initially be reserved or even hostile to a new PM. This is only natural. Usually, meeting with them one-on-one, listening to their concerns, addressing the ones that you can, and asking for their help in moving the project forward leads to them becoming allies instead of opponents. Ensure they participate in the replanning effort, and they will help communicate the plan to others on the team.

In a similar way, there will be key influencers external to the team. More than just the Sponsor and Business Owner, there are key stakeholders that can impact the overall success of the project. This can include end customers, regulators, inspectors, vendors, executives, etc. Try to make them allies instead of opponents or obstructors. For example, as a house is being built, the local building inspector will come to the job site to ensure that building codes are being followed. This can be viewed as a hindrance, potentially adding work and expense to the project. Or the inspector can be treated as a trusted advisor, helping the construction team get things done right. If an issue comes up, an objective discussion about what is needed and why instead of an argument will get better results. Which approach is more likely to result in a stop work order? At this stage of the project review, it should be clear who the external influencers are. Go to them and seek their input and support. Identify any concerns they may have, and assess their commitment to the success of the project. Try to increase that commitment and get them to state their support for you and your project.

There are likely challenging personnel issues that need to be addressed as well. If the project has been struggling, there is probably a need for changes to the team. This may include bringing in a few star performers to address complex and difficult issues, but it may also include dismissing members that are not contributing to the team.

When projects start to struggle, there is often a tendency to put more people on the team. Not only does this make it harder to manage the team due to the need to train the new members on the specifics of the project, but it also increases the amount of communication that must be done. In many cases, the people are added because they were available or inexpensive, not because they had the right skills and experience. These additions hurt the project in three ways—they don't produce, but they add costs, they reduce the productivity of other team members, and they take up management time. Try to get these people off the project as soon as possible (see Chapter 7).

Can We Meet the Deadline?—Results

The review was completed on time, with the significant exception of meeting with client team members. At the last minute, client managers decided to prevent the planned interviews and instead responded to questions provided to them in writing. This was less than ideal and highlighted a critical issue that the review team had identified. There was poor cooperation and communication between the two client organizations involved and between both of them and the contractor's team. In addition, there were disputes between the two client organizations over business processes, application requirements, team work schedules, and more. It was clear that the joint team would not succeed if things continued as they were. The project review team presented a number of recommendations to change processes, tools, and team dynamics to improve project performance and settle the outstanding requirements issues. The review team also suggested requesting relief on the target date for the regulatory changes from the governing body.

A number of the recommendations were implemented, and cross-team relationships were temporarily improved. Unfortunately, the guiding regulations from the external governing organization continued to change, with no change

---

to the previously defined end date, right up until a few weeks before the new regulations went into effect and the system had to go live. The result was a poorly performing system, with the new business organization having significant challenges of its own. After a few months of continued struggles, the client and contractor parted ways.

There are some issues and challenges that cannot be overcome, even when they are identified and corrective actions are recommended. In this case, there were causes both internal and external to the organizations directly involved that led to the unsatisfactory conclusion of the project.

We've covered a lot in this chapter, and the information gathered should provide insights into the project, its current status, the delivery team, and key stakeholders. There is probably a need to update project plans, perhaps in a major way. We'll cover how to do that in Chapter 8, but before we go there, we may have some urgent issues that need to be addressed. Particularly with a project that is in Red or Yellow status, there may be a need for immediate action. Chapter 7 will address identifying and acting on these immediate needs.

CHAPTER 7

TAKE REQUIRED
IMMEDIATE ACTIONS

"There is an old Cajun saying; It's hard to remember the objective is to drain the swamp when an alligator is chewing on your butt."

Anonymous

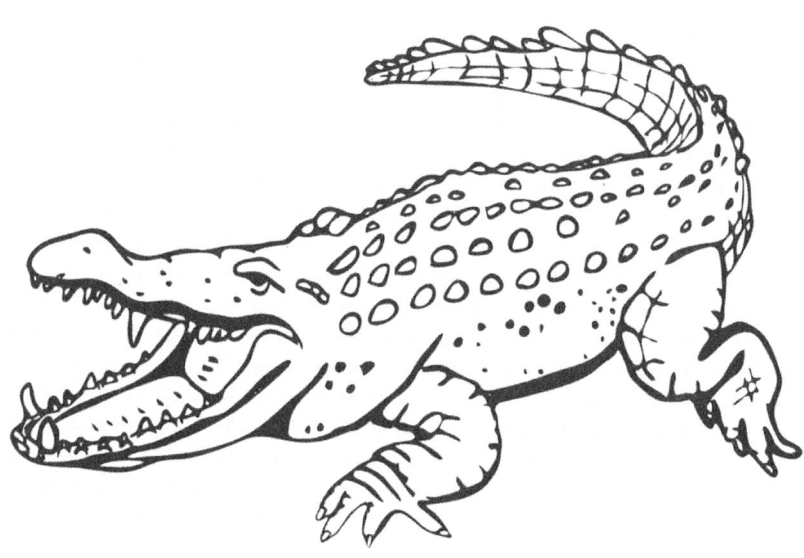

The cartoon is a humorous way of emphasizing an important point—there may be urgent issues that need to be dealt with immediately. Ideally, the incoming PM and project team can update project plans, including schedules, budgets, and scope. Unfortunately, reality is seldom that simple and neat. Experience has shown that in most cases, there will be issues that need to be addressed quickly, often without the opportunity to develop an optimal or ideal solution. Just as the new sheriff may be faced with a rowdy bunch of cowboys breaking up the town, we may need to resolve a number of problems and issues quickly. In other words, stop the alligator before focusing on the swamp. That said, there are often ways to address urgent issues that support the longer-term approaches to getting the project back on track.

> *Without awareness of error, learning is*
> *very difficult, if not impossible.*
>
> Dr. Russell Ackoff

Very few people enjoy pointing out problems, particularly if it means other people have to correct them, change the way they are working, or redo work that has already been done. As Dr. Ackoff points out, if we don't identify and acknowledge a problem, it is unlikely to get corrected. If we have found problems that need to be corrected, we should prioritize them and consider how to address them. Some can be handled as part of updating project plans, work processes, team structure, etc. Others may demand more immediate action, and we'll focus on these in this chapter. Project Managers are expected to have a bias toward action and the courage to make decisions that may be difficult, recognizing that postponing those actions, decisions, and conversations will ultimately be worse for the project, project team, and the organization overall. A common saying that fits is, "Bad news does not get better with age." While we do not want to jump to conclusions without supporting facts, there are going to be things that require immediate action if they are present. We'll cover some of these below.

If the project is Ugly (Red), try to get schedule relief for replanning (scope, schedule, and resources). This usually involves meeting with the Project Sponsor and Business Owner first, so they can ask questions and provide their input before taking the request to the ESC. This is likely to be a negotiation, so be prepared with a realistic assessment of the time and effort to conduct the replanning exercise. Does it make sense for the delivery team to continue working while the replanning is ongoing? If not, what should they work on? What is the impact of the replanning on the overall schedule? Any cost impacts? Answers to these questions will influence the willingness of these key stakeholders to allow a pause for replanning or to provide a period to keep the project going while replanning occurs in parallel. For example, asking for two to three days to develop an updated project plan is more likely to get approved than asking to suspend work for two to three weeks for planning purposes. The scope and complexity of the project, as well as the current status, will influence the time required. Be prepared with supporting information, and avoid padding your estimates. If you were called into a floundering project, the need to replan was probably expected, and requesting time to do so demonstrates your professionalism and willingness to put things on the right track.

As noted in the "Toy Story" in Chapter 3, there may be cases where the project can't be saved or shouldn't be saved. Again, hold informal discussions with the Business Owner and Sponsor before meeting with the steering committee to kill the project. Provide objective facts and figures, potential alternatives, and justification for ending the project. In some cases, this may be so a new project can be established to meet the desired objectives with a fresh start and better plans. Or there may be alternative ways to achieve the desired objectives. In other cases, the original business reasons for the project may no longer apply, the project may not be technically feasible, breaking it into smaller projects may be appropriate, the project is more likely to succeed following a different methodology, and so on. Agree on a plan to end the project, re-assign team members, etc. It may be appropriate to complete some artifacts so the organization can benefit from them in the future. Be sure to conduct Lessons Learned, complete final status reports, and get member performance review inputs completed as well. We discuss ending the project in more detail in Chapter 12.

If the project is close to a required delivery date, there may be little flexibility to change plans, resources, team members, etc. Identify what needs to be changed to make achieving the delivery date more likely. This may include additional support from outside the delivery team, removing obstacles to progress, and potentially suspending some activities that do not directly contribute to meeting the delivery date. In conversations with the ESC and key stakeholders, emphasize the requirement to separate the "required" from the "nice to have." For example, can updating artifacts to reflect the as-built wait until later? Are there activities not related to project delivery distracting the delivery team that can be suspended? For example, postponing required HR or security training until after the delivery. If team members are assigned to more than one project, can their responsibilities on the other projects be removed? Can the process for reviewing and approving artifacts and making necessary decisions be streamlined? Think creatively and ask team members to identify any tasks or issues that may take time and energy away from completing tasks for your project. Take steps to address and remove these obstacles.

Working to meet an upcoming delivery date is a good time to manage project scope. Remove anything that is not absolutely vital to go live now. For example, if rolling out a new or updated software system, it is unlikely that the quarterly, semi-annual, and annual features and reports are needed on Day 1. Move those to a subsequent release to focus effort on what is vital for Day 1. This should be done rapidly and via the Change Management Process, with accelerated review and approval. Another example is getting a new house ready for the owners to move in. It may be possible to get the certificate of occupancy approved while delaying completion of an outside deck or landscaping.

Be open-minded and creative when considering which items are truly must-haves for Day 1 and which can be delayed. There are likely to be cost implications to the delays, but these should be less than the costs to the organization of missing the delivery date. If not, that provides additional support for delaying the delivery date. When adjusting project scope, keep in mind potential impacts on related projects or systems and impacts on the broader delivery organization. Will keeping members on the team longer than originally planned impact the start of other projects? If so, which impacts are least harmful to the overall organization? This may require a meeting between sponsors or ESCs to reach a consensus.

In many cases, the delivery team may already be working overtime to get the project back on schedule or to "crash the schedule" to meet deadlines. This may be necessary, but it should not be the first option considered. Team performance is going to suffer from long hours and a lack of rest and recovery time. Canceled or postponed vacations impact not only the delivery team members but also their families and friends. In addition to morale issues, this can lead to poor quality work due to people rushing to get things done, communication issues, and greater levels of rework. If this continues too long, people will seek to leave the project or even the organization.

Losing experienced team members hurts in two ways. Their knowledge and expertise related to this project are lost, and if they are replaced, another team member has to take time from their project work to bring the replacement team member up to speed. Carefully consider if overtime work is really needed. There are usually other options, including reducing scope, identifying and eliminating work that does not directly contribute to the delivery of project objectives, and providing additional resources to the team. For example, if there is a machine or instrument that is a bottleneck in the workflow, consider adding more of that equipment, even if only on a temporary basis.

Assess the resources available to meet the goals of the project within the constraints of scope, budget, and schedule. Does the project have the right combination of resources needed? Are there any glaring deficiencies? Most importantly, does the project have the right mix of members given the unique characteristics of the project? Are there specific knowledge, skills, or experience missing from the team? Are there enough members with the desired characteristics to meet the target dates? Will these members be available when needed? These can be the most serious gaps and may take some time to remedy. Work with your team leads and identify who and what is needed, then work with them to get the members needed. This may require changing team membership, adding new members, and letting some members go. Understand the impacts that this will have on team performance and potentially morale, and do your best to factor those impacts into your updated plans. If the resource gaps are so major that the project no longer appears feasible, then concern needs to be brought to the Sponsor and ESC to determine if the project should be terminated or have adjustments made to make it feasible again.

Be careful about "flooding the zone" with additional people. This is seldom the right answer when trying to speed up delivery. As noted above, each new member added to the team will need to be trained on the specifics of the project, tools, processes being followed, etc. This will take the time and attention of existing team members away from working on their deliverables, further slowing overall progress. In addition, there are the team issues addressed in Chapter 5, pushing the team back to the "Forming" stage as new members join. Additional team members also require more communication paths between members, which requires more time to be spent on communication within and external to the team. More time spent on communications means less time spent on productive work, so the rule of diminishing returns applies.

Experience has shown that new team members tend to make more errors, impacting overall quality and the time required to test and fix the product. This is due to new members not having the full history of the project, and they may not know some of the informal policies, decisions, methods, etc., that have been made up to this point. As the PM, you should carefully consider the costs and impacts of adding new members before proceeding to enlarge the team, even if there is management pressure to throw people at the problem. It is often better to bring in one or two senior experts to aid the team instead of adding a lot of junior or less expensive resources. As noted in Chapter 6, this may also be the time to release some members from the team. If there are members that are not contributing enough value to the project to justify their costs, both directly and indirectly, move them out. This can provide some immediate budget relief and may free up the budget needed to bring on the "stars" that are really needed to turn the project around.

There may be some good opportunities to add the right members to aid the team. As described in the "What's the Buzz" story in Chapter 2, adding an expert with the knowledge and skills needed can actually improve team performance. In particular, organizations using Agile methodologies can benefit from assigning Agile Coaches with deep experience in the specific methodologies and tools being used to support the project teams at multiple levels. Adding coaches to assist at the team, Business Owner, and program levels to ensure consistent advice is being provided at all levels has been shown to be very effective. On the opposite extreme, bringing in senior managers to closely monitor the team and provide additional reporting to executive management is usually not at all helpful. Base your immediate resource requests on what you discovered in your team interviews and artifact reviews. If possible, complete the replanning effort described in the next chapter before adjusting the resource plan. This should keep all the plans in harmony and ensure that only critical additions are made.

Whether tied to looming delivery dates or continuing to deliver against the current plans while going through the replanning effort, be sure to set clear expectations with the project team, the ESC, and key stakeholders. These expectations should include what the current schedule and deadlines are, quality requirements and checkpoints, what resources are needed, and how communications will be handled. For example, there may have been too much interaction between end-users and the delivery team, leading to unapproved changes being made, rework, and a lack of progress. These need to be shut down immediately while establishing proper communication channels and a visible change management process. While this is more common in software development projects, it can also occur in other types of projects. If the homeowners are showing up at the house construction site and requesting changes from the electricians without the prime contractor being involved, the likelihood of increased costs, schedule delays, and impacts on other trades is greatly increased. Whenever possible, communicate these expectations in multiple ways—in meetings reinforced with meeting minutes and e-mails, with visible materials such as schedules, Kanban Boards, and other Agile charts and tools, and in changes to supporting tools and systems.

In addition to adding members to the team, there may be other team changes needed. At this stage, these changes need to be well thought out and should not be done hastily. There may be members who appear to be problems, but it may be due to a lack of knowledge, skill, understanding, or resources. Ensure that these aspects have been considered before removing someone from the team. If a team member is overly critical, negative, and impacting other members and team morale, the first step should be to meet one-on-one and determine what their motivation and issues are. Request the behavior that you want to see from them and ask for their help in moving the project forward. Their response, and the tone of the conversation, will guide your next steps. After considering the viable alternatives, along with the costs and benefits of cutting the member from the team, you can make a logical decision. Although it may cause issues with the remaining team members (remember Maslow), these are the types of decisions that require courage to take for the benefit of the project and the remaining team members (see the "Why Did You Fire Our PM?" story in Chapter 2).

There are seldom benefits to delaying these actions, but in some cases, it will be possible to bring in a new member with the desired knowledge, skills, and attitude to get a hand-off from the member who needs to leave the team. Take this approach when possible, encouraging the departing member to be cooperative for the benefit of the other team members and the overall project. In some cases, a member is just not suited for a project that they have been assigned to, so these changes should be made without harming their reputation or career.

I Can't Work for This Guy Anymore

In the early stages of a mission-critical software development project, the Project Director was confronted by the QA Lead. Her frustration was clear, and it was also clear that she expected immediate action.

"The consultant they brought in to teach us the new QA process and tools is driving me crazy and is slowing down our work. We can't meet the schedule unless you do something today."

"What is the problem?"

"He reviews everything that we do in detail, which has become a bottleneck. I've got 10 people working on this project, and he wants to micro-manage every aspect. He doesn't tell us how to do things the right way; he just tells us what is wrong. Yes, he's experienced and usually makes good suggestions, but I can't work for this guy anymore."

"Okay, I'll talk to him and see what we can do."

The PD met with the QA Consultant on the issue that afternoon. The consultant looked haggard and tired and was clearly stressed out. As they discussed how things were going, it became clear that the QA Consultant had been moved up from a QA Lead role and had never worked in a coaching role before. He felt that he had to review every artifact from the team in detail, which was too much for any one person. They agreed on changes that were needed, but after a few days, it was apparent that the QA Consultant couldn't change his approach. The PD met with the onsite manager for the consulting company and the internal QA Practice Manager, reaching an agreement to replace the QA Consultant with someone more experienced in the role.

The QA Consultant was moved to another engagement, and the QA Lead successfully built a 50-person team that implemented the new tools and processes. Years later, the QA Consultant met the PD when both were at another organization, and he thanked the PD for helping him recognize that he was not ready for the role he was in at the time. The QA Consultant had more success with other engagements and had gotten promoted twice in the intervening years. Sometimes difficult personnel situations can lead to better results for everyone involved over time.

There may be immediate actions required with some of the stakeholders. For example, there may be end users responsible for defining project requirements that are unable to agree, unwilling to commit and make a final decision, or are not participating in requirement discussions. While these issues are more common with software projects, imagine the situation with building a house. If the family members can't agree on what colors to paint the walls, what can the contractor do? Or if they keep changing their minds on paint colors long after the time the paint needed to be ordered? Or if they wait until the room is painted and then state that they never agreed to the color selected? Obviously, the project cannot proceed on time with this type of behavior. There can be other negative stakeholder behaviors impacting the project as well. These should become apparent during your project interviews and artifact review. Separate out the ones that can be addressed over time and those that need to be addressed immediately.

The approach to handling these will vary with the type of engagement, the relationship of the Sponsor and Business Owner to the stakeholders in question, and the delivery methodology. In some cases, try to discuss the issues and work out how to deal with them in coordination with the Sponsor. This is usually appropriate when the troublesome stakeholders are in another part of the organization or in the customer organization with a contractor delivering the project. It is best for the stakeholders' own management team to work with them to correct the issues. If they are customers of the organization running the project, it may be appropriate to go through the customer liaison team. For example, for an insurance company rolling out a new auto insurance program, the Underwriters and Agency Management Teams should address any issues with independent insurance agents that will use the new program.

There can be cases where a stakeholder's behavior is particularly harmful to the project. This should be handled via the Sponsor. Usually, a direct, factual conversation about the goals of the project, the importance to the organization, and the behavior that needs to change is sufficient to get the desired result. There may be cases where the stakeholder may need to be removed from the project team or even the organization itself. These situations can be politically sensitive and should be carefully worked out with the Sponsor and management before taking any action at the project level.

You Can't Make Me

The President of the Personal Lines Insurance Division was meeting with the CEO over his concerns about a new auto insurance product that was being developed. It was a radical departure from how the company had underwritten policies before. Having come up through the underwriting ranks, the President was convinced that the new approach was too radical to succeed.

"As the President of the Personal Lines Division, you can't make me approve the new underwriting guidelines."

"You're right, I can't make you approve them, but I'd like your support for this project, which is needed to make our auto insurance competitive in the marketplace."

"I don't agree with your assessment. I've had 35 years of success with this company; you've only been here a year. You're just wrong."

"I may be wrong, but as CEO, it's my decision to make. You won't have to approve the changes since I'm accepting your resignation and request to retire today. Thank you for all the great work you've done for the company over the past 35 years."

Word of the "retirement" of the Personal Lines President spread through the building like wildfire. Vocal opposition to the new underwriting guidelines died down immediately. The new course had been set in a decisive manner.

---

*"You can lead a horse to water, but
you can't make them drink."*

Old English Proverb

> *"Shoot a few horses, and the rest get thirsty."*
> *Mike Quinn, Organizational Change Consultant*

What if there are issues due to the Sponsor's behavior? For example, not attending ESC meetings, failing to handle Sponsor-level activities, off-the-cuff comments, and directions that impact the team, etc. These are best handled through a direct discussion with the sponsor one-on-one. Point out the actions and impacts in a non-threatening way, using the third person when possible. For example, "When the Sponsor regularly misses ESC meetings, the other participants may feel that the project is no longer important, and their commitment to the project lessens. This makes it harder for the project to succeed. Can I get your commitment to attend future ESC meetings, or if there is a schedule conflict, let me know so we can reschedule the meeting to when you can attend?" If it becomes clear that the Sponsor is unwilling to change their behavior or continue to support the project, the situation is much tougher. Ask if the Sponsor wants to terminate the project or hand over sponsorship to someone else. Either result is better for the project team and organization.

In some cases, the Sponsor may have lost confidence in the project due to its current status, or the business need may have changed. It is better to end the project and free up resources than to continue to limp along. There may also be another executive who is more committed to project success that can step in as the new Sponsor. If the Sponsor is unwilling to give up their role or end the project and the negative behavior continues, it may be necessary to bring it to members of the ESC privately and request their support in making changes. Be sure to note concrete risks and issues resulting from Sponsor behavior and decisions in the Risks and Issues Log as objectively and professionally as possible so mitigations can be planned with the delivery team. This scenario is very risky, so don't hesitate to get senior management support.

There are other difficult issues that may need to be addressed at this point. Is the selected technology suitable for the project? While this is more likely to be an issue with a technology-based project, such as software development or designing a new computer, it can also apply in other circumstances. A new welding technique may not be suitable for submarine construction, or the selected materials may not work for a new product design. The incoming PM needs to depend upon their own expertise with similar projects, the industry, and the information they have found out so far. If there are concerns, check with available experts and prepare a recommendation for consideration by the project team. In some cases, it may be necessary to bring in technical experts to conduct a technology or architecture review to get an objective assessment of the viability of the current technical approach. Ideally, develop some alternatives before going to the ESC with the issue. The worst approach is to continue with a technology that you do not have confidence in, or that is clearly failing. It is much better for the project team and the organization to recognize the issue and take action, even if that means canceling the project.

A similar challenge arises if the delivery methodology is not suited for the project. Particularly in IT organizations and projects, there is a tendency to use the latest methodology and to get caught up in the hype. Depending upon the organization and project team's experience with the methodology, the characteristics of the project, and the tools required for the methodology, the fit may be good or bad. Again, the incoming PM should depend upon their familiarity with the methodology in question, the industry, the characteristics of the project, and the results to date when assessing the suitability of the methodology. If there are concerns, check with the project team, methodology coaches (if available), and local experts. If there is a better methodology recommended, roughly assess the impacts on budget and schedule, as well as impacts on related projects. Discuss these options with the ESC and determine the next steps. In many cases, it is better to wrap up the current project, preserve artifacts and what has been done to date, and start up a new project that will use the recommended methodology. This provides an opportunity to develop appropriate plans and ensure that the team is trained in the new methodology.

In other cases, the problem may be that the project team is not familiar enough with the methodology and/or tools that they need to use. In these cases, bringing in coaches to provide training and support will usually correct the issues over time. Use these coaches during the replanning effort to ensure their inputs aid in developing a realistic plan. Often pausing delivery for a few weeks to accomplish the training and set up required tools is more productive than trying to limp along with training and development going on in parallel.

So far, we've focused on issues that need to be addressed quickly. Although it may be difficult, look for opportunities for quick wins as well. Is there an upcoming milestone that is important to meet? A critical feature that key stakeholders are looking to get? A project review that must be successfully navigated? Maybe there is an achievable outcome that can be presented as an important step forward? Identify opportunities for accomplishments that demonstrate that the project is making progress and that things are going well. Push to achieve them, and celebrate the achievement with the team. Communicate the success and the importance of the success outside the team as well. Not only will this encourage the team, but it should also provide some political capital or breathing space for the PM and team. Use this space to fully develop revised plans for the project and gain support for those plans.

We've covered a number of urgent risks and issues that may need to be addressed before the replanning effort is complete. A key point to keep in mind at this stage is to not overcommit the team. Particularly with projects that are Yellow/Red at this stage, there will be pressure to quickly get to Green. The new PM is expected to make immediate changes, push the delivery team harder to make up for lost time, correct any deficiencies, and so on. This is usually more than can reasonably be done. It is easy to slip into "Heroic Project Manager" mode and to try to single-handedly save the day. That is not your real job! *Your job* is to get the project delivered without destroying the members of the delivery team. This is in the long-term interests of the stakeholders, the organization, the project, and yourself. You may need to have discussions with the ESC, the Sponsor, and the Business Owner to get these points across. The information gathered through the process described in Chapter 6 and the immediate actions that you have taken should demonstrate that you are increasingly

110

knowledgeable about the project and current circumstances, that you are willing to take appropriate actions, and that the project is in capable hands. Point to the replanning efforts that are ongoing and the improved communications to get the time you need to come up with an achievable plan.

In the next chapter, we will go over the work you will do with the project team and ESC to update plans, improve communications, and keep the project on the path to success. The information you've gathered up to this point will inform and guide these activities, but remember that additional information is going to emerge, and things will occur that may require modifying plans. Planning is an ongoing activity, never a "one and done." Continue to listen, communicate, and work with your team to move the project forward together.

Tip: Create or revise the Communication Plan and follow it— you cannot over-communicate at this stage.

CHAPTER 8

REVISE THE PLAN

**"Plans are worthless, but planning is everything.
If you haven't been planning you can't start to
work, intelligently at least."**

--President Dwight Eisenhower

We've developed a view of the overall project, its current status, the project team, and key stakeholders. If there were urgent issues that required action, we've initiated and hopefully completed those actions. Now we need to work with our team and stakeholders to update and revise our plans to align with the current status and reality of the project and describe the path to a successful project completion. We are not going to cover how to plan in detail since there are plenty of project management textbooks that do that, and experienced PMs know how to plan. Instead, we are going to note the key planning items that need to be revised and important considerations when revising them.

As noted earlier, it is likely that project delivery will have to continue while plans are revised. Establishing time to replan may be difficult, but it must be done. Avoid the temptation to go off in the corner and update the plans yourself; the team needs to be involved in the plan to be committed to it, and better plans will result. Set up a series of planning meetings with the core attendees needed so there will be revised plans to work from. As with any plan, it cannot be static, but it will have to be continuously updated based on actual results. Remember to include remote team members in planning sessions and to coordinate with outside teams that interact with your project (suppliers, technical specialists, infrastructure, coordinating projects, etc.). Including members in planning activities that involve them is the best way to ensure that they are committed to the plan and project, improving the odds that the project will be successful.

Commitment

The difference between "involvement" and "commitment" is like an eggs-and-ham breakfast: the chicken was "involved" – the pig was "committed"!

In western movies, this is the point where the new sheriff gathers the posse to help them clean up the town. Remember that the PM can't do it alone—take the steps needed to build a supportive team, and request additional resources if needed. Now that you've met the team and assessed their commitment and skills, are there any concerns? Most projects require a mix of talents. Do you have the right mix? While it is unlikely that you will have top experts in every category, are there any gaps that jeopardize the project? Will part-time assistance from an expert or a coach fill the gap? Is there time to provide training to team members that may need to level up in certain areas? As you work with the team and key stakeholders to revise the current plans and identify the path forward, include these considerations. Sometimes it is more efficient and effective to take a pause for training or to get expert assistance than to carry on without the knowledge and skills needed. It may require a discussion with management to get approval, but a properly explained case can make all the difference.

Interviewing Is a Skill

The requirements gathering and analysis phase of a critical project was already two weeks behind schedule. The Business Analysis Team for the organization had more than doubled in size during the quarter and was going through a major methodology change with the assistance of a consulting firm. The Program Director noted a number of deficiencies in the methodology roll-out, in particular a lack of emphasis on fundamental BA skills. After sitting in on a few requirement-gathering sessions, it was clear that there was a wide variance in BA skills since the BAs had come from many different organizations. In particular, most of the BAs did not know how to prepare for, conduct, or follow up when doing an information-seeking interview with stakeholders. The consequences rolled through the other steps in the requirements process, contributing to the delays and rework that were already occurring.

The Program Director went to the ESC and noted the observed issues and insisted that more training in some specific skills was needed. Having previously taught BA courses for a well-respected IT training firm, the Program Director had the credibility needed to convince both the ESC and the consulting firm that the need was real. Although four days of training was requested, the compromise was two half-days, with consulting firm coaches sitting in so they could provide one-on-one support to the BAs later. The training was well received, and the BAs were happy about getting the training and supporting materials. Improvements were noticed immediately, and the training was rolled out for BAs on other project teams over the next few weeks. Although the issues had contributed to an overall three-week delay in completing the requirements phase, the delays did not increase, and the quality of the requirements was improved.

As planning sessions are held and plans are revised, this is the time to build relationships with the stakeholders and team. This is not trivial and takes time, so allocate time and effort to plan how to build these relationships. Depending upon the current atmosphere and performance of the team, taking time for team-building exercises may be worthwhile if there are team issues. Including the Sponsor and Business Owner as well as other key stakeholders in these team-building events is usually beneficial, as it should increase their familiarity with the team and improve their confidence in the team members. These activities do not need to be elaborate or held offsite. Sometimes a pizza party or a few simple team-building exercises is all that is needed. If there is an Organizational Change Management (OCM) expert around, or someone within HR with the desired skills, getting their help in planning and executing these activities is beneficial. Another key step is updating the Stakeholder Map and Communication Plan, which we will address later in this chapter.

Replanning needs to start with your team. Get them together and briefly review what you've discovered up to this point. Be sure to praise the team for the "Good" results, focusing on concrete accomplishments that have laid the foundation for long-term project success. Be careful not to rehash history—there is no "way back machine" to change decisions that were made or events that occurred. Focus on the road forward—identify the Bad and Ugly issues that can be fixed and seek the team's suggestions on how to fix them. Keep the discussion focused on realistic solutions; keep the tone positive. If there are limitations or external issues raised that team members see as blocking improvement, do not make promises to fix them unless you have the authority to address them. Instead, make a note of the issues, promise to seek management support to resolve them, but ask for solutions that assume the issues will not be resolved.

Tip: Be cautious when revising plans. Don't change more than is really needed to keep the project moving forward. There are likely to be things in the project that do not follow your preferred way of doing things. Carefully consider whether it's *really necessary to change them or whether you can live with things the way they are. Don't push for changes just for the sake of change or to put your personal stamp on things. Not only will this take time and effort that the project probably does not have, but it may also alienate team members.*

The team is probably under pressure to accelerate the project, add scope, perhaps rotate some members to other projects that need specific skills, etc. These pressures are especially present in matrix organizations where different managers are bringing their needs to members that report to them in one way or another. Communicate the need to resist external pressure to add scope, accelerate dates, etc., from any of these sources. These requests, or demands, all must go to the sheriff! Updated plans can easily be undone by members responding to these external pressures, wanting to make everyone happy. Unfortunately, members may not have the full picture or fully understand the impacts that a seemingly simple accommodation or favor may have on the overall team or project. Members need to feel comfortable bringing these requests to the PM so the PM can handle them appropriately, whether that means going through the change request process, escalating to the Sponsor or ESC, or just denying requests that fall within the authority of the PM.

As you meet with the team, look for opportunities to "pick some low-hanging fruit." There are probably some issues that fell into the "Bad" category that provide opportunities for quick wins. These may be reducing overtime work, at least temporarily, or deferring outside requirements for training or mandatory meetings. Ask your team what obstacles they face and what solutions they suggest. Many will be easy to implement, especially in the "honeymoon period" that is often available for PMs joining a project. For example, having the Sponsor or Business Owner join a few team meetings to stress the importance of the project for the organization and their appreciation for the hard work of the team can raise morale. Training sessions similar to those mentioned above for the BAs not only solve skill issues but also raise morale because it shows team members that the organization is investing in their skill development and career growth. These quick wins can also help politically, showing management that progress is being made and that project performance is headed in the right direction. Do not forget to ask about opportunities to do things better or differently. Team members deal with obstacles and issues every day and probably have some good ideas on how to do things better. Encourage them to bring them forward and implement the ones that make sense.

During the planning sessions, listen to suggestions, be open, be objective, but be firm in meeting revised goals and schedules as they are developed. As with any project planning effort, be alert to members or sub-teams padding estimates and hiding slack in their schedules. There is probably management pressure to meet previously established target dates or to accelerate revised dates that are not acceptable to management. While the PM and team need to be realistic in revising dates, use overall experience and performance to date to determine what is achievable. However, once those targets have been agreed to, the team needs to work to meet them. This is no different than the discipline applied to any project. Delivering something Monday morning when it was promised for Friday is not acceptable. Commitments need to be met unless there was advance agreement among the parties making the agreement to revise the target. This discipline is even more important to maintain in situations with a new PM taking over to demonstrate that there is a new sheriff in town, commitments are taken seriously, and they will be met. This builds confidence in the PM and team and signals to stakeholders that the project is moving in the right direction.

Where do you begin the replanning effort? Since the plans will continue to evolve over time and most plans will impact other project artifacts and plans as they change, there is no one right answer. Every project will be different. However, experience has shown that having an up-to-date and accurate Stakeholder Map and associated Communication Plan is not only a good place to start, but they also help prevent surprises and issues in the future. If there is not a Stakeholder Map, create one, even if just a simple form. Update and revise it as you learn more about the project, and review it with the team, the Sponsor, the Business Owner, and ultimately the ESC to ensure that all stakeholders are identified and their needs are considered (remember the "Why Did You Fire Our PM?" story). There is a simple Stakeholder Map template included in the Appendix and online materials. Note that there are different stakeholder types with different degrees of involvement and communication needs. Mapping these out allows us to update the Communication Plan.

Sample Stakeholder Management Grid

Stakeholder	Organization	Location	Impact on Project	Impacted by Project	Change Readiness Now	Desired Change Readiness	Power	Interest	Notes
Underwriters	Personal Lines	Home Office	L	H	R	S	H	H	Emphasize WIIFM, benefits to company and Agents
Customer Service Representatives	Personal Lines	Home Office	L	H	U	S	H	L	Must be trained and see benefits of new rules
Agents	Various	IL, IN, WI	L	H	U	S	L	H	Provide training and WIIFM
Agent Training Team	Personal Lines	Various	M	M	N	L	L	H	Include in requirements reviews, training development, and testing

The Communication Plan can be very basic, and it is often contained with the Project Management Plan. As long as it identifies stakeholders, their communication needs, and how those needs will be met, that is sufficient. We've included a simple template in the Appendix, with a sample shown below. There are many different formats for Communication Plans, so select one that is suitable for the organization, industry, and methodology of the project. Again, develop this with the project team first, then review it with the Sponsor, Business Owner, and stakeholders before presenting it to the ESC. Think of the Communication Plan as a promise to communicate with these stakeholders and keep them informed. It should also address communications within the team and from outside the team. As an information roadmap, it sets expectations and simplifies communications. The purpose of meetings and expected results should be clear as well as when and how they are conducted. If there were reports done that do not have a clear purpose or a benefiting stakeholder, eliminate them. Be sure to estimate the time and effort required to develop these communications, hold meetings, etc., so they are factored into work plans and schedules. At this stage of the project, it is best to ensure frequent steering committee and team meetings. Keep the ESC and team aligned and informed of changes as they occur, and maintain consensus on the current path to successfully completing the project.

Teams should establish communications plans that include:

- Frequency of communication
- Modes of communication (and when they are appropriate)
  - IM
  - E-mail
  - Phone
  - Face-to-face
  - Web meeting
  - SharePoint or team website
- What to communicate
  - Regular reports
  - Status information & updates
  - Emergent issues and tasks
  - Team information
- Established expected response times to avoid cross-cultural disconnects

A very simple communications plan sample is provided below in what is sometimes referred to as an information map format. The goal is to quickly and easily communicate the desired information without any extra text to clutter or confuse the message.

Team Communication Plan (Sample)

Purpose   The purpose of this document is to establish guidelines on communication standards for PROJECT meetings and reports. Guidelines are included for
- Meetings - communicating information
  * Scope and timeliness of regularly scheduled meetings at all project levels
- Project Reporting - establishing documentation
  * Automated and manual reporting methods
- Methods of communication - establishing distribution lists
  * Alternative methods of communicating (e.g., bulletin board, e-mail, and issue tracking) project status to all project levels.

Objective   The objective of this document is to provide a communication framework that *minimizes*
- missed project deadlines;
- cost overruns;
- production errors; and
- high project personnel turnover.

Meeting Schedule

The following meetings are held on a regular basis. Team members should determine which meetings they should attend and plan their schedules accordingly.

Sponsor Meeting
  Attendees: Business Sponsor
Sponsor designees
Program Director

Schedule:	Weekly
Time:	Wednesday 1:00–2:00 p.m. EDT
Place:	TBD and videoconference
Purpose:	General status update
Facilitator:	Program Director
Scribe:	Project Manager

Team Leads Meeting

Attendees:	Project Leads
Schedule:	M/W/F
Time:	9:00–9:30 a.m. EDT
Place:	Project Team Room and videoconference
Purpose:	Current project status and issue update meeting
Facilitator:	Project Manager
Scribe:	Assistant PM

Meeting Schedule

Meeting	Mon	Tue	Wed	Thu	Fri	Notes
Sponsor Meeting			1:00 – 2:00 p.m.			
Team Leads Meeting	9:00 – 9:30 a.m.		9:00 – 9:30 a.m.		9:00 – 9:30 a.m.	
Program Leadership Meeting			10:00 – 11:00 a.m.			
Technology Steering Meeting						Monthly as scheduled by PMO

Project Reports

Project Status Report

When:	Weekly
Originator:	Project Manager
Audience:	Sponsor
	Program Director
Purpose:	Formal project status

Game Plan

When:	Monthly
Originator:	PM
Audience:	IT Organization Leadership
	Operating Committee
Purpose:	To provide a coordinated view across all subprojects contained within the project

Executive Steering Committee Communications

When:	Monthly
Originator:	Project Sponsor
Audience:	Senior Leadership
	Operating Committee
Purpose:	Disseminate project information

Although we are not going to go into detail about creating and updating specific project planning documents, we are going to highlight some specific considerations. The overarching one is to replan based on where the project really is now. You have had an opportunity to gauge productivity and progress, identify issues, and develop a view of what the current project team is capable of. Bring those views to planning sessions, and challenge the team if unrealistic assumptions are being made. Use your experience in the industry and with similar projects to keep the team focused on what is needed and what is achievable.

Work with the Sponsor and adjust scope if required to meet the cost, schedule, and quality constraints. As noted in Chapter 7, there may be lower priority items that can be removed from the current project or phase, and there may be others that can be deferred because they are not required on Day 1 of go-live, such as annual reports. Team members should participate in identifying requirements, epics, user stories, etc., that can be deferred or eliminated. The final decisions should be made by working with the Sponsor and Business Owner, taking into consideration the impacts on all stakeholders. When changes are being made, ensure that they are clearly communicated to the impacted stakeholders and reflected in the associated artifacts and plans. They should also go through the change management process as a Change Request (CR) so they are fully documented and approved.

Another approach to adjusting the workload on the delivery team is to modify the quality requirements. For example, there may be a number of typographical or graphical issues noted in screen layouts or printed reports. If they do not impact the ability of the user to perform their tasks or get the information they need, correcting these issues may be deferred or given a lower priority in the backlog. They should not be simply dismissed. They should remain in the tracking system as defects requiring correction, being deferred to a later phase of the project, or handed off to the maintenance team. Again, these should be tracked and reviewed in the hand-off to a maintenance team if the delivery team is not going to correct them. In some cases, extending the warranty period when the delivery team is still responsible for correcting these issues allows the primary delivery to occur on schedule while ensuring that the customer does not have to pay extra or live with the defects. For example, it may be acceptable to have paint and finish problems addressed after the house has been occupied.

There may be cost and schedule impacts related to quality issues that occurred earlier in the project or related to the updates being made to project plans. Working with the team, guided by the interviews and artifact reviews that you have done, determine if the preceding work needs to be redone (e.g., fixing poorly done requirements). Previously completed artifacts, such as the architectural plans, may need to be adjusted to reflect the current reality. A software package may not provide the promised capabilities, system throughput may be much higher than originally estimated, there may be geographical issues with the home site that require shifting the location and design of the foundation, etc. In some cases, it may not be possible to correct existing artifacts and deliverables, requiring the team to live with the current state, but be sure to properly record the issues. If possible, include them in the backlog for future sprints, warranty period work, a future project, or correction by the maintenance team.

As scope and quality are being revised, work with the delivery team and reschedule the project. Identify changing resource needs, changes in task duration and sequencing, any additional potential scope changes, member assignment changes, and so on. The key is to be realistic and objective, so we can avoid additional schedule slips in the future. As noted earlier, there will be a tendency to pad time and resource estimates, especially if the project is behind schedule or having other issues. The PM needs to clearly communicate that it is OK for estimates to come with their uncertainty noted. In fact, using the PERT approach (Program Evaluation Review Technique) of optimistic, pessimistic, and most likely estimates for each task is preferred, if possible, to develop them. Any slack or reserve time (and budget) should be explicitly identified and held by the PM.

There are different scheduling approaches used by different methodologies. Ensure the selected approach is appropriate for the methodology and provides a way to project future schedule performance, not just track past performance. The driving a car down a road analogy fits—it is better to steer based on looking out the front window than looking out the back window. Avoid using "schedules" that only track activity, not progress—from a schedule point of view, knowing that 80% of the planned labor hours have been expended is not as important as knowing that only 50% of the task is completed when it should be 80%. Although we'll use both facts to adjust our plans and budgets, in terms of the schedule, we are behind. Also, be careful when using Gantt Charts for scheduling and tracking progress.

If they do not show the sequencing and interdependencies of tasks, they can provide a false picture of progress. Be sure to monitor the critical path of tasks and milestones as plans evolve. Progress by the team may shift the critical path to include different tasks and place additional pressure on the schedule.

As scope, quality, and schedule are adjusted, that is going to impact resource plans. Keep these updated to reflect ongoing work as well as the revised plans. It is unlikely that work will be paused while replanning goes on, so "actuals" need to be factored in. For example, with agreements to reduce scope, it may be possible to reduce staffing. Until the scope reductions go through the approval process and the staff reductions are made, there will be continued expenses incurred for those resources. Ideally, they will contribute to tasks that still need to be done, but the resource plan and budget need to reflect their continuing assignment to the project. Note that resource plans should also include resources other than people. These can include equipment, communication lines, office space, etc. For example, the project may need to continue paying for a test environment that is no longer needed until the resources can be allocated to another project or customer.

When looking at resources, identify ways people and resources outside the team can help. This can range from bringing in specific expertise, coaches, or support staff, to getting relief for members who are assigned other responsibilities outside the project. For example, a senior architect who is split across multiple projects may be able to more rapidly complete an architectural review by being dedicated to this project for a few days. Work with team members to identify outside resources that can benefit the project and ask for them. Press to get the resources desired, stressing the benefits to the project, especially if there are key external dependencies.

Exercise: List the things you can do to identify resource gaps and fill them.

All these changes are going to impact the budget. Depending upon the planning approach being used, the budget may be updated as plans are updated or may be done separately once the scope, quality, schedule, and resources have been adjusted. It is very unusual to have projects with unlimited budgets, so budget considerations should never be left until the very end of a replanning effort. As noted with scheduling, there is a tendency to pad budget estimates and provide some slack for individual tasks and teams. All estimates come with some uncertainty, and this can be noted as part of the estimate, but it needs to be explicit. As the project budget is revised, any reserve should be held by the PM, not hidden across a number of tasks. It is a truism that work will expand to fill the time allocated for it, and the same will happen with budgets.

Question the estimates received and ensure that you are comfortable with them. Are they realistic? Does the effort match the expected value of the end result? Were current performance and conditions factored in? While the PM cannot be an expert in all the technical areas involved, and budget estimates need to come from the team members and leads, the PM is expected to question the estimates and verify that they were properly vetted by the team(s) involved. When these actions are completed, there will be an updated budget target and contingency. These need to be regularly maintained, updated, and reported with the help of the delivery team. If working with a PMO, ensure the revised values are reflected in their reporting systems as well.

As the replanning proceeds, identify any key dependencies, especially if they are outside the delivery team and not under the direct control of the PM. Seek formal acknowledgment of commitments and target dates with external teams and providers supported by the ESC. Track the progress of these related efforts and escalate any issues as they appear. For example, if an interface to another system should be available at a specific date to allow development and testing to continue, work with the team developing the interface to track progress and verify that it will be ready on time. Most projects require deliverables to be reviewed and accepted by a customer, whether there is a contractual requirement, milestone review under waterfall delivery, or acceptance of work at the end of a sprint. Get formal agreement from the customers to promptly review and approve deliverables as they are completed to avoid project delays or rework if a deliverable is subsequently changed, impacting downstream items. Monitor this going forward to prevent backsliding on the agreements. Emphasize that the revised plans and agreed targets were based on prompt reviews and acceptance, so delays will cause target dates to be missed.

One of the most difficult situations for an incoming PM is when the delivery methodology needs to be changed. There can be many reasons for this to be necessary, usually a combination of the ability of the broader organization and delivery team to follow the selected methodology, availability and use of proper supporting tools, and the constraints of the project itself. For example, if there is a hard deadline that must be met with specific scope and quality, Agile methodologies are unsuitable. If the requirements are unclear and likely to change, waterfall is unsuitable. If the project review and interviews have demonstrated the need to change the methodology, this needs to be discussed with the Sponsor, Business Owner, and ESC. If it is agreed that a new methodology is needed, the existing project will usually be stopped and a new project started, planned from scratch, probably with a new team. If the decision is made to continue the existing project with the same delivery team but change the methodology, try to get a pause to review the new methodology with the team, replan the project to align with the methodology, and get approval from the key stakeholders before restarting work. This is a lower risk than trying to revise the methodology with the team while still delivering under the old methodology. If this cannot be done, note the issue, and be ready to handle additional challenges as the project proceeds.

Throughout this process, keep the Risks and Issues Log updated, making sure it is based on reality. Avoid the temptation to pad the log with typical project risks. Focus on the ones that are unique to this project and the current circumstances. Do not use the R&I Log as a tool to provide excuses if the project is not successful. Focus on the ones that matter and that can be addressed. The R&I Log should be reviewed at all status meetings, obtaining updated status on planned mitigations and responses to issues. Provide the R&I Log to the ESC and other key stakeholders, highlighting the most urgent and those that require action or support from the meeting participants. Used properly, this can be a valuable tool in highlighting areas requiring management attention and gaining needed support for the project.

Revised plans are no good if they are not accepted by the delivery team and the key stakeholders. Developing and updating the plans with the delivery team and stakeholders should ensure their commitment to the latest versions and lead to formal acceptance. Be wary about situations where there are multiple draft plans prepared but none of them are formally accepted as the new plan. Draft plans allow parties to pretend that they did not agree to the changes, even if they are following the draft plan in many respects. This can be especially dangerous in a contract situation. Get a formal agreement on the revised plan, preferably in writing. The plans will change, they always do, but the possibility of future changes is not an excuse not to accept the current plans, which are the best available at that point in time. If approval cannot be obtained, this must be escalated to the ESC for a quick resolution.

Tip: *The replanning effort is an iterative process for all but the shortest of projects. Include additional planning efforts in the project plans going forward.*

In this chapter, we provided some key considerations and tips when replanning an ongoing project. The exact form that the plans will take will vary with the methodology in use and the standards of the organization. Including delivery team members and key stakeholders in the replanning process is critical to ensure their commitment to the revised plans. Seek opportunities to adjust scope and quality targets if schedule and/or budget are fixed. Support team members in identifying support needs and opportunities to improve processes and tools and in overcoming obstacles that they face. Keep the Sponsor, Business Owner, and ESC informed and involved in the replanning effort to avoid surprises and gain their support. Take the time to review and update the Stakeholder Map and Communication Plan to identify any hidden stakeholders and ensure that required communications are being conducted on a regular basis.

All this activity has probably been occurring while work on delivering the project continued. In the next chapter, we'll provide some guidance on executing the revised plan, including the additional management challenges that an incoming PM has with an ongoing project and existing project team.

Exercise: List specific things you will do and tools you will use when replanning an ongoing project.

CHAPTER 9

EXECUTE THE REVISED PLAN

"To succeed, planning alone is insufficient. One must improvise as well."

--Isaac Asimov, writer and professor

As noted in the quote from Isaac Asimov, as we execute the revised plans, we will have to make changes. Ideally, these will be minor adjustments as we go, and the project will stay on track. There are a number of things that we can do while executing the revised plan to reduce the probability that major changes or disruptions can occur. These include good communications, commitment from the stakeholders, tracking and reporting progress, and keeping the delivery team focused on successfully delivering the project. We'll cover these tasks in this chapter, while the next two chapters will cover some leadership tips and keeping the project on track for success. Keeping the project on track does not mean that there won't be changes to the revised plans, just that suitable progress is being made to get to the agreed-upon finish line.

Research and Development Is Not Steady State

A navy engineering team had designed a new deployment and retrieval system for a towed sensor system. The design looked good on paper, and all the calculations indicated that it should work. Approval was received to build and test a prototype. Limited testing onshore had gone well, so sea tests needed to be done. The lead engineer was struggling to complete the sea test plan, so the PMO was called in to help. Within a few days, a PERT schedule was completed, along with a project plan, budget, and Risks and Issues Log. The test team was briefed on the plan, and revisions started coming in. The ship assigned for testing was no longer available at the desired time, fabrication of test rigs was behind schedule, and test equipment calibrations were behind schedule. In short, the usual issues that can come up in this type of project.

Although some key stakeholders had downplayed the necessity of a detailed plan, since R&D is a lot more variable than steady state work "you can't plan it," the value of the base plan soon became apparent. As each issue arose, the impact on other tasks was readily determined, as well as the impact on the overall schedule. When negotiating new commitments, reference to the plan and overall schedule was made, helping the PM get the desired results. The equipment was installed on the new test ship, and the tests ran smoothly. Thanks to the planning that had been done, all the required engineers, equipment, and supporting materials were there. The tests were successful, and the system was put into production.

*Don't let the probability of future changes
prevent creating and maintaining a plan.*

Unless you are planning to take over the world, secret plans do not work. Take the plans that the delivery team and key stakeholders have developed and communicate them broadly. Ensure that supporting and coordinating teams understand any revised dates and expectations, including the fact that you will keep them informed of your progress and that you expect them to keep you informed of their progress and readiness to meet the agreed-upon dates. If there is going to be slippage on either side of the agreement, the earlier both teams know about it, the more options there are to handle the issue. Open and honest two-way communication is an important step in not only advertising the revised plans but getting commitment to them.

If possible, set up a "War Room" or team area where the schedule and project metrics are posted for all to see. Update these as progress is made, and celebrate milestones and little victories. In addition to helping team morale, this also reinforces the public commitment that the team has made to the current plan. If anyone has questions about where their tasking fits into the overall scheme of things, they can easily see it. Progress, or the lack of progress, is also readily apparent to the entire team and to key stakeholders. This increases the commitment of members to meet their obligations and not let the team down.

When possible, hold team meetings in the team area and refer to the posted materials. Use them when reviewing progress and issues since they are the road map the team is using to get to their destination together. Don't hesitate to bring the Sponsor and Business Owner into the team room and review progress with them and the team to ensure that everyone has the same understanding regarding progress and challenges, making it more likely that they will communicate the same story to people outside the project. It is better to prevent rumors and misinformation from spreading instead of having to correct the information once it has spread. War Rooms can also be online, and this is required when working with remote and virtual teams. While these are very innovative and necessary, don't forego the opportunity to have a physical War Room if possible. Even with dispersed teams, there are benefits to having a dedicated team space.

As noted in the R&D story above, changes are going to happen. They may be minor, they may be major, but be sure to communicate those changes to all impacted parties. Use the Communication Plan that you've developed to identify who needs to get the information and the best way to get it to them. The roles and responsibilities of the stakeholder will determine the impact of changes on them and determine the urgency of the communications. Be prepared for feedback from outside the team that may require adjusting plans. For example, a user testing period may have shifted to a week that is already overloaded for the users, such as an accounting team that has to do quarterly reporting that week. Work out accommodations as needed, ensuring that appropriate members of your team are included in the discussions. There will be some things that you can change without impacting the overall schedule and others that will have a big impact. Be flexible where you can, but be firm when you have to be. Bring your Sponsor and Business Owner into the discussions when necessary, and escalate to the ESC for particularly impactful issues. Remain alert for opportunities to compress schedules, reduce effort, and save resources when they provide benefits without stressing the team. These small wins can be helpful when not-so-good changes need to be made to plans.

Why the emphasis on communication? We need to get commitment to the revised plans and the inevitable changes that are going to occur. Very few project teams can "go at it alone"—most need support from other teams, other departments, contractors, suppliers, and other organizations. The team also needs support from managers and executives within the organization. Each of these people and groups has different views of our project, some favorable, some not favorable. There may be rumors going through the hallways (or over the net), and these may negatively impact our project. Clear, easy-to-understand, and consistent communication is the best way to prevent miscommunication and misperceptions about our project. In addition, once it is understood that information about the project, its plans, and its progress is readily available and shared, people are less likely to go to the "rumor mill" to get their information. They will feel comfortable going to the PM or team members with questions or concerns and also with updates from their areas that may impact the project. Wouldn't it be nice to get an unofficial heads-up about a potential delivery delay that could impact your schedule? This is more likely to happen when communications from the project team have increased the commitment of external groups to the project plans and success of the project.

As the inevitable changes occur, we need to maintain commitment to the revised plans. There are likely to be changes that will negatively impact other teams. For example, a Building Inspector moving up an inspection date may require the electrician and plumber to work over a weekend to complete their tasks prior to the inspection. If they are not committed to the success of the project and informed of the change as early as possible, they may not be willing or able to accommodate the change. You need to have a bias towards communication and action to stay on top of situations similar to these. PMs cannot sit content with a "perfect plan" and wait for updates. Demonstrate your commitment to the project and plans by being proactive and interested in daily activities, and expect the same from your team. You have to demonstrate your commitment, not just talk about it. Set similar expectations with your leads and team members, and address any shortfalls as they come to your attention.

Gaining and keeping commitment to the project and project plans isn't just enforcing discipline. Take advantage of opportunities to celebrate successes, praise members and accomplishments, and recognize support provided from outside the team. For example, when the infrastructure team worked over the weekend to set up the SIT environment three weeks early (see the "Not All Risks Are Bad" story in Chapter 6), the PM and QA Leads brought in pizza and ice cream for the infrastructure team on Saturday. The infrastructure manager and his leads joined the Monday afternoon project status meeting and were given a standing ovation by the project leads and the Sponsor. This further cemented bonds between the teams and fostered greater commitment to project success. It also led to closer ties for future projects in the program and much better communications across the teams. If a member or team puts forth extra effort to meet a commitment or exceed expectations, take time to recognize it, even if all you can do is send a thankful e-mail (be sure to copy their manager on the e-mail). It's the right thing to do, and it demonstrates your leadership and commitment to the team. A reputation as a committed and supportive leader will last far beyond a single project and will lead to future success and career growth.

How do you know what to communicate to the team? Although we'll cover metrics and quality measures in more detail in the next chapter, having appropriate and reliable metrics is the foundation for your communications. The number and type of metrics will vary with the type of project, industry, and methodology involved. By this point, you should determine which metrics are available, which ones are useful, and any additional ones that may be needed. If the data being collected does not provide the information needed to make decisions about the project, then the metrics should be revised or dropped. For example, the scheduling process being used should allow progress to be tracked and determine if tasks and the overall project are ahead of or behind schedule. The critical path, or chain of dependencies, should be clearly identified, along with key milestones. Updating the schedule to show progress to date should facilitate identifying which tasks are ahead or behind schedule and if there are any impacts on the project completion date. If not, then another scheduling process and/or tool are needed.

In addition to tracking and reporting on the schedule, metrics tied to the other project constraints also need to be maintained and consulted. Is project scope stable or changing (e.g., Is the number of requirements changing? Are there a lot of Change Requests being submitted? Are defect reports being used to mask what are really Change Requests?)? What is the quality of what is being developed? Is the quality improving or decreasing? How do actual and projected expenditures compare to the budget? Are the expenditure trends going in the desired direction? How is software development going if it is a software project? Are we tracking activity (hours spent) or progress (requirements or function points completed)? All these inputs should be used to update project plans and provide the status in reports. They are also needed when working with the delivery team to determine status and adjust plans going forward. Metrics allow the team to focus on facts, not opinions or feelings. Objective, fact-based team discussions lead to better planning and maintaining a commitment to the project.

As we go through the metrics collected and assess progress with the delivery team, we will need to summarize this information and report it to the Sponsor, Business Owner, ESC, and supporting teams. As with metrics, we need to provide the information that these entities need to inform their decisions and actions, so there may be more than one report format needed. Reporting may need to follow an organizational standard. If there are shortcomings with the standard template, work with the controlling activity to update the template. If this is not possible, there should be a narrative section where additional details can be provided. At a minimum, report what was planned to be accomplished, what was actually accomplished, and what is planned for the upcoming period. The Risks and Issues Log should be available to management and key stakeholders, but it can also be helpful to highlight separately the top few issues and risks that are being attended to by the project team.

While monitoring progress, maintain control of your reserves—slack in the schedule, budget reserve, etc. Do not allow these to be frittered away without thought. As the PM, these belong to you and only you. If a task is running late or extra budget is required, the member or lead involved should let the PM know as soon as the issue becomes apparent so the potential impacts can be assessed and alternatives examined. Spending slack and reserves is likely to be needed, but be careful to use it wisely. Make sure the entire team is aware of the need for the PM to control slack and reserves and enforce the discipline needed to keep it under your control. It is unlikely that time lost or budget spent can be replaced, so do not spend it too early.

There's Plenty of Time Left

A three-year contract to design, develop, build, and install a revolutionary new test facility for specialized military hardware was given to a small engineering company that had the required expertise and manufacturing capability. An overall schedule and budget were prepared, working backward from the contract end date. The effort and budget estimates were optimistic, and due to it being a fixed-price contract, profit margins were estimated to be higher than normal for the company.

The project team proceeded to purchase new office equipment and expensive computers, attend professional training conferences, and conduct other activities to enjoy work while preparing to focus on the project. Progress was slow, and milestones were delayed. This developed into a pattern. Software development was slow, and required hardware design drawings were not provided to the fabrication shop when expected. Other teams working with the core group expressed concern when commitments were delayed and expressed doubts about the commitment of the core group to meeting the schedule.

With 18 months left to go, the customer was finally worried enough to conduct a detailed project review, leading to a revised project plan with updated schedules and budgets for each team. Not only had all the schedule slack been used up, but the forecast profit margin had also dropped by 50%, and due to unforeseen design challenges, it was estimated that another 24 months were needed to finish the project. New project management was brought in, along with staff for project administration. The core team and supporting teams had to work overtime, including multiple weekends for months, to try to maintain the revised schedule. Schedule slips continued, and costs soared. Many of the original team members left the company, and recruiting new members was difficult as news of the troubled project spread through the organization.

The test facility was eventually up and running over two years after the original target date, with a budget overrun of many millions of dollars for the government and a net loss of close to $3 million for the engineering company. All because the budget and schedule reserves to account for development issues were frivolously spent at the beginning of the project.

The "There's Plenty of Time Left" story provides a good lesson on why the PM needs to carefully control schedule and budget reserves. As the delivery team proceeds with the revised plan, take advantage of opportunities to conduct Lessons Learned sessions or retrospectives. These should be done at the end of each Sprint if following a Scrum methodology, but they should also be planned into the schedule for other delivery methodologies. For example, at the end of the requirements phase, after software has been moved into a test environment, or when the house foundation is completed. Review what went well, what went not so well, and what should be changed in the future. Look at what is coming next and what improvements can be incorporated. Review what worked well that should be continued.

Unfortunately, too many teams look at lessons learned as only useful for the next project and miss the opportunity to apply them to their current project. For example, was there adequate communication? Did everyone get the information they needed when they needed it? How are the processes and tools working out? Are changes needed? These are all legitimate topics to cover in a Lessons Learned or Retrospective session. Be sure to include capturing tacit or implicit knowledge and information as well during retrospectives. This can be beneficial during the current project and phase as well as later on. For example, documenting why a particular change request was postponed until the next project will be very useful if there is a new request to add it to the current scope. The reasoning behind key decisions can be very helpful to other PMs and teams as well, so consider where it makes sense to document that information.

We'll cover some tips on how to conduct Lessons Learned in more detail in the second section of Chapter 12. Go ahead and jump there if you can't wait. We've also provided some supporting materials for Lessons Learned in the Appendix and online at our website.

The revised plan has been completed and communicated to all the stakeholders. The team is moving the project forward, progress is being reported, and plans are being updated as needed. Things are going better than before, and the project is headed in the right direction. The hard work is done, and to use the old phrase, "It's Miller Time!" ... Not exactly! While the immediate crises may be over and the project improving, there is still a lot of work to be done. The "honeymoon" period that the new PM may have been granted is definitely ending, and there are going to be rough days ahead. The next two chapters cover some of the issues likely to arise and why there are still likely to be challenges different from a regular project that had the same PM from beginning to end. While regular PM activities, disciplines, and tools are needed, there are additional warning signs and potential issues that need to be covered.

CHAPTER 10

MOVE TO THE FINISH LINE TOGETHER

"Leadership consists of nothing but taking responsibility for everything that goes wrong and giving your subordinates credit for everything that goes well."

--Dwight D. Eisenhower, 34th US president

Get Me off This Project!

The project was Red, and it was getting redder. Despite working closely with the client team for over three years, the project was going badly. Client requirements kept changing, with the client claiming they were defects. Changes and fixes were made, but the client delayed testing and accepting them. Client meetings sometimes turned into blame sessions. The delivery team was tired, frustrated, depressed, and burnt out. The incoming Project Director had recommended terminating the contract and reaching a settlement with the client. Despite

---

this recommendation, the managing VP directed that work continue in an effort to complete the contract.

While meeting with each team member individually and as a team, the PD heard about the history of problems and learned that all the team members wanted to get off the team. The members had unique knowledge that was required to finish the project, so the team had to hold together. As a first step, the PD stopped all direct communication between the client team and the delivery team to reduce noise and confusion. This was presented to the client as necessary to control the flow of information so client management had better control. Regular status meetings and reports with the client were formalized, using a more detailed format. Responses to client requests were promised within 48 hours, and as these deadlines were met, client comfort and confidence improved. All this was done to reduce the noise aimed at the team and the pressure they felt.

Additional members were added to the team from the bench to support the core team. Working hours were reduced for the entire team to the regular 40-hour-a-week schedule, and some members were allowed to attend technical training that had been requested but delayed for months. A series of team-building sessions were held, including "working lunches" to demonstrate value and regard for the members. An overdue promotion was pushed through. In client meetings, the PD pushed back on unreasonable client requests and did not allow derogatory comments about members to be made. Despite some initial pushback by client management, the tone of meetings became much more professional, and members no longer dreaded them.

By the end of the first month, morale improved, and significant progress was made on the project. Although still Red overall, a number of problem areas were improved, and the morale of the delivery team was much better. Jokes were told in meetings, and member events were celebrated, such

> *as birthdays, work anniversaries, and so on. All the transfer requests were voluntarily withdrawn, and several temporary team members asked to be assigned full-time. The PM, who had been pulled into the project when the first PM abruptly left the company, had taken over a number of responsibilities from the PD and was clearly developing into a much more confident and capable PM. Senior management was confident enough in the PM, and current progress, to appoint the PD as the lead PD on a major new program with a new client without stopping their work on the current project.*
>
> *The swamp had not been drained, but the water level was receding, and the alligator had paused his chewing, at least for now.*

The key takeaway from the above story is that we have to keep moving to the finish line together. No PM can deliver a project by themselves, nor can they drive the team to be successful by force of will. The PM has to bring the team along with them. In westerns, the sheriff gathers a posse to help him or her track down and capture the bad guys. Many of the steps we've already taken were designed to keep the team together, foster commitment to project success, and build team spirit. These efforts need to continue as we work on the revised project plan and deliver the project. We also need to bring all the key stakeholders along, so we'll cover some actions that support that goal after focusing on the delivery team itself.

Gather the Posse

A key component of the updated project plans is the staffing plan. A PM doesn't deliver a project alone; they must have a team with the right skills that is committed to successfully delivering the project. When a PM joins an existing project, there should be a team in place, but it is also likely that team changes will be needed. In most cases, the current team needs to continue making progress on the project while the PM and team leads adjust resources to meet the updated staffing plan. This includes evaluating the knowledge and skills of existing team members and identifying any shortfalls. There may be other factors driving changes to the team as well, such as replacing higher-cost team members with lower-cost members who can perform the required tasks, rotating members who are needed on other projects, replacing traveling members with local members, and replacing members that have been promoted to other roles.

Do not hesitate to request resources if needed, using the revised plans that have been approved for support. Using facts and coherent plans to demonstrate resource needs objectively will be more successful than unsupported requests for help. Be as specific as possible when requesting members with required knowledge and skills, but understand that it is unusual to get a member that matches the request perfectly. There will always be a need to bring them up to speed on the specifics of the project, including their role, processes, and tools. Be sure to factor this into staffing and resource plans, budgets, and schedules. Work with HR to determine a reasonable estimate of the lead time required to identify, interview, and assign new team members. Do not assume zero lead time or that new members will be productive immediately. Those assumptions immediately invalidate your plans, something that should also be looked for when reviewing project plans and project recovery efforts.

Most projects require a mix of talents. Do you have the right mix? While some gaps will have been identified during your preliminary research, others will only come to light as time goes by. Follow up with your leads and key team members to get their assessments. Sometimes this requires being objective and decisive. If a member is clearly struggling to complete tasks on time, repeatedly has quality issues, or requires too much help from other members, that issue needs to be addressed. In some cases, coaching will work; in others bringing in a more experienced member to directly supervise the member on a regular basis or providing training in particular areas is more effective. In other cases, the member may need to be replaced on the team. This should not be a decision to separate the member from the organization; that is outside the purview of the PM. Instead, the tack should be that the member is not in the right role within the current project, and they would be better suited in a different role on a different project.

Work with HR and management, including the member's direct manager, if in a matrix-style organization. Stay objective, and highlight the member's strengths as well as weaknesses. If there are knowledge and skill gaps, suggest how those might be addressed once the member leaves the team. Then take action with HR and management to remove the member from the team. Be prepared to meet with the individual and have a difficult conversation, as well as to communicate to the team why the member has moved on. These are important steps to ensure that you continue to be trusted by management and team members and that you are seen as having the best interests of the team and project in mind. Member changes should never be vindictive, personal, or hasty.

There may be cases where a member is acting in a manner that is harmful to the team and the project. Especially when members have been working long hours and are under a lot of pressure, this stress can lead to unsuitable behavior. Work with HR and the member to correct the situation, but if the member is unable or unwilling to change, work with HR to quickly remove them from the team. Do not let the larger team be negatively affected by one member, and communicate this to the team when the member is removed (see Chapter 2 story "Why did You Fire Our PM?").

From the project review, and as the project evolves, there are likely to be additional resource gaps. Identifying and filling these gaps should be done with your leads and team members as project plans are updated. For example, a decision by the homeowner to use marble tile for the bathroom floor may require the addition of tasks to select and purchase the tiles, find and hire a tile installation expert, and make adjustments to the schedule and budget. These impacts should be included when estimating the cost and schedule impact of the change request and approved as part of the change order.

Other resource needs may occur as part of the plan, for example, needing organizational change experts to help roll out new software within an organization. These should be included in project plans, including time to obtain the desired resources. In some cases, expert advice from outside the team may be needed to aid in determining the knowledge and skills required, estimating the effort involved, and selecting the right resources or member. Do not be reluctant to request this help, and work with the broader organization and ESC as needed to get the support required. If there are likely to be challenges in getting the support required, note this in the Risk and Issues Log, track it, and change it to an issue before it becomes a critical gap impacting the project.

Some PMs and leads are reluctant to delegate tasks to members or to take the time to train members as needed for the project. There are many assumptions that cause people to fall into this trap, "It is easier to do it myself," "We don't have time to train them," "They aren't ready for this responsibility," etc. I've made this mistake myself. What I've found, and is usually the case, is team members will surprise us with what they are really capable of. Give them the opportunity to accept additional responsibility, learn new skills, take a burden off an overworked member, and fill gaps in the team. Most members are eager to learn new skills and want to advance their careers. Seek opportunities to help them do this while providing the training and support they need. It may take some extra effort in the near term, but it will pay off in the long run, as well as demonstrate to the member and the broader team that you have their interests at heart. This may also require monitoring and working with your leads and technical experts to help them break out of the "do it themselves" habit and get them to do more to develop their members. As members become more skilled, they can more readily fill gaps that may appear in the team and ultimately benefit the project while improving their career opportunities.

Exercise: List the things you can do to identify resource gaps and fill them.

We noted the likely need to conduct team-building exercises during the early phases of taking over a project. These efforts should continue throughout the project. They may be more subtle and less formal but include them in your plans. These can include some fun activities in team meetings, team get-togethers, celebration of milestones and key wins, and even just praising members who have done well. If members are leaving or joining the team, additional team-building activities may be required—remember Forming, Storming, Norming, Performing. Do not assume that new members will automatically blend with the team and be productive right away. Ensure that new members are properly inducted into the team, and follow up with them and other team members to learn how it is going. If a large number of members are being added to an existing team, taking a pause for specific team-building activities is usually a good use of time. It should speed up the formation of the new and larger team and pay productivity dividends that will more than make up for the time spent on team building.

In Chapter 5, we discussed Maslow's Hierarchy of Needs as a useful mental model when working with members and teams. There are likely to be issues and events within or even external to the project that push some members, or the entire team, to lower levels of the pyramid. For example, there may have been layoffs in the broader organization. Even if no one on the team was laid-off, they probably know someone who was. Don't ignore the impacts of the event. Taking time to meet with the team, discussing what happened, discussing member feelings and concerns, and reassuring them that no further layoffs are planned in the near term will help them get over the event and move back up the pyramid faster. Keep Maslow's Model in mind, and use it when deciding on a response to events that impact member or team morale.

Keeping the project team together and focused requires leadership, not just management. PMs need to be leaders to be effective, despite their role being called "Project Management." Some organizations use the title "Project Leader" instead of "Project Manager" to emphasize the leadership aspect. There are many, many schools of thought on leadership and thousands of books on it. A model that I have found particularly useful when taking over existing projects is also used by the U.S. military, where changes in command are regularly expected.

The model is called Situational Leadership, and we will very briefly cover the key components of the approach. If you are interested in learning more about it, please check the numerous online and published resources on the topic. If you want to see a great example of situational leadership in action, watch the movie *12 O'Clock High*, starring Gregory Peck. It is a fictional story of an officer taking over a troubled unit in World War II. You will see him take the unit through all four stages described in the Situational Leadership model.

> **"Leadership is a difficult, but not impossible, quality to acquire. Any individual who really wants to be a leader can be one. It takes hard work. It takes knowledge. It takes enthusiasm. But it can be done."**
>
> --Admiral Arleigh Burke, Chief
> of Naval Operations

The Situational Leadership Model

The Situational Leadership model is based on the work done in the 1960s by Blanchard and Hersey and described in their book *Management of Organizational Behavior*.[4] Although they later continued their studies and writings along different paths, their basic views remained the same. The key concept is that the effectiveness of a leader's style depends upon the situation in which it is used. For the best results, match leader behavior to the maturity of the organization (or individual) and the

---

[4]   Paul Hersey, Kenneth Blanchard, and Dewey Johnson, *Management of Organizational Behavior*, 10th ed., Pearson, 2012, New York; also see Stephen P. Robbins and Timothy A. Judge, *Organizational Behavior*, 15th ed., Pearson, 2013, New York (p. 376); Stephen P. Robbins and Mary Coulter, *Management*, 11th ed., Pearson, New York, 2012 (pp. 466–467); Don Hellriegel and John W. Slocum, Jr., *Organizational Behavior*, 11th ed., Thomson-Southwestern, 2007, Mason, OH (pp. 221–225); Rodney C. Vandeveer and Michael L. Menefee, *Human Behavior in Organizations*, Pearson-Prentice Hall, 2006, Upper Saddle River, NJ (pp. 96–98).

task at hand. The same individual may require little leadership for one task but a lot more on another. As the team maturity level increases, leader behavior requires less structure (task) and more interpersonal communication (relationship). Eventually, both task and relationship communication needs will decrease. What is meant by task and relationship communications? How are they different?

- **Task**—The leader's behavior in defining the relationship with the team, communication channels, and delivery processes, along with an emphasis on mission completion. This should also include the transformational aspects of the project or mission, communicating the vision of the broader organization and team status after the project is successful (e.g., auto insurance sales will grow exponentially because our premiums will be more competitive).
- **Relationship**—The leader's behavior in terms of friendship, mutual trust, respect, and warmth with the team. This aspect also relates to the Servant Leadership school of thought.

When assessing the Task-Oriented Maturity level of a team, look at the following areas:

- Capacity to set realistic and challenging goals
- Willingness and ability to take responsibility for the successful completion of the task
- Task-related knowledge, skills, and experience
- Understanding and definition of work processes and tasks (e.g., Is this a new process?)
- Length of time Leader and Team have worked together

When assessing the Team Relationship Maturity level of a team, the following areas should be considered:

- Extent to which the leader engages in open dialog with the follower and actively listens to the follower
- Recognition/reinforcement for task-related progress

Here is a diagram of the Situational Leadership quadrants, relating team maturity from low to high for Task Orientation and Relationship. Note that the style used by the leader will vary based on the relative maturity levels of the team or individual involved. It will also vary with changes in tasking, team organization, and events inside or outside the team. For example, if the broader organization has layoffs, the leader will likely need to revert to a more directive style until the team members recover from the impact of the layoffs, even if no one on the team was laid off (remember Maslow again).

Figure 10-1: Situational Leadership Model

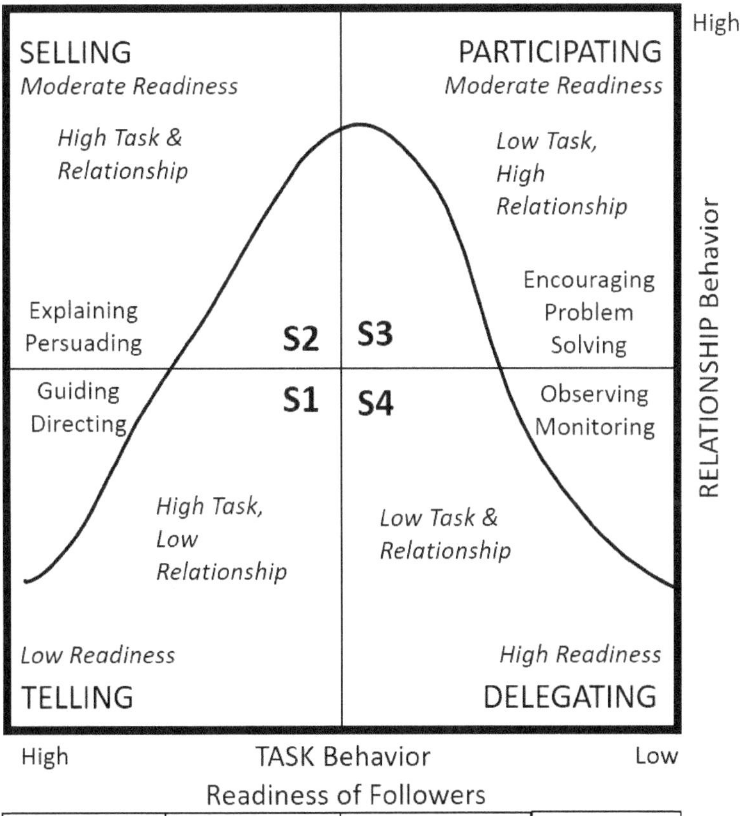

R1 (Low)	R2 (Moderate)	R3 (Moderate)	R4 (High)
Unable, Unwilling or	Unable but Willing or Confident	Able, but Unwilling or Insecure	Able, Willing and Confident

Here are some key characteristics of the four leadership styles.

Telling

This is often the starting point, particularly for a PM joining an ongoing project that has been struggling. The initial orientation is High-Task (focus on moving the project forward) and Low-Relationship (not as much focus on building warm relationships with team members). Due to time constraints and the need to accomplish specific goals, there is primarily one-way communication from leader to team. The leader defines the roles of members, although this is often already set based on member knowledge and skills. The leader tells the team what, how, when, and where to do tasks. Note the absence of "why." In some cases, "Dramatic Acts" may be needed and can be effective in communicating to the team that there is a new sheriff in town and that things are going to be different going forward. These can range from stopping overtime work while replanning is going on, standing up to an abusive member, or even dismissing a troublesome individual from the team.

Dramatic Acts

The new Project Director (PD) and existing Project Manager (PM) were attending the first Executive Steering Committee (ESC) Meeting with the senior client executive and his technical advisor since the PD had joined the team. Unfortunately, the consulting organization VP had to attend the meeting via telephone. As soon as the meeting started, the client executive started shouting at the consulting team and VP about the VP not being there. He stood up, his chair flying back against the wall, and pounded his fists on the table, demanding that the VP immediately approve all the open Change Requests, without cost to the client, roughly $750K in value. Sensing that the client executive was acting up to bully the consulting team, the PD stood up and placed his fists on the table as well.

"We're not going to be intimidated by shouting, and this won't end the change request discussion! You can deal with me, and I'm right here!" shouted the PD.

The room was silent as the client executive and PD looked each other in the eye. The client executive smiled and said, "Okay, if you're here, and you're the one who I need to deal with, we're fine." He calmly retrieved his chair and sat down. So did the PD. The rest of the meeting was polite and professional. The dramatic act by the client executive was to see if he could continue bullying the consulting organization VP to get what he wanted. The dramatic act by the PD showed that he was not going to be bullied and that those tactics would no longer work.

Although the PM was horrified at the time, when the story was repeated to the project team later that morning, they cheered. They realized that a new tone was being set with the client, and they had a manager that would stand up for them.

Selling

As the team moves forward, the leader will move to selling the team on the need to perform the tasks and often the processes to follow. This is shown as High-Task/High-Relationship. The leader still provides most of the direction, but providing the "why" to the individual or team becomes more important. The leader attempts to get members' psychological support for what must be done. Two-way communication and emotional support are required, and this usually takes more time. There is more discussion about what needs to be done and how to do it, but final decisions are still made by the leader. For example, if working over the weekend is needed to meet an intermediate deadline, the PM may explain the need to maintain the schedule and not get behind at this stage. Alternate approaches may be discussed, but if working over the weekend is the best way to stay on schedule, the PM will make that decision.

Participating

As the team continues to mature and they demonstrate more commitment to achieving project goals, the leader will adjust their style to Participating. This is shown as High-Relationship/Low-Task. Low Task does NOT mean less emphasis on achieving organizational goals—it means less effort needs to be spent defining how, when, and where to do the task. In other words, processes are well defined and followed. There is shared decision-making and extensive two-way communication. The leader may be seen as more of a facilitator. This is often the relationship described for the Scrum Master and Scrum Team in Agile-Scrum methodologies. The Scrum Master removes obstacles for the team and coordinates with other teams and management for the team.

Delegating

Ideally, the team will continue to mature and move to a point where the leader can adjust their style to Delegating. This is shown as Low-Task/Low-Relationship in the diagram. The team members "run the show," making decisions about what will be done and how it will be done. The team and members are mature—they are willing and able to take responsibility for their behavior. They self-organize, and business processes and team roles are well understood. The leader can delegate all but setting goals or missions for the team. This is the Performing stage of the team life cycle described earlier. In Agile terms, the leader is likely to be seen as the Business Owner or Business Owner's representative, setting goals and priorities for the team while allowing the team to determine how to achieve those goals in priority order.

There are some challenges when trying to apply the Situational Leadership Model to real people and organizations. First, the leader must be careful to keep longer-term goals and overall strategy in mind when making leadership decisions. Too much focus on dealing with the current situation can lead to suboptimization of the overall project. This is an easy trap for inexperienced managers to fall into and is often noted by academics without management experience who have studied situational leadership. Second, there is a human tendency to want to be liked, which may cause a leader to put more emphasis on relationships instead of the task than is warranted at the time. Third, leaders usually have a preferred leadership style that they are comfortable with. It is easy to default to that style, especially when under stress. Leaders need to be trained and practiced in situational leadership and recognize that they need to shift styles to obtain better results. Finally, it can be challenging to recognize the maturity levels of the team or organization. The tables below provide some help with this.

Table 10-1: 12 Low Maturity Indicators

1. Team members working overtime—all the time
2. Team members leaving early—all the time
3. Inexperienced team members (availability is not a skillset)
4. Team members seem apathetic about mission/deadlines
5. CYA (cover your a**) e-mail trail has started
6. Leads/Managers not sure of the real project task status
7. Intermediate progress points missed, but no adjustments made
8. Missing or out-of-date planning documents
9. Team relationships are problematic
10. No initiative shown by the team—any problem leads to a dead stop
11. Only a few key members are contributing effectively
12. No knowledge transfer, coaching, or training going on between members

---

Table 10-2: 12 High Maturity Indicators

1. Team takes initiative to solve problems
2. Issues/changes/status communicated up the chain without prompting
3. Team takes responsibility for integrating new members— knowledge transfer (KT), culture, and teaming
4. Team accepts responsibility for setting and meeting objectives
5. Team monitors/disciplines members
6. Team work schedules vary with progress, problems, and deadlines
7. Members identify training needs and seek opportunities to correct them
8. Leader tasks increasingly focused externally to the team
9. Leads/Managers familiar with real project task status at all times
10. Intermediate progress points hit or adjustments made without outside prompting
11. Members do not compete, they collaborate
12. Members comfortable letting other members handle their own tasks without interfering

This was a very brief overview of Situational Leadership. It has been shown to work, particularly in cases where a PM takes over an existing team. If you are interested, there are plenty of online resources and training opportunities available so you can explore Situational Leadership further. If you are comfortable with a different leadership approach, that is fine too. Just recognize that some approaches are more effective than others when dealing with different organizations, teams, methodologies, and events.

Get Support From the Town

As important as having a strong, hard-working delivery team is, that is not sufficient to have an overall successful project. Just as a new sheriff needs support from the townspeople, the new PM needs support from key stakeholders. These include more than the Sponsor, Business Owner, and ESC. What groups are going to be impacted by the project? What groups have influence over the project? Are there any other project teams or organizations that are connected to this project, for example, the infrastructure team for software projects, regulatory agencies for construction projects, end customers for new product developments, and so on? These groups should be explicitly identified, their goals and needs identified, and plans established to involve them to the degree necessary to maintain their support for the project. Many organizations will use a formal stakeholder plan; other organizations may do it informally. The nature of the project and organization will strongly influence the number and type of stakeholders involved and their relationship to the project team. Stakeholders should have been identified in the Communications Plan, along with their preferred communication channels. Keep this updated as the project evolves and as the effectiveness of the communication processes and tools are assessed. Ask for feedback from the stakeholders and act on it.

The PM needs to build relationships with these stakeholders, which is usually not trivial and takes time, so it is better to plan for it and include the effort in project estimates. In addition to team building exercises with the delivery team, it may be worthwhile to extend team building outside the delivery team. This is especially true if there are external teams that the delivery team relies on to complete the project. This often includes key users, customers, or suppliers. For example, an automotive firm designing a new hydraulic transmission included sales engineers from a key supplier to ensure that they would use standard components in the design that met the desired specifications. That would eliminate the need for custom and more expensive parts once the new transmission was in production. Consider how the project fits within the overall organization and bigger picture when determining who the stakeholders are and how closely they are tied to the project. If possible, get assistance from an Organizational Change Management (OCM) expert, if one has not already been assigned to the team. The larger and more complex the project, the more likely OCM needs to be a part of the plan.

When dealing with people outside the immediate delivery team, the PM needs to demonstrate leadership and good communication skills. These are even more necessary with a PM taking over an existing project. Expectations were already set with the prior PM, and it is likely that people are comfortable with the way things were going. In other cases, there may have been problems with the prior PM, and the new PM will have to demonstrate that those problems are being addressed and that the path forward is better for all involved. This is not easy and will take time, so allow for it. A key step to resolving issues, preparing the path forward, and maintaining good relations with people external to the team is having good communications with them. Let's look at what that means in more detail.

Communications

The incoming PM needs to focus on effective communications and collaboration within the delivery team, with key stakeholders, and with the broader stakeholder community. The most important thing to do is to communicate to all *honestly*. The new PM needs to establish trust in their leadership, and honest communication is mandatory. This does not mean sharing every bit of information with everyone but providing the information that is needed by that person or group to them when needed. This will likely require more frequent communications than before, even if the project is not in trouble. Since there is a new "sheriff," there is a need for people to learn more about the sheriff, what is changing, what is not changing, what they can expect from the new PM, etc. It is better to intentionally communicate this information than to let it happen randomly. Use these communication opportunities to reinforce that there is a new "sheriff" and that it is not business as usual. Using the Communication Plan developed earlier, provide the information needed to each group, and confirm that the type and frequency of communications planned for that group meet their needs. Adjust the Communication Plan as required while being careful not to overload the team with communication requirements.

When taking over a project and updating project plans and commitments, frequent communication will be required, especially with the ESC and management. Once the updated plans are in place and are being executed, the project should settle into the new routines. That will allow dialing back the frequency of communications and should allow a reduction in the number of reports. For example, if a project is in Red status, daily or weekly meetings with senior executives may be required to keep them informed and to demonstrate positive progress. As things improve, these meetings should be dialed back and possibly eliminated so the PM and team can focus on delivery.

There are likely to be reasons to change report formats, to ensure meaningful metrics are used, and that the right people have the right information needed to make decisions. Some reports may be eliminated if they no longer have value. Different reports may be needed for different delivery phases, for example, Daily Test Reports during testing. Focus on providing the information required in a format that makes it easy to understand and interpret. Usually, graphics are better for showing trends and forecasting future results if things are left unchanged. There are plenty of project reporting examples and textbooks available, and most organizations have established their own formats. Work with management and the delivery team to determine which are appropriate for the project. Don't be afraid to introduce new report formats and retire others. Keep in mind the effort required to compile and format the report and how it will be used. The benefits should outweigh the costs. Finally, there should not be any secrets. Honestly report progress, defects, risks, and issues as they become known. Don't hide problems while trying to fix them. You are probably missing important management support that could help solve the problem. It is true that bad news does not get better with age!

In terms of bad news, it is not appropriate to rehash history or allocate blame; focus on the current facts. There is no "way-back" machine to allow the PM or team members to go back in time and change decisions that were made or events that happened. Accept the facts as they are now and focus on moving forward. If it is necessary to help a member understand how a poor decision was made or that a process needs to be changed, it is best to do that privately. The team needs to feel that they can bring problems and issues to the PM without being shamed or blamed. Encourage open communication and group problem solving to keep information flowing to you. In the same spirit, keep management informed of problems as well as progress; seek help and support when needed.

> **Tip:** *Frequent, factual reporting to stakeholders will increase their confidence.*

There is a caution regarding open and honest communication. If things go very badly, all internal communications may be subject to legal disclosure. This includes unofficial and official communications and artifacts. Things such as e-mails, online chat, text messages, recorded video calls, handwritten notes, and so on are also subject to legal discovery, not just formal artifacts and deliverables. Carefully consider what is being communicated before hitting the Send button.

An experienced customer once explained his approach to e-mails, calling it the "Boston Globe Test." Never put anything in writing that you would not want your mother to read connected to you on the front page of the Boston Globe newspaper. Nowadays, "in writing" involves a lot more than the printed page, memos, or e-mails. This includes notes that you may be taking for your own use, never intending to share them. Sensitive information is best discussed verbally and privately.

Although we discussed conducting a stakeholder analysis and developing a related communications plan earlier, this is a good time to note some of the additional considerations when dealing with remote and dispersed teams. The Covid pandemic accelerated the move of work outside of central offices and the increasingly diverse membership of teams. It is very likely that projects include members from diverse regional, social, and national backgrounds. While this diversity provides many benefits to the project team and the project overall, it can also increase communication and coordination challenges. There are many papers, books, and training courses that cover working in and managing diverse teams, so we will just review a few key tips here. The most important point is to recognize that people are different with diverse communication styles and backgrounds that are likely to impact how they understand the information that is provided to them and how they act upon it. It is important to ensure that the desired information has been received and understood as intended, so maintaining two-way communications is vital. In many cases, communications will need to be tailored for the intended audiences instead of just blasted out without regard to the recipients of the messages.

Remote teams generally tend to take longer to go through the formation process (forming, storming, norming, performing)—allow for it in your plans, including re-establishing communications with the Project Manager. As a vital link in project communications, having a replacement PM is going to temporarily impact communications within and external to the project team. Include these considerations when updating and executing communication plans. In collocated work, a lot of the attention of a PM can be on supporting the delivery of tasks. In virtual and remote working, more focus must be placed on communications between the dispersed members of the team. Clear communication and clearly defined outcomes are a foundation for this. However, ensuring clear communications with remote and diverse teams is not always simple.

Accepting that there are differences between national and regional cultures is an important factor in working today. The impact of these differences is hard to quantify but mainly shows up in communication problems and management style differences. Unfortunately, this can be seen as an increased risk to project team performance, and ultimately success, when it should be seen as a benefit. Diverse people bring different approaches to solving problems. Viewing a problem or opportunity from a new angle can lead to additional options and ideas, while groupthink can stifle creativity and problem recognition.

Organizations that value diversity tend to have members who are more creative, motivated, and productive, with better communications within and across all groups.[5]

Workforce Diversity describes differences among workers in gender, race, age, ethnicity, religion, sexual orientation, and able-bodiness.

There are three levels of cultural differences—Superficial, Societal, and Fundamental. Most of us are familiar with examples of superficial cultural differences since they are the easiest to see. For example, different ways of dressing, speaking, favorite sports, etc. These are often the easiest to accept as well since they appear to be personal preferences. The next level is more difficult to identify and accept. Societal level differences are more deeply rooted within each culture. They appear as the right and natural way to do things, causing people from that culture to question why anyone would do things differently. Encountering people from another culture who do not conform to your culture's "right and natural way to do things" can be upsetting since it seems that they are not doing the "right thing" or behaving in the expected way. The least accessible level includes fundamental cultural differences. These are so internalized that we do not even realize that these thoughts exist. For example, how we view and experience time. In the Euro-American view, time is linear. Some African cultures have no word for the future beyond tomorrow. In some Asian cultures, the view of time is circular. These different views can affect how we negotiate and respect schedules and deadlines without understanding that members from other cultures may not have the same understanding of a deadline as we do.

In addition, linguistic and written language structures affect how we think. For example, the structure and vocabulary of the German language encourage very precise statements. Chinese has numerous

[5]   John Schermerhorn, *Management*, 11th ed., 2010, John Wiley and Sons, Hoboken, NJ.

homonyms—words that sound similar but have different meanings. Different views on the relationship of the individual to society are also likely to impact team communications and behavior. America is strongly individualistic, and Americans expect a greater degree of autonomy and control over their work, while Japanese are strongly group and socially oriented. If circumstances change during a project, Americans are likely to adjust and adapt without communicating to the PM or the rest of the team what has changed. A Japanese team member is more likely to communicate the change in circumstances and wait for a team decision on how to adapt. Each member feels that they are doing what is "expected" based on their cultural background. Such deep differences are almost impossible to recognize in ourselves but can lead to issues within the team.

Typical problems encountered in building diverse teams can include:

- Different levels of experience and education
- Different ways of communicating (e-mail, texting, face-to-face, etc.)
- Different views of how things work and how they should work
- Dispersal across multiple locations and potentially time zones
- Value systems and motivations usually varying
- Primary languages possibly differing

Three key steps for PMs and members of virtual and diverse teams will go a long way in resolving these problems and gaining the benefits of diverse teams:

- Recognize that diversity exists.
- Research specific characteristics of the cultures you are dealing with.
- Understand that your own culture and biases may affect how you interpret what you see,

The diagram below highlights that successful teams need to create and enlarge the intersection of all three aspects that impact team communications and performance—People, Culture, and Processes. Early identification of potential differences and challenges across the team and stakeholder community and addressing them through team building and the communications plan will get the team into the sweet spot earlier and keep the team there as changes and challenges occur.

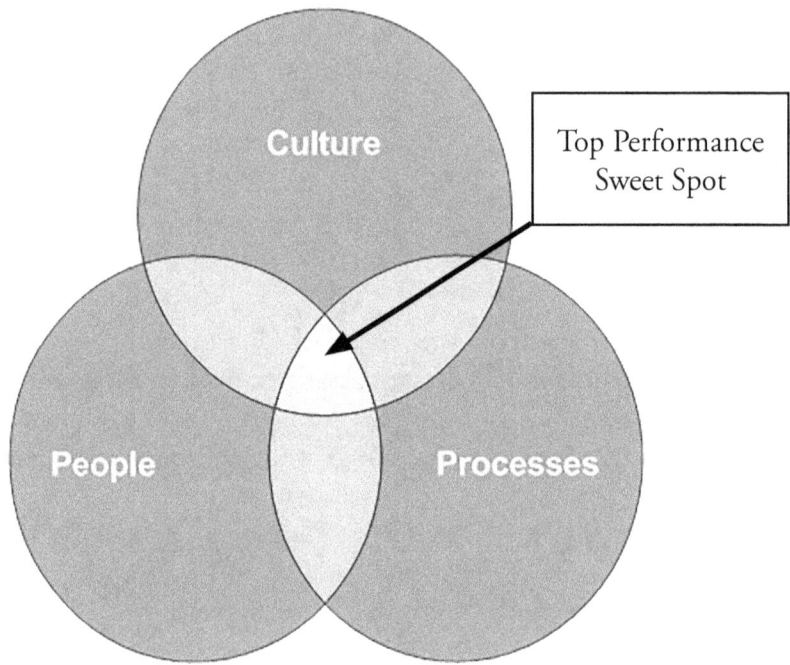

At this point in taking over the project, the revised plans are in place, the delivery team is working the plan, and management and key stakeholders are being kept informed. Things should be moving smoothly. As noted in this chapter, there is plenty more for the PM to do, especially since projects seldom move smoothly for long. There will be new changes and challenges that arise, and just because the new PM has taken over the leadership role and improved communications does not mean the hard work is done. We'll address keeping the team and stakeholders together and focused on the project in the next chapter, along with providing some key tips on how to spot early signs of trouble within the project.

Get Me off This Project!—Results

Ultimately, the project was not successful. During legal settlement proceedings, internal client memos revealed that they had decided a year earlier to end the project and get as much money back as they could. Their behavior was aimed at getting the contractor to cancel the contract so the client could sue for a full refund. (Remember the caution about communications and the Boston Globe Test!) This weighed against them in arbitration, and a settlement was ultimately reached.

The PM and project team members went on to other projects, a number of them requesting assignments on teams with the PD. The bonds formed while working together on this difficult project lasted long after the project was over. The skills and experience gained also aided their career development and positively influenced future assignments. Lessons Learned from the engagement were documented and communicated throughout the organization so that future issues of this type and scale could be prevented.

Even unsuccessful projects can have some benefits.

CHAPTER 11

RIDE HERD AND
AVOID A RELAPSE

"This is not a business where you can hand off
and run by remote control."

David Neelman

Don't Worry, We're Making Progress

*A global telecommunications equipment manufacturing
company had brought in a consulting firm to supplement
their struggling development and maintenance team to get a
major update completed and into production. The intent was
for the consulting project team to complete the delivery and
take over maintenance while the corporate team shifted to a
new technology project that was also delayed. The consulting
company PM did an in-flight project review as his team was
assembling and getting knowledge transfer (KT) from the
existing team. Although there were some troubling issues, the
PM felt he could overcome them with the new team and a
revised methodology. There was an immediate improvement
in the pace of development, and testing showed that quality*

---

issues were rapidly being resolved. Members of the corporate team were transferred one by one to other projects. Things seemed to be going smoothly.

The regional manager for the consulting company arranged for a half-day status review prior to an upcoming ESC meeting with the client VP for Development. A review of the last few status reports from the offshore portion of the team indicated a problem. The completion percentage on a number of tasks was going up very slowly—80%, 81%, 83%, 84%, etc. This was significantly different than earlier reports that followed the existing standard for reporting progress on tasks (10% credit at start, then report achievement of 25, 50, 75, and 90%, only get to 100% when the task is accepted by the client). A series of tough phone calls and escalations with the offshore management team established that the team had actually stalled at 50% completion, and they faced a number of technical challenges that they were unable to overcome. Instead of reporting the issues, they thought they could work through them internally. The onsite PM knew that these issues needed to be reported, and project schedules were adjusted.

Reports to the client PM and VP were corrected, and additional engineering support was obtained from the client's R&D Center. It turned out that the technical issues were due to the hardware design and could not be corrected via software changes; firmware changes were also needed. These were implemented, and software development continued, but an additional six weeks were lost. Due to the nature of the issues found and the wording of the contract, the two organizations agreed to split the extra costs. Needless to say, none of the executives were happy.

Ride Herd

As the example above shows, just because a project seems to be going well, we can't relax. Sometimes we let up once the immediate crisis is past; it is only natural to do so, but we can't. Ideally, we have set up routines with the project team that are being followed, and those routines should reduce the likelihood of new problems arising. We also need to have quality assurance processes and tools in place that are being used, coupled with meaningful metrics that provide a clear picture of the project status. These metrics and reports should not only show us what has been accomplished and where we are, they need to show us what the trends are and where we will be if these trends continue. As described in the example above, a change in trends or the tone of reports may be the first indication of an issue. As the PM and project team shift from transitioning in the new PM and possibly project recovery mode to business as usual, they need to ensure that their processes, tools, and reporting are appropriate to keep the project on track.

As we briefly covered in the section on Situational Leadership in Chapter 10, the PM needs to adjust their management style as results come in, and they learn more about the team. In addition to team maturity, which should guide selection of an overall leadership style, the team members and leads will also demonstrate different levels of maturity, expertise, and commitment to project success. One-on-one interactions with them should be adjusted to account for their individual styles and characteristics. These relationships will continue to evolve and develop as time goes on and as new challenges arise. The PM will learn how to handle each member.

If possible, set up regular one-on-one sessions with key team members to get their true feelings on project progress, issues, and concerns. Don't be all business in these sessions. Get to know the members better, and let them know more about you. This is part of team building and developing a team that has confidence in itself. It is vital that these efforts also include team members that may belong to other organizations, be working remotely, or be working from home. Out of sight should never mean out of mind when dealing with project team members. This takes extra time and effort, but it needs to be done. The result will be a well-functioning team that doesn't keep secrets from the PM, and that will work together to address problems as they arise.

Trust the experts on the team, but verify their recommendations and watch the results. Although the PM is not expected to be an expert in every aspect of the project, especially when dealing with technology projects, they are expected to ask questions and dig further if something sounds strange. Sometimes asking simple questions of a technical expert can help them review their assumptions and possibly lead to a better solution. There is no need to pretend to have expertise that you don't or to act as if you have all the answers. Be humble, express your lack of knowledge when appropriate, but do not hesitate to ask meaningful, relevant questions. Assume that you will have to go to your management and explain the decision being made, the problem that was encountered, or why the team is pursuing a particular path. The old saying "trust but verify" applies. Some PMs hesitate to ask questions since they feel they do not have the technical expertise required. As the story below shows, asking the technical experts how they reached their conclusions is not challenging their experience or expertise, it is giving them an opportunity to demonstrate it. Sometimes the discussion leads to different solutions or options that may be better for the overall project or for other teams.

We Need This Part

The two leading electronic technicians approached the PM with a purchase order for several expensive parts that couldn't be delivered for three to four weeks, likely delaying completion of repairs beyond the scheduled period. Although the PM was not an electronic engineer, he asked the technicians to return with the system schematics and walk him through the troubleshooting they had done to determine that the circuit boards were bad. As they went through the signal flow, the PM would ask how they knew it was good up to that point.

The technicians thought it was funny that the PM was "so stupid," but they explained things as they went. A few steps in, they realized that there was another circuit that could have an impact that they hadn't checked. Scrambling, they returned 15 minutes later with a pile of torn-up paper. They found the problem actually was in the other circuit, and they had already repaired it. Laughing, they dropped the torn-up purchase orders on the floor, stating that they didn't know the PM really was a tech. While the PM laughed with them, admitting that he didn't know 10% of what the techs knew, he cautioned them to check their assumptions before coming to him. At the next team meeting, the lead tech handed the bad circuit card to the PM, noting to the entire team that the new PM asked good questions and that they needed to step up their own work.

The team went on to have the best system performance and availability in the entire region and won the excellence award that cycle.

As the two stories in this chapter show, objective, factual communication internal and external to the team is still critical. Continue to follow the communication plan, updating it as necessary. The goal is to keep the consensus that has been gained both within the team and, more broadly, across the stakeholder community. As the community understands that they are getting the information they need in the form they need it, and when they need it, they gain confidence in the PM and the delivery team. This should lead to fewer ad hoc requests for briefings, status reports, and extra reporting, especially when a project was in Red or Yellow status before. The project may not be Green yet, but objective reporting of the true status, coupled with improving trends, is usually enough to move the project out of crisis mode in the minds of executives. This should take that pressure and concern off the PM and delivery team, allowing more time and energy to focus on the real problems that need to be solved. As we will discuss later in this chapter, the team needs to communicate factually to the PM, and there need to be appropriate metrics in place to track the true status of the project. These are likely to need adjustment as the project proceeds. Some metrics will work, and some won't. As the project moves through different phases, different metrics are likely to be needed. The delivery methodology will also determine which metrics make sense. So, continue to review what is being communicated to each stakeholder and adjust as the project evolves.

Just as cowboys on a cattle drive need to continue to ride herd and watch for rustlers, the incoming PM needs to watch for time bandits. Time bandits rustle away time better spent on delivering the project, delaying task completion, distracting the team, and taking PM focus off the project. Although there are some non-project tasks that must be done, make every effort to limit them. For example, if there is mandatory HR training that must occur, can it be delayed until after a sprint is completed or a test period is done? Schedule optional training for periods between projects. Review the communication plan for the project for less profitable meetings, and see if there are other meetings for team members that may no longer make sense for them. Ask members if they feel there are activities that take their time but don't add value, and work with them to see if they can be eliminated. Identify metrics and reports that can be consolidated or eliminated without reducing the flow of important information.

As the team and PM get into a rhythm, meetings should go more quickly. Expectations have been set, a routine established, and everyone knows what information is needed. For example, on one project, the initial daily test status meetings were 45 minutes to an hour long. Within a few weeks, they were down to under 15 minutes, and a few weeks later, they took 5 minutes. How did this happen? In addition to having a standard agenda, the PM started the meetings on time every day—same time, same location. Team leads quickly learned to show up on time with the required information from their teams. Second, when there were issues that did not require the entire team to resolve them, the meetings were adjourned early so the team leads involved could stay in the room and resolve the issues themselves (with the PM if needed). Third, the daily test status reports were adjusted based on what was discussed in the meeting, so all the relevant information was presented in a manner that was useful to the entire team. The reports were distributed early each morning with the overnight results so that information was available before the meeting instead of delaying the meeting to verbally transmit it. Team leads learned to read the report and come prepared with questions and answers for the meeting. Finally, instead of using up the entire meeting time because it was scheduled, the focus was on sharing information, making joint decisions as needed, and dismissing the team to do their regular work. The PM demonstrated that they respected everyone's time and that it shouldn't be wasted. The team responded, and the culture evolved to a point where members felt free to question assignments or requests that they felt would waste their time.

Another time bandit is when key members of the team are assigned part-time to other teams or are pulled to help with other activities. Again, there will be cases where that is the best answer for the overall organization, but this should not be the default decision. Ensure these requests come to the PM, and the PM should push back on them to determine how serious they are and if there are alternatives that might work equally as well. For example, perhaps a more junior architect can review the plans for another project and then have the senior architect from this project review the conclusions of the junior architect with them. Requests such as these are more likely to occur with a smooth-running project, especially if the team has developed a reputation for good results. While dispersing the knowledge, skill, and methods more broadly through the organization will be good for the organization, it will negatively impact the project. The PM needs to weigh the impacts and have a frank discussion with management about distracting or transferring key project members. These transfers and part-time assignments should be noted in the Risks & Issues Log, initially as risks, and elevated to issues if there are real impacts on the project. Be cautious when a key member is assisting outside the project in their "spare time" since this can lead to over-burdening the member and impacting their health and well-being or leading to stealthy time losses on their primary project.

Exercise: *What is the most important thing for you to do to keep the project moving?*

Before leaving the topic of time bandits, there is one use of time that is not wasteful—celebrating successes. Take advantage of opportunities to celebrate team successes. This can range from taking time during a meeting to applaud someone or the team as a group. These may be accompanied by small tokens, company logo items such as coffee cups, or free pastries. Team lunches, pizza parties, and even dinners are all important ways to improve team spirit, recognize accomplishment, and motivate the team for the next challenge. While they may take time away from working on tasks, these celebrations can actually aid productivity. Team members believe that their hard work and dedication are being recognized, leading them to be more willing to continue their efforts. Members see that the team is successful and the project is moving forward, so they are more intent on keeping that progress going. Instead of seeing a troubled project as the Titanic going down and looking for a lifeboat, they look for ways to save the ship and bring it into port.

There is usually a "cheerleader" within the team who is good about knowing when members have birthdays and how to organize social events. Try to identify them and get their help in maintaining team morale and holding suitable celebrations for team success. In most cases, management will support a small budget for these events. If not, it is often worth the PM funding the event themselves to improve morale. Buying a few pizzas and bringing in some donuts may be the difference between on-time and late delivery—what is it worth to you?

Team celebrations and rewarding success are more difficult with remote and dispersed teams, but that makes it even more important to do them. All members need to feel that they are part of the same team, even those that are remote. Due to the Covid pandemic, there is much greater use and acceptance of video conferences, chat rooms, and other remote communication methods. Take advantage of these, and be creative. Video "happy hours" provide an opportunity for the team to meet informally and discuss things other than work. While not a full replacement for in-person offsite meetings, they can help fill the gap. Send gift cards and other small rewards to remote members, especially when the onsite portion of the team is getting rewarded. Get help from remote managers as well. For example, if having a pizza lunch for the onsite team, arrange with an offsite manager to do something similar for the remote members in their location. If possible, schedule team celebrations at times when the entire team can participate. For example, one organization had a pancake breakfast for the USA portion of the team with the team in India having an ice cream social simultaneously over video. By checking the Internet, you will find that there are many creative ways to keep the team together despite working in multiple locations. Discuss some options with your team leads, and experiment to see what works best with your organization and team.

Keep 'em Secure

Keeping the project on track with the revised plans also requires close monitoring of scope and change management. As noted earlier, there are many ways that scope changes can creep into a project, especially with Agile methodologies. They may come in as reinterpretations of requirements or changes classified as defects or a use case or user story being refined. Depending upon the methodology being used, there may be minor changes that are acceptable without going through a formal change request process. Even so, these need to be tracked and managed, so the entire team is aware of the change that is being implemented, so they adjust their work accordingly. For example, the architect may decide to move a window over by a few feet before the wall has been constructed, so the cost and schedule impact is negligible. The plumber and electrician need to know about the move as well as the carpenters, since it may require them to reroute pipes or wiring.

In most cases, changes must go through the change management process, so they can be properly defined, estimated, reviewed by the team, and approved or disapproved. If approved, plans must be adjusted to reflect the changes. Note that the proper review of changes will take time from the delivery team, as well as management attention, so there should be time budgeted to do so. If the number of change requests is excessive, this is an issue that must be raised with the Sponsor and Business Owner and potentially go to the ESC. Some organizations will have change requests go through a two-step approval process. The first step is to roughly define the CR and evaluate the time it will take to fully define and estimate the CR. This is brought to the Change Control Board (CCB), and a decision is made on whether to continue pursuing the CR or to stop it or defer it to another project or period. For example, there may be a new user story identified during a sprint that is relatively rare. The decision may be made to defer work on that user story to a later sprint or until after the next production release. If the CR is approved for a full investigation, those results are also brought to the CCB for a final decision on when or if the CR will be implemented. The two-step approach can save time for the delivery team by quickly ending activity on CRs that should be canceled or deferred.

Prior problems with scope may reoccur, especially if a project was in Yellow or Red status when the new PM joined the team. It is usually easier to push back on scope when trying to get a project back on track. Once the project seems to be going well, the requests to change scope will come back. Usually, they come in as minor changes, correcting "defects" or reinterpreting requirements. As noted above, these need to go through the change management process and should be identified as change requests. The entire team needs to be sensitized to how these changes to scope can creep in and that they need to go through the formal process. Again, depending upon the methodology being followed, the change process may not need to be time-consuming and painful, but it needs to be followed so that everyone from the Sponsor on down knows that a change has been approved and what the impacts are. Keep the plans up to date and communicate changes to the broader team. Refer back to the approved scope of the project, and when this changes, ensure that adjustments to schedule, budget, and potentially quality are also made. As we have all heard, there is no free lunch, and there are no free scope changes.

There are going to be times when things do not go as planned, and estimates turn out to be wrong. Although we sometimes get lucky and tasks are done sooner than planned, they usually take a bit longer. When delays hit tasks on the critical path, the overall project will feel the delay. It is only natural that there is more attention paid to these and greater effort to get these tasks completed on time. This means ensuring that targets are hit, even if it means overtime for the team. Ideally, these issues should be identified before the task is due so the impact on the team is spread out and a crisis is avoided. Similar discipline is needed for tasks not on the critical path.

Often there is a feeling that there is some slack in the schedule and being a few days late is OK. This attitude needs to be changed! As the PM, you own the slack, no one else. Only the PM has the authority to decide when and how slack will be used. This can be especially critical when working with dispersed teams. For example, an onshore development team is due to move their latest software into the test environment at the end of the day. They decide that they want to wait until first thing the next morning to do so since the member who usually handles migrations left early for a medical appointment. Unfortunately, this means the offshore team that works overnight will not be able to do their smoke tests and start testing the updates, losing an entire shift of work for the team. The PM needs to intervene with the development lead to ensure the migration takes place as planned. This may require the member to come back to work in the evening or other members to take responsibility for the move. Sometimes members will need to work overtime to meet commitments or complete tasks on time. It is better to do so as these issues occur instead of looking back later and seeing that a new critical path has emerged due to cumulative delays, and it is too late to take action to avoid impacting the overall schedule.

There may also be opportunities to regain slack. By creating a team mindset that pays attention to schedules and slack, there are likely to be some tasks identified that can finish early or where task dependencies can be altered. The experienced PM response to the question, "How did the project get behind schedule?" has been "one day at a time," is also the answer to how slack can be regained or a project brought back on schedule. Once the team internalizes the philosophy of time management, they can bring ideas and opportunities to compress time to the PM. For example, a software development team may decide to put in a little extra time and migrate their code into the test environment on a Friday instead of the following Monday, so the offshore team that works Sunday evening can get an extra day to test. If a system interface with another team won't be ready for a few days, perhaps there is testing that can be done before that, which doesn't require the interface to be present. If a software module is being updated to fix a defect in this sprint, perhaps an upcoming change can be put in at the same time. Work with the team to identify these opportunities and take advantage of the ones that you can. In addition to regaining slack that may be needed for unforeseen issues that may come up in the future, it may also be possible to complete the project a bit early. The PM needs to set the tone and provide an example to the team, looking for positive opportunities as well as watching out for negative impacts.

Metrics and Monitoring

> **"If you can't measure it, you can't manage it."**
>
> --Peter Drucker, Management Guru

As the project continues, adjustments to plans are going to be made to reflect actual progress, approved changes, and events that occur. This is inevitable. As noted in the quote from Peter Drucker, we can't foresee or manage these changes if we don't have appropriate metrics available. When joining an ongoing project, there should be existing metrics that are already in place and updated regularly. If not, useful metrics will need to be identified and implemented. If there are metrics being used, they need to be reviewed to see if they are the right metrics. In this section, we will briefly review the steps to take to evaluate the existing project and sub-team metrics and how to determine if they should be kept, replaced, or simply discontinued. This is not meant to be a full-on metrics discussion but a guide to assist the incoming PM in determining which metrics are appropriate. There are many books that cover the subject. Appendix C includes some recommended metrics for different project types and methodologies, and even that is not an exhaustive list. There may be constraints on the metrics that can be used due to the methodology in use, the nature of the project, or what is available within the organization. There may also be opportunities for the incoming PM to introduce new metrics that are required to properly track and manage the project, so do not hesitate to suggest new metrics where needed.

There are some terms that we will use when discussing metrics, and their use varies widely across different industries. Here is what we will use going forward:

- **Dashboard**—A set of organization-specific metrics pertinent to project delivery that *enables managers to manage by exception*[6]
- **Rearward View**—Data that shows results, typically numerical or financial, against original or "baseline" plans
- **Forward View**—Data that shows projected results, based on actual results to date, and revisions to original plans

Table 11-1 provides the key reasons that a PM needs to use metrics. These reasons apply regardless of the project type or methodology being used. They should be kept in mind when evaluating the metrics being used and if there are any information gaps with those metrics and dashboards.

---

[6] Gartner Research Note SPA-18-9766, emphasis added

Table 11-1: Reasons to Use Project
Metrics & Dashboards

Control the Project	Monitor activities and results to catch issues early and predict future outcomes (i.e., *prevent surprises*) Foster *communication* between teams to improve productivity Establish realistic, documented *goals* to drive higher performance
Improve Engagement Performance	Substantiate Lessons Learned by *measuring results* and quantifying process improvements Improve estimation accuracy for future delivery engagements
Achieve Client Satisfaction & More Sales	Quantify outcomes in areas including quality, effort, schedule, and cost to win more work; demonstrate that we are in control and working to improve results
Increase Member Satisfaction	Early *identification of trends* to minimize crises and the need for long hours will raise member satisfaction, help prevent attrition, and reduce recruitment efforts and costs
Improve Communication	Ensure all relevant stakeholders have the information they need to understand the current project status and have trust in the accuracy and relevance of the information they are provided Provide management and coordinating teams the information they need to identify issues, concerns, or actions that need their involvement

Dashboards in particular can be very helpful for PMs. A good dashboard supports the rapid assessment of project progress and future results (will it meet objectives?) for the PM and management stakeholders. When compiling and reviewing a good dashboard, it also forces the PM to examine progress and trends, not just day-to-day issues. In other words, focusing on the path through the forest instead of the next fork in the path or tree in the way. The dashboard aids in identifying where Program Manager and Executive support may be needed to address challenges and obstacles. From a PMO or senior manager view, dashboards support cross-project analysis and Project Portfolio Management (PPM). This can be vital in identifying future challenges to one or more projects that have dependencies.

When assessing the adequacy of the current project metrics, the PM should be able to answer the following questions throughout a project, regardless of methodology:

- Are we on schedule? If not, what is the forecast completion date based on current progress? Are there specific activities or teams having challenges?
- Are we on budget? If not, what is the forecast cost to complete based on current expenditures? Are there cost drivers that need to be managed?
- Is the quality as expected at this stage? If not, what are the potential quality issues at completion? What are the key contributors to quality issues?
- Is project delivery as efficient as forecast at this stage of delivery? If not, what are the issues, and how can they be resolved?
- Is project scope being managed effectively? Is the number of change requests in line with the original forecast? Is the number of changes impacting any of the areas listed above?
- Are the sub-teams using the right metrics? Are they tracking their progress, efficiency, and quality on a regular basis? Have they been reviewed and verified (spot checked) by the PM (trust but verify)?

Although the relevant metrics to use will vary with industry, project type, delivery methodology, and with organizational standards, there are some common key principles to consider when assessing the adequacy of current metrics or the need for new metrics:

- Metrics and dashboards should support management by exception, providing a focus on decisions that must be made.

- The information required for the metrics should be gathered once and at its source.
- Seek to minimize data collection and analysis tasks, especially if the PM will be required to do them. Usually, metric reporting and analysis are below the PM level, but remember that every metric has a cost associated with it. Carefully weigh the costs and benefits of each metric.
- The information presented should be of real use to the Project Manager, Program Manager, and Executives.
- Work top-down to define the right metrics for the project, focusing on the information to be provided and decisions to be made based on that information. Document the details of metrics data collection and calculations in the Measurement Plan or an appendix to the Project Plan.
- Incorporate the metrics into the work process, not as something separate. Include metrics in status meetings, retrospectives, etc. If they are not useful in meetings and for decision-making, do the metrics have any value?
- A picture (graph) is worth a thousand words (or numbers).
- Metrics and dashboards should look forward, not just backward. They should provide a forecast based on actuals. Unless actions are taken, the future results are unlikely to change from the forecast. But remember that no trend goes on forever.
- The information presented must be meaningful to ALL. This requires that common definitions be formalized and published. There should be standard collection and processing systems. The type of data needs to be clear (i.e., Budget, Forecast, or Projected). Identify where the data is from (i.e., accounting system, scheduling system, resource management) and how it was manipulated.

When analyzing metrics and dashboards, the PM should follow some basic principles and be looking to answer some key questions based on what they see. Are the results showing an exception or a trend? For example, if there was a holiday last week, does that explain the drop in productivity or progress that occurred? What has changed since the last report? Are these positive changes or negative changes that need further investigation? Is what caused the change clear? What will change by the next report? Are those changes desirable or undesirable? Is there action that needs to be taken to support a favorable change or to reduce the likelihood (or impact) of an undesirable change? Are there any leading change indicators that need to be taken into account? For example, a member going on parental leave without a replacement will probably reduce the pace of progress on their tasks. Finally, is the target still achievable? Keeping in mind the goals of being on time, on budget, on quality (scope), and with delighted customers, is the project making suitable progress in meeting these goals? If not, what action should be taken to get back on track, and when should the results of those actions be apparent in the metric and dashboard reports?

Some of the common problems that we find with project metrics are too great a focus on accounting results or finances instead of project progress and quality. Many metrics or reports can show us where the project was at some point in the past, but not where we are now, or where we'll be in the near future. Other metrics or indicators may be too qualitative (e.g., what is the difference between Yellow and Red, and who decides which it is?). Some data may require too much time and effort to collect compared to the benefits to the PM and project team. There can also be dashboards that present too much information; they are too complex to understand or use on a regular basis. Sometimes there are great reports and metrics, but they are not available when needed for timely decision-making. For example, if a monthly report is not available before two weeks into the next month, the PM has lost another two weeks before taking action to correct a problem or trend.

Speaking of trends, many tabular reports do not show trends, just the current numbers, which severely limits their usefulness. Trends also need to be projected into the future, based on the results to date. This is especially true when looking at budget expenditures and completion percentages. Some reports may contain raw data instead of the meaningful information needed to make decisions and draw conclusions about progress, quality, and cost. Finally, there may be data or metrics that are useful for team members but are at an incorrect level for decision-makers. Although it may be necessary to keep tracking this data within the team, providing it to executive stakeholders may just confuse them or lead to unproductive discussions. Carefully filter out information that may just be "noise" when received at an executive level.

In summary, project dashboards can be a valuable tool if they help us steer going forward. Identifying who, why, what, when, and how for the dashboard helps determine the correct information to be displayed.

- WHO needs the information?
- WHY do they need the information?
- WHAT decisions will they make with the information once they have it?
- WHEN do they need the information to make timely decisions?
- HOW will the required information be gathered, manipulated, and presented?

Don't be afraid to ask these questions about metrics that have been gathered in the past to determine if they are still needed going forward. Provide training and completed examples of dashboards, with supporting definitions, to facilitate adoption by the delivery team and by management stakeholders that will also receive them. Do not assume the recipients will be able to understand and interpret the metrics and reports the same way that you do. Whenever possible, test new or revised dashboards before fully rolling them out. Work with the PMO, if there is one, to get their recommendations and experience with similar metrics or reports. They may already have something suitable or know what failed in the past. Whatever metrics are being used or get introduced, do not be afraid to change them if they aren't worth the effort. Finally, ensure your reporting, and potentially your metrics, also allow the tracking of external dependencies and related projects. This may simply involve exchanging summary reports with other PMs or coordinating with the PMO to ensure your project team is aware of progress and events outside of the project that may impact you.

The next two tables provide some tips to keep in mind when considering which metrics to use and how they are used on your project.

Table 11-2: Tips for Metrics Success

1. Take action on reported results and metrics; PMs are not bystanders!
2. Track progress regularly, at least weekly.
3. Ensure metrics are focused, reliable, worthwhile, balanced, and constructive,
4. Include future projections based on results to date as much as possible (moving averages often work).
5. Discard metrics that are not meaningful.
6. Share metrics with all teams; keep them involved in interpretation and decision-making.
7. Ensure "Done" is measurable and defined upfront.
8. Don't ignore "soft" issues and focus too much attention on numbers.
9. Use metrics to support decision-making and resource requests—facts speak louder than "feelings."
10. Be proactive—ask questions and hold people accountable.

Table 11-3: Signs of Poor Metrics Use

1. Unclear goals or requirements for metrics
2. Metrics routinely generated late or irregularly
3. Metrics selected based on ease of generation
4. Team does not understand metrics or their connection to successful project completion
5. Metrics do not allow forecasting future results

6. Metrics are not shared with the delivery team
7. Metrics are used to push or punish the delivery team
8. Metrics provide conflicting views of progress and future results
9. An external group is used to generate metrics is seen as disconnected from the delivery team
10. Metrics only generated or updated when a crisis occurs

Maintaining Quality

One of the challenges when riding herd and preventing a lapse in performance is maintaining quality across the project. When there is pressure to compress a schedule, control costs, or achieve a milestone, there is a tendency to cut corners, work faster, and let things slip. While it is bad enough when team members fall into this mode, it can be very harmful when PMs go into "just get it done!" mode. This can be compounded when taking over an ongoing project if quality considerations were already shortchanged, or absent, in the existing project. The critical first step is to ensure that quality requirements and processes are built into project plans, either from the beginning or in the revised plans that have been created as part of the new PM joining the team.

We'll cover some of the quality basics that should be included in the plans and some tips to ensure that quality isn't an afterthought. Remember that there may be some occasions where conscious decisions are made to allow specific defects or quality issues to be deferred. For example, it may be agreed with the key stakeholders that a software application goes into production, despite there being some typographical errors on some screens. Or a quarterly report may not function correctly at go-live, but it will be corrected before the quarterly reports need to be run in production. Another example could be proceeding to get a certificate of occupancy for a new house, even though there is a room painted with the wrong colors. These are all explicit agreements on how a quality issue will be treated, not something that just happened to sneak through.

Despite the schedule pressure that most projects are under, the schedule should include time for critical quality tasks. For software and other development projects, these should include Requirement Reviews (also ensure Architecture, Development, and QA participation in the reviews), Design Reviews (ensuring BA and QA participation), Peer Code Reviews, Code Walkthroughs, Unit Testing, and formal Sign-Off Reviews. While the type, nature, and number of reviews and other quality activities will vary with the type of project and the methodology being used, be sure to schedule them in. Allow time to prepare for the reviews and conduct follow-up activities, as well as for the review itself. Avoid the trap of scheduling the next phase or activity immediately after a review or quality gate; allow time to address the issues and defects that are likely to result from the reviews. For example, most building inspectors will find something that they want changed during building construction. Making these changes will pull the tradespeople from their planned activities for hours or days. Build time for these efforts into the schedule. If they are not required, that will provide additional slack into the schedule or perhaps shorten the critical path.

Since there has been a noticeable drop in software and application quality across the world, this section is going to focus on some specific actions that have been shown to improve software quality. Many of these techniques also apply to other industries as well, so do not skip over the next few paragraphs if you are not a software PM. These guidelines apply to all methodologies as well, since many Agile projects have quality issues in production.

A first step is to have clear coding standards to ensure development and maintenance developers have the same expectations. In the building trades, the equivalent would be building standards and trade-specific codes, such as the Electrical Code. Most organizations have coding standards developed for multiple development environments and languages. These should form the basis for project standards and can save time when determining the applicable standards when joining an ongoing project. If working with a client, they are likely to have coding standards that must be followed, so check for these and verify applicability to the project. Take time to review the standards with the

Architects, Designers, and Developers to ensure their understanding of the standards and to identify and resolve potential issues upfront. If the standards are not sufficient, work with the Architects and Designers to create supplemental standards that apply to the project and ensure that Developers joining the team are briefed on them. The standards should ensure that proper comments are included in the code—these can be critical to the maintenance team.

> **Tip**: *Without quality standards, anything goes—would you want to maintain "wild west" code?*

The PM should regularly monitor the quality of what the project is producing and verify that the quality processes put in place are being followed. One issue to watch out for is a shortage of business process and current system knowledge within the team. We would not expect a new person off the street to be an expert carpenter, but we often expect team members with no prior experience with the industry, organization, business process, or application to know what to do. Knowledge transfer to team members is vital, especially with remote teams. When joining an ongoing project, check for this knowledge and understanding when doing reviews, and include time for KT in the revised plans when needed. Depending upon the state of the project when joining, frequent meetings between the PM and QA Manager on quality tools, issues, processes, and current quality state may be needed.

There are some good quality habits that should become a regular part of the project. During testing periods, there should be daily test meetings. Insist on them if there is pushback. These meetings should be supported by standard status reports with applicable numbers and graphs—just the facts that are required to gauge test progress and project quality. The PM needs to push for aggressive defect resolution in these meetings, keeping a focus on defects until resolved. As defects arise, ensure they are tracked to resolution—no "it always works that way" responses. If making updates to an existing application and existing production defects are discovered that are not in project scope, do not close them until the production support organization agrees and the customer says they can be deferred to post-release maintenance or warranty. If using an Agile development methodology, the Daily Stand-Up Meetings should *not* become Daily Test Meetings. These meetings have separate goals and should be kept separate to ensure that their respective goals are met.

As the project progresses, ensure test planning stays in step with requirements and software development. All the relevant sub-teams should review test plans (customer, SMEs, BA, Development, Architecture, QA, PM) to ensure their needs have been considered and that what is being built and how it will be verified is clear to all. When they are needed, be sure to define test environment needs early to get them built and tested before you need them (or plan on losing time due to environment shakedown delays). Plan for and use a shakedown period upon entry into each environment—if completed early, you have some extra margin. If the application includes output that can be printed, even if that is not the primary form that is meant to be used, be sure to check printed output in printed form. There have been issues even when software changes were not expected to impact the ability to print or the printed results. It is also important to remember downstream systems that may not have had any code changes. They need to be tested anyway—their data feeds may have been impacted.

Tracking quality as the project proceeds will be much easier if Daily Test Reports are complete, accurately reflect test progress as well as defect status, and are issued early in the day—every day! Daily Test Reports should support all the sub-teams in determining their priorities for the day. The PM should institute the 24-hour rule— a team has 24 hours to take action on a defect or issue passed to them, or it needs to be escalated. For example, if a defect is assigned to a developer, and the developer has not had time to review the defect in a 24-hour period, then it should be reassigned or escalated. It should not sit in someone's queue indefinitely.

While conducting testing, there are some specific areas for the PM to focus on. Review the open-closed-open-closed cycle for defects that are recurring—this indicates troubled modules or other issues that need additional attention. Look for bottlenecks in the defect process (e.g., a backlog with a particular team), such as defects building up with the BA Team doing their investigations and defect confirmation. The PM should also look at which modules, developers, etc., have a large number of defects, take longer to fix defects, fail in the retest, etc., to identify areas for further study and action. There are probably some areas or features of the project that are more challenging and require additional attention and support. More experienced and skilled resources may need to be shifted to these components to get them resolved and keep the project on schedule.

> **Tip:** Shift your attention and resources according to what is happening as the project evolves. Be a Driver, not a Passenger!

There is a lot for the PM to do to keep the project moving smoothly. Although many of these activities are a normal part of keeping a project moving forward, there can be additional challenges for an incoming PM. The required tools, processes, and *attitudes* may not be in place, so they need to be implemented while delivery continues. The delivery team members need to adapt to these changes and turn the revised work processes into habits. The PM needs to be diligent about enforcing the new standards while coaching members to adopt them. Depending upon the duration of the project, and the state of affairs when the PM joined, the additional activity level may be short or last through the end of the project.

The PM should be cautious about taking on additional responsibilities or getting another project assignment just because the replanning and stabilization efforts appear to be over. There are plenty of issues that can arise and plenty of work that still needs to be done before the project is completed. With this in mind, the PM still needs to plan for a successful finish to the project, which is usually more than just getting the software into production, the new product released, or the new building ready to be occupied. Chapter 12 will describe the activities needed to ensure a successful project finish.

CHAPTER 12

FINISH SUCCESSFULLY

"Some people dream of success, while other people get up every morning and make it happen."

Wayne Huizenga

They Can Just Flip a Switch

The State of Florida had decided to remove an auto insurance coverage requirement that was especially prone to fraudulent claims. Due to the politics involved, the executives at a mid-sized insurance company didn't think the change was going to really happen, so they delayed starting a project to update their software, underwriting rules, rates, etc. With just over 90 days to go and the regulatory change still due to take effect, they had to start an emergency project. They assigned a Project Director with experience delivering crash projects and got started. With a lot of support for the project team, deadlines were hit, and everything was on track for an on-time production release. The PD was driving home Friday evening when a call came in from his VP. She told him to pull off the road and park. Fearing bad news, the PD did so.

"The governor of Florida just approved a bill that requires the coverage to stay in place. You have to undo all of the code changes and retest the system without them."

"We're going into production at 7 a.m. tomorrow. The coverage was supposed to be removed by the 1st of the month; that is only six days away. How long do we have to make the change?"

"There isn't supposed to be a gap in coverage, so the change has to be out before the 1st."

"That's crazy; no company can change their systems that much and test them in less than six days."

"The governor was asked that question by a reporter. He replied, 'It's easy; it's all on computers. They can just flip a switch.'"

Laughing instead of crying, they agreed to a meeting with the executive team on Saturday morning.

As he got back on the road, the PD realized that despite everything that was done to make the project successful up to that point, unless they could undo the software changes and meet the deadline, the project was not going to be seen as a success.

Finish Successfully

The project is stable, and things are going well, with the inevitable problems and changes being handled smoothly by the team. What else should the PM do to ensure the project remains on track? Are there any warning signs that new problems may occur? If the right metrics and reports are in place, these questions should be easy to answer. Continue to follow the rhythm that has been established, adjusting your leadership style as the team matures and the project proceeds. There may be upcoming milestones or events that require extra attention; continue to be proactive in preparing for these. There may be opportunities for team members to take on additional tasks or responsibilities to further develop their careers. Ideally, the framework you have set up will allow this with processes, tools, and leadership that they can adopt going forward.

Exercise: *What actions should you take to ensure your project stays on track for a successful finish? Are there any warning signs that should be addressed?*

Ideally, the revised plans you developed with the project team will work, leading to a successful project conclusion. PMs who can assume ongoing projects, or rescue failing projects, are highly respected and considered for promotions and additional responsibilities. In addition to helping your career, successfully meeting the challenges of taking over an ongoing project also help you improve your knowledge and skills. Remember that you did not achieve this on your own. Be sure to share the credit with the team and support their career growth. Supporting and promoting team members is a characteristic of successful leaders and is expected by most organizations. The "Member Support" section below will cover supporting team members in more detail.

All projects must prepare to end, whether that is completing the construction of a house and turning it over to the owners, launching a new product in the market, or putting new software into production. If the project was poorly planned or encountered difficulties along the way, planning and preparing for the "Go-Live" (completion) and post-production period may have been skipped or poorly done. The current PM needs to review these plans in light of the revised project plans and schedule and be proactive in updating plans for go-live and any post-release activities. Do not wait until the last minute to address this, as there may be organizational change management, training, advertising, and other activities that need to be put in place before the release. Chapter 13 will cover handing the project off to another manager or handing off project results to another team, such as an application maintenance team. There are some key considerations for properly finishing a project, which we'll cover below.

Most projects require a warranty period where the Delivery Team is responsible for correcting any issues that arise. Ensure all teams agree on warranty duration and roles/responsibilities during warranty. Some organizations will require a formal warranty plan, coupled with a transition plan for the support team that will handle the results of the project long-term (building maintenance, sales team for a new product, application maintenance team, etc.). Following good industry practices up to this point will reduce the likelihood of defects at the time of release. Continue to enforce these good practices during the warranty period, including updating any supporting documentation to reflect the "as-built" state of the building, product, or software.

The release and hand-off to the long-term support team will be eased by establishing post-release support plans with the teams involved prior to the release. Ideally, include the support team in post-release planning and warranty activities to assist their learning about the details of the product or software. Having support team members shadowing delivery team members during warranty defect correction is especially helpful. Be sure to conduct walkthroughs with the release and support teams, as well as key stakeholders. For example, this would include the local building inspector for home construction, the sales and promotion teams for a new product, and the maintenance team for software.

The warranty period can be problematic, depending upon organizational norms and expectations. Clearly spell out the defect triage process (who, what, where, when, and how—see below) so that all members and teams involved are clear on what their responsibilities are and how the communications will work. Be aware that the project team is likely to ease off at this point, which may be a problem with defect correction and getting good knowledge transferred to the support team. The project team has been working hard, especially if the project was Red or Yellow at some point, and they may feel they need a break. They may also be getting involved with their next project assignment, so the PM needs to be alert to these issues.

Triage Planning Questions

- WHO is responsible for each triage level? WHO assigns severity and priority levels to issues?
- WHAT action is taken by each team? WHAT are the criteria to pass it on to the next team or level?

- WHERE are the triage teams located? (WILL there be time zone issues?)
- WHEN are issues supposed to be resolved, based on their severity and priority?
- HOW are issues tracked and communicated, both internally and externally?

Plan ahead to ensure adequate coverage for issues that may arise during the move to production or in production. Agile methodologies, in particular, seem to have problems identifying and correcting problems that occur in production, although this is supposed to be a core tenet of Agile. The "fail fast" mantra should always be accompanied by "fix it faster." Monitor production results to ensure that any defects that may have slipped through are caught early. With software applications, there are some key areas to focus on during the warranty period:

- Issues with the first batch run (delays? stoppages?)
- Issues with production printing
- Excessive kick-outs for manual processing
- Problems interfacing with other applications or organizations
- Monitor performance indicators such as response times, batch duration, and exception processing to identify problems early

There are going to be focus areas for other project types as well, depending upon the industry and nature of the project. Have the team brainstorm a list of them based on their experience as part of the project preparing for production release and warranty, then ensure that the release and warranty plans can handle them. Keep in mind that the maintenance team does not want to clean up problems left by the Development Team, and their opinions will influence how the project is viewed.

Tip: Everyone is likely to be tired at this point, so leadership by example is needed to maintain process compliance.

Lessons Learned

Providing objective Lessons Learned will reduce the chances of future project problems, so they are especially important when a PM has taken over a struggling project. In those cases, try to frame the project as a learning experience. Conducting Lessons Learned sessions as the project progresses not only provides mid-course guidance for the current project but also sets the tone for the end-of-project lessons learned events and summary report. There are many books and articles on how to conduct lessons learned, so this section will just focus on tips that apply when a PM has taken over an ongoing project.

Lessons learned sessions should be conducted at each phase end and at project completion, even if the sessions are informally done with small teams. Ensure the lessons learned format is usable by following teams; for example, the lessons should be grouped by project phase, sub-team, impact on the phase or project, etc. During the information gathering sessions, seek out what went right as well as what could have gone better. Especially with projects that were in Red or Yellow status for a period, there is a tendency to focus on what went wrong, so the PM needs to set a proper tone during the session. Seek opportunities to point out what went well, even if they were corrections to problems that perhaps should not have occurred.

Do not wait more than four to five weeks after the project goes into production to conduct the lessons gathering session, or key members may not be available. Time heals all wounds, but it also blurs memories and details of what happened and what was done in response. Some PMs combine a lessons learned session with a project wrap-up party. Be creative. For example, have a pizza party for the project wrap-up, with each member needing to bring 3x5 cards with a positive lesson and a negative lesson to get in. Afterward, the leadership team can determine the best lesson in each category and provide a prize to the member who submitted it.

Lessons learned should also contribute to risk management for upcoming projects and, if available, should be consulted when taking over an ongoing project. In addition to reviewing any lessons learned compiled in the project itself, look at lessons from similar projects for ideas on what to do or not to do when replanning the project being taken over. Try to determine when the action should have been (or was) taken (e.g., having the Maintenance Team Lead Business Analyst (LBA) review requirements in the Delivery Team walkthrough with the Business Owner). As the team prepares to enter another project phase or specific tasks are coming up, review the lessons that should be applied in that phase as well as the lessons that could impact that phase.

Agile delivery methodologies should include a retrospective at the end of each sprint. These can be very beneficial if done correctly and are not artificially limited. Product quality, performance in production, and coordination with other teams need to be reviewed as well as how the sprint went internally. Defects should be reviewed along with correction and prevention measures that will be applied going forward. Issues with processes and tools should be shared across Agile teams so the overall organization benefits from the lessons learned.

Well-conducted and documented lessons learned are the mark of an experienced and disciplined PM. They take planning and time to do correctly, but they provide important benefits to the project team and to the overall organization. Ensure plans for lessons learned collection are included in the updated project plans. One caution when dealing with a project that changed PMs is to be careful not to blame individuals, including the prior PM. There are objective and professional ways to handle this. For example, documenting, "Original project schedule lacked task relationships and dependencies, making identification of the critical path impossible" is better than, "Schedule from the prior PM was unusable." Many of the checklists and top 10 lists in this book were derived from project lessons collected over a 40-year period across a variety of project types and organizations. The lessons you collect are a valuable tool to have in your PM tool kit.

Table 12-1: Sample Lessons Learned

#	OBSERVATION	GOOD/BAD	SUGGESTION	AREA	PROJECT IMPACT	PRIORITY OF LESSON	TEAM AFFECTED	TEAM FOR ACTION	PHASE AFFECTED	PHASE FOR ACTION
1	Prior to implementation day, testers developed a thorough plan of exactly what was to be tested and what the expected results were.	Good	Do it again	Testing	High	High	BA	QA/BA	Testing	Test Planning
2	Test director entries needed to have more detail - specifically many were missing quote #'s which caused extra phone calls or delay in resolution.	Bad	Ensure everyone gets TD training prior to the start of Testing	Testing	Low	Medium	BA	QA	Testing	Testing
3	24 / 5 development compressed calendar time – worked well	Good	Continue 24/5 software development	Development	Moderate	Medium	Development	Development	ALL	ALL
4	Having a designated single point of contact in code development area simplified and sped defect analysis and correction	Good	Provide a single POC for Development during Testing	Testing	Moderate	Medium	Development	Development	Development/ Testing	Development/ Testing
5	Daily testing meetings are crucial to success	Good	Continue focused Daily Test Meetings	Testing	Moderate	Medium	QA	QA	Testing	Testing
6	Running test cycles between shifts was beneficial (evening US time)	Good	Run Test Cycles to minimize interference with work schedules	Testing	Moderate	Medium	QA	Development	Testing	Test Planning
7	Test Director works great for test management	Good	Continue to utilize Test Director	Testing	High	Medium	QA	QA	Testing	Test Planning/ Testing
8	Multi-site test coordinators worked well	Good	On-site/Offshore Coordinator model worked well, continue it	Team Mgt	Moderate	Medium	QA/Dev	QA/Dev	Testing	Test Planning/ Testing

Member Support

As noted earlier, the PM did not complete the project by themselves. The project is successful due to the efforts of delivery team members and other contributing stakeholders. The PM should ensure that the project wrap-up includes proper recognition for team members—whether local or remote, employees or vendors. A good leader takes care of their members, and properly wrapping up a member's time on the project is part of that. Depending upon the type of project and the duration, some members may leave the project before it officially ends, going to another project or wrapping up their tasks. The departure considerations described here still apply and should be done in each case. If possible, the PM should meet individually with each departing team member to thank them for their contributions and briefly discuss performance, any feedback on the project, and the next steps for the member. In addition to being the right thing to do, this also benefits the employee and the organization by supporting the professional development of the member. Members remember PMs who take an interest in them and are more likely to join the PM on future projects, even ones known to be in difficult circumstances.

Most organizations will require member performance reviews, or at least inputs to a performance review from a PM, even in matrix-style organizations. Follow the organizational guidelines when completing these, and if possible, review them directly with the members before submitting them to the member manager. There shouldn't be anything in the review that the PM is not willing to discuss face-to-face with the member. In particular, project difficulties should not unfairly taint members who did nothing wrong. When members have picked up new skills on a project, be sure to include those accomplishments. The member should also update their resume to include their accomplishments, as well as their assignment to the project itself.

As noted in Chapter 7, there may be cases where a member needs to be removed from a project. In many cases, the member will benefit by moving to a different role more suited to their skills and experience. In these cases, member reviews should focus on what the member contributed to the project and how they can contribute to future projects. If the member can benefit from specific training or coaching, include those suggestions.

There may be members who have demonstrated knowledge and skills that could benefit the organization if they provide coaching to other members. Include these suggestions, as well as cases where a member could benefit from coaching or skill development in the next project. If the member is working on making their next career step, discuss what that may be and if there are any tasks or responsibilities on the current project that can help them make that step. In some cases, working with the member manager or a prospective PM for the member to help them get a suitable assignment will be helpful. For example, a BA that has done well on this project may have been given opportunities to shadow the Lead BA, and now they are ready for a Lead BA role on their next project. Reaching out to the prospective PM may help make that assignment happen.

When taking over an ongoing project, the incoming PM may not have enough time with some team members to form an objective opinion and write a performance review. If possible, reaching out to the former PM may help, but the current PM is responsible for whatever they put in the review. In some cases, noting that there was inadequate time to evaluate a member's performance may be the best way to go.

Consider the departure evaluation for members as a required project activity. The project is not complete unless these are done and done well. Just as the members supported the project and PM, the PM needs to support the members. Putting member evaluations on the schedule is just as important as any other project task, and it should be supported by appropriate planning and follow-through. High-quality departure reviews are the mark of an experienced and professional PM.

As noted in earlier chapters, it is important for the PM to take care of team members during project delivery. This includes recognition and rewards throughout the duration of the project. Set aside some time to meet with member managers to discuss their members' contributions, strengths, and development opportunities as the project progresses. Not only is this important for the professional development and careers of the members, but it also establishes a stronger bond with the member managers. This bond can be very helpful if difficult circumstances arise, such as needing additional support from them or their members. Do not fall into the trap of assuming that these activities can wait until the project is completed.

Wrapping Up

As the project wraps up, there are a number of tasks that may not get the attention they need. Ensure they are included in the schedule, even if they occur during the warranty or post-production release periods. Although it will vary with the industry, type of project, and delivery methodology, there will always be documentation required. Work with the team to conduct reviews and walkthroughs to verify that the project documentation is complete and accurate, reflecting the "as delivered" or "as-built" results of the project. This especially applies to Agile projects, where creating documentation may have been neglected throughout the project. Project retrospectives should include reviews of the documentation from that phase or sprint.

If proper quality assurance processes and tools were put into place, there shouldn't be any lingering quality issues, but some additional steps may apply for some projects. The intent is to ensure that quality is on target and that any gaps are identified along with plans to address them. For example, a new product may require specific testing to receive a consumer safety certification, or a new house may require a final walkthrough with the owners. Include these in the schedule, along with time to correct any issues that may require correction before final acceptance. In cases of software development, the software may need to go through a code analysis tool to ensure it meets minimum industry and organization standards. If so, try to run these scans periodically through the development and testing phases, instead of leaving it to the end and potentially getting a bad surprise. Ensure these final steps are included in project plans and schedules and work with the team to identify ways to reduce any risks associated with required reviews and inspections.

They Can Just Flip a Switch—Results

Due to the Florida changes being coupled with software changes from other projects, the Florida changes had to go into production with the overall release that Saturday. All the tests went smoothly, and the Florida changes were in place. The coverage removal would only affect policies that originated on the 1st of the month or later. The executives crafted a notice to the Florida Insurance Commissioner stating that due to the last-minute change in the regulations, policies would be issued without the required coverage, but it would be retroactively added once the software was updated. The project team was given until the 15th to reverse the changes.

The Executive Sponsor joined the Monday morning project team meeting to personally thank the team for their hard work and successful release. Expressing confidence in their ability to be just as successful in reversing the changes, he noted that his door was open for anyone needing help or an approval to keep things moving.

The team mapped out a new plan and proceeded to get things going. Working 18-hour days, the target date was met, and the software changes were pulled out without impacting any of the other projects that had been in the original release. The other project teams had to extend their warranty period work to retest their software as the Florida team pulled out their changes, and these teams also supported the second production release.

Everything was completed according to the revised schedule and adjusted budgets, with no quality issues. One key to these successes was that the PMs involved understood that projects need to be carefully managed through to their conclusion and that problems can occur even at the last minute. Using a baseball analogy, "Keep your eye on the ball until you feel it in your mitt."

There are additional tasks required when handing off the project to a support team or to another PM that we'll cover in Chapter 13. PMs that are skilled at rescuing troubled projects often get reassigned once the troubled project is stable. The hand-off should be smooth and easy for the incoming PM. In other cases, the project development team needs to hand off the completed results of the project to another team for long-term operation and maintenance. This can range from a software development team passing the updated software to a maintenance team, to a house being turned over to its owners, or to a new ship being handed over to its crew. All these cases have some basic similarities and a few complexities added in cases where there was a PM transition during the project. Chapter 13 will address these considerations before the PM rides off into the sunset in Chapter 14.

CHAPTER 13

HAND-OFFS

"Every person in a leadership position must
know when it's time to hand over the reins."

Eddie Compass

We're Not Going to Take It!

*The massive software project that was required to save the
company was in its ninth month. With six weeks left to go
before the production release and warranty planning well
underway, the Program Director set up a brief meeting with
the Production Support Manager (PSM) to ensure a smooth
hand-off. The key leads from both teams met in the designated
conference room, amicably chatting over coffee and donuts.
The PD got the meeting started and thanked the maintenance
team for their support in sorting out existing production issues
during the test phase, and asked the PSM to say a few words.
What came next was a surprise.*

*"We're not going to take responsibility for this application
after the warranty period. You've made massive changes to
the requirements and design, with hundreds of thousands of*

> lines of code altered by a team of almost 200 developers. My entire team is only 30 people, so we can't handle the revised application. You'll have to figure something else out. And thanks for the donuts and coffee; our budget isn't big enough to afford that stuff."
>
> The room went silent. Resisting the urge to say, "You have to take it," the PD asked the PSM and her team to describe their concerns and turned the meeting into a brainstorming session to identify what was needed to support the maintenance team so they could take over support for the application. Time ran out before solutions were identified, but smaller follow-up meetings were set up to address the concerns of the production support team.
>
> A new issue was added to the Risk and Issue Log that had not been identified as a risk before. "Maintenance Team not prepared to assume support at the end of the Warranty Period." The PD and Development Team had more work to do and not a lot of time to do it.

Although the story that opened this chapter focused on handing a software application off to a maintenance team, this chapter will look at other types of project hand-offs as well. These can include handing the ongoing project to another PM, transitioning project responsibilities to another delivery team (such as may occur when outsourcing work to a supplier), and transitioning the results of a project to another team. While the theme of this book is taking over an in-flight project, which seems to overlap the topic of this chapter, there are different assumptions. While we would hope that the incoming PM has the advantages provided by the processes and tips we provide in the chapter and throughout the book, we have assumed that they did not. Now that the incoming PM has the project running smoothly, there is a planned transition, either due to the project reaching a concluding stage or there is a management decision to bring in a new PM or team since the project is in good shape.

The intent of this chapter is to describe how to hand off a project in a manner that works for the departing PM (and team) as well as the incoming PM (and team). The guiding philosophy is to treat the incoming PM and team as you would like to be treated when you receive projects. While it may not be possible to follow all the processes and steps described below before the transition occurs, the gaps should be noted as risks or issues and steps worked out to cover those gaps. The intent is not to provide a step-by-step methodology for transitioning projects; that would be a book in itself. Instead, we are going to highlight some key steps and considerations to help guide the participants on both sides of the change to conduct a satisfactory hand-off.

Handing-Off to Another PM

There can be many reasons why ongoing projects are handed off to different PMs, as we covered in the early chapters of this book. For the purposes of this chapter, let's assume that the project was challenged, and a different PM was brought in to stabilize the project. Things are going smoothly now, and the organization wants to move the current PM to a different assignment. The goal is to have the incoming PM take over the project and keep it running smoothly to the end. The current PM has worked hard with the delivery team to get the project on an even keel and is working their plan to finish at the agreed time, with the updated scope and budget. It can be difficult to let go of something that has taken so much time, energy, and talent to get to this stage. That shouldn't interfere with the hand-off to the incoming PM, and every effort needs to be made to set up the incoming PM for success. After all, isn't that what we would want when taking over a project?

How should the transition start? With a plan, of course! When notified of the decision by management, explore the reasons for the change and the timing. It may or may not be possible to push back on the decision, but the reasons and timing for the change will impact the plan for the transition and, potentially, the thoroughness of the transition. Ideally, there will be a week or two to work with the incoming PM to ease the transition for them and the team. Once there is a preliminary agreement on the timing, try to meet with the incoming PM one-on-one to learn about each other and discuss any initial concerns and needs. Even if you have worked with the incoming PM before, take time to meet over coffee or in an informal meeting. There may be specific aspects of the project that may be challenging for the incoming PM. It is better to uncover these early, so they can be addressed as part of the turnover plan.

Create a list of information to share, following Chapters 3 and 5 from this book as guides for what the incoming PM needs to know. Use the Communication Plan as a guide to develop a list of introductions that should occur, making sure to include key stakeholders and not just the delivery team. Meet with the incoming PM to review and jointly update the information list and meeting plan. Jointly develop a schedule to address the items in the plan, including meetings where both PMs brief management on the progress of the transition. These can be brief sessions over coffee to keep the Sponsor or key manager informed of transition progress and any concerns that may have come up. It is also important that the Sponsor or key manager gain confidence in the ability of the incoming PM to be successful. Keep this additional goal in mind.

There is likely to be a mix of information-sharing sessions and stakeholder meeting types. For example, joint meetings with both PMs and certain stakeholders can ensure that current understandings, guidance, and assumptions are properly communicated and reinforced. In other cases, what started as a joint meeting should end with the incoming PM having a one-on-one with the stakeholder or team so they can start building a personal relationship. There will also be situations where the incoming PM will benefit from meeting one-on-one with stakeholders, establishing their relationship and communicating that they will be the point of contact and PM going forward. Communicating the current PM's experience with each of these members or groups can be especially valuable at this point, but be careful about interjecting personal feelings or politics into the mix. There have been plenty of cases where different PMs have had different experiences and relations with specific stakeholders. Many times, I have found "difficult customers" easy to deal with once I understood where they were coming from (what their true objectives were).

Once the joint turnover plan has been set, execute it. Provide all the relevant materials to the incoming PM, supported by opportunities to go through them with the relevant team members. Do not feel that the outgoing PM needs to be in every meeting or personally hand over every item to the incoming PM. The goal at this point is to ensure the project can continue to succeed without YOU! The outgoing PM may need to be reminded of this as the transition occurs. Try to avoid a "lingering transition" where the former PM comes back for ESC meetings or gets involved with future deliverables. Not only does this distract the former PM from their new assignments and responsibilities, but it also undermines the incoming PM. The signal is being sent that the former PM does not trust the current PM with the project and that they are not fully capable of handling their responsibilities. Is that a message you would want communicated about yourself?

When possible, the outgoing PM should brief management, including the Sponsor, Business Owner, and ESC, on the transition to the new PM. The goal is to reassure management that a proper hand-off has occurred, the incoming PM is fully prepared to take over the project, and that no additional issues are expected due to the handover. If there are any open action items or issues, these should be discussed, including the agreement the two PMs have on how the issues will be handled. In addition to providing a good start for the incoming PM, these departure briefings also demonstrate that the outgoing PM has not let things drop but has worked to ensure a smooth turnover to the new PM. Not only is this the right thing to do, but it also adds to your reputation as a thorough professional with the best interests of the organization at heart. Even if you are a consultant PM leaving a client, there is always the possibility of returning in the future for other assignments.

If possible, establish a formal turnover date and have a meeting to do so. This "change of command ceremony," whether formal or informal, is an important signal to everyone involved that "there's a NEW Sheriff in town." Depending upon circumstances, this may be coupled with a team celebration of a project milestone or a warm send-off for the departing PM. Sometimes referred to as "hail and farewell" parties, these ceremonies are an important part of maintaining team spirit and morale, so do not dismiss them as "fluff." Even with dispersed teams working remotely, a formal hand-off and accompanying ceremony are important. Do everything possible to avoid having the former PM depart in the dead of night, as this sends some troubling messages to the team. It can start rumors and conjectures about the circumstances of the change, the status of the project, and the job security of other team members. As noted earlier in this book, we do not want to "spook the herd" during a transition.

Be sure to provide all the tools and materials that the PM has been using to the incoming PM. If appropriate, provide contact information for the departing PM for any follow-up questions that may occur. If the departing PM was a consultant, there are going to be client-owned materials and information that must be left behind or destroyed. Include these actions in the turnover plan. Congratulate the incoming PM on taking over a good project and delivery team, and ride into the sunset (see Chapter 14).

> *Tip:* Act as you would like to be treated when you receive projects.

Handing-Off to Another Team

Depending upon the industry, organization, and type of project, it may be required to hand off the project to another team. This may be due to an organization passing a project on to another organization when a project reaches a specific stage, such as moving from research and development to preparing a system for production. Or an organization may outsource specific aspects of a project, such as testing or the entire project. More common is handing off the results of a project to a customer organization or maintenance team. This section will focus on the latter case since it encompasses the other cases as well. As noted earlier, companies that specialize in outsourcing have playbooks that cover this in detail. Essentially, the transitions are projects in themselves. This section will not go into that level of detail. The intent is to highlight some activities that should be included in project plans to prepare for and ease hand-offs to other teams.

Although many transitions go smoothly, there are many examples of ones that have not gone well. Table 13-1 lists some of the transition problems observed by the author over the last 40 years in project management across multiple industries and project types. As Agile project methodologies become extremely common across multiple industries and organizations, additional transition challenges are being observed (see Table 13-2). The processes and tips described in this section are intended to reduce the problems encountered by triggering the PM and project team to incorporate transition considerations in their ongoing project plans.

Table 13-1: Typical Project Transition Problems

1. Knowledgeable team members depart before transferring information
2. Lack of current documentation
3. Estimates made based on current methods, not documented methods
4. Negotiated gating rather than documented approvals
5. Inaccurate or out-of-date information and documentation
6. No direct contact between the teams transferring responsibilities
7. No feedback loop to verify that receiving team has understood the knowledge being transferred and is able to perform tasks
8. Receiving team does not have appropriate skillsets
9. Receiving team not appropriately staffed at the time of transition
10. Receiving team does not have access to application/environments/data during transition

---

11. Inadequate time for Knowledge Acquisition (KA)/ Knowledge Transfer (KT)
12. May have multiple components from different teams (i.e., Commercial off the Shelf (COTS) owner, interface team, mobile app team—all following different processes and standards)
13. Delivery and/or support processes not documented or understood by the support team

Table 13-2: Additional Transition Challenges With Agile Methodologies

1. Agile emphasizes "try and fail," while production maintenance often emphasizes "do not fail."
2. Requirements and requirements changes are often not documented.
3. Design changes may also lack documentation.
4. Architectural standards may be lacking or not followed.
5. Agile teams often fail to document "as-built."
6. Agile tools may not be used by the O&M team—decisions are needed:
   - Transfer the tools and data to the O&M Team?
   - Transfer/translate data into the O&M Tools?
7. Test cases and tools may not be transferred with the code.
8. Agile Team members may not be available for KT.
9. Non-standard Agile methods may have been used for development that do not work for maintenance.
10. Clean Up Sprints may not have been done to address the above issues.

Tip: Consider adding a "Transition Sprint" in the schedule to ensure a proper hand-off to the O&M Team.

In order to have a smooth transition, start with a plan, then work your plan. Don't wait until the end of the project to plan the transition, and recognize that there are going to be points during project development and execution where the transition team will need to be involved. The delivery team will also need to take steps during their work to prepare for ongoing work by the support team after the transition has been completed. These will be further detailed below. Execute the transition plan as the project proceeds, ensuring that all teams are informed and involved. Good two-way communications, including formal checkpoints, sign-off of key artifacts, and candid feedback, will keep both teams aligned and informed.

Although the types and amount of documentation can vary greatly based on the type of project and the delivery methodology, ensure that the documentation is available to both teams. If it is kept in an online repository, make sure that the repository has these characteristics:

- Easy to use and search
- Inventory listing that is clear, accurate, and complete
- Clear document versioning and "as of dates"
- Document ownership that is clear and noted when it changes

Preparing for the transition should start before the release to production; in fact, it should be considered at project initiation. If possible, the Project Manager should meet with the Maintenance Manager at the *start* of the project. In that meeting, cover the following areas:

- Identify potential issues and concerns affecting the future hand-off and ongoing maintenance—agree on how to handle them.
- Determine how the maintenance team will be kept informed of project progress and challenges.
- Agree on the documentation that will be provided to the maintenance team and how it will be reviewed and accepted by that team.

- Agree on a cross-team communications plan.
- Agree on a schedule for interactions and progress tracking.
- Establish checkpoints, gates, etc., through the course of the project.

Short-cutting this preparation *will* lead to missteps and stumbles later. As an incoming PM, if these steps have not been done and there is going to be a transition at the end of the project to a support team, completing these planning actions should go on the project planning and "to-do" list. While there may be bad and ugly issues that need to be addressed right away, be careful about pushing transition planning too far down the priority list. It may pay dividends to have a preliminary meeting with the support manager and solicit their help in planning and perhaps leading the drive to get ready for transition. Make them an ally instead of an obstacle.

With a plan in place, be sure to track transition progress regularly with tools and the right metrics, just as for any other project task or sub-project. Through the planning meetings with the support manager, "Done" should be measurable and agreed to. Use checklists and joint reviews as the project progresses to track progress against "Done," flagging risks and issues as they occur. During reviews and transition meetings, be proactive—ask questions and hold people accountable. The success of the transition to maintenance or support is an important and often highly visible component of overall project success. Planning and working together with the maintenance team can be crucial in ensuring that they "own" the future support of the application. Table 13-3 highlights some of the missteps leading to a poor transition; we've just covered ways to address all of them.

> *Tip: Managers must avoid both "throw it over the wall" and "no acceptance without perfection" attitudes within the teams.*

Table 13-3: Missteps Leading to a Poor Transition

1. Lack of a transition plan
2. Waiting until the end of the project to start on transition tasks
3. No agreement on what "done" looks like
4. Assuming the support team has what they need without ever asking them
5. Support team wanting "perfection" in everything before acceptance
6. Not updating application documentation to reflect "as-built"
7. Throwing documentation "over the wall"
8. Not obtaining sign-off when the transition is complete
9. Documentation of known issues and outstanding commitments to stakeholders does not exist or is not passed to the support team

Tip: Get agreement on what "Done" looks like **now** so you can plan how to get there.

While we established that an overall transition plan should be agreed to and in place, the following paragraphs will highlight some of the items that should be addressed within project plans and some transition considerations. Note that many of these apply early in the project, which is another reason to include transition and long-term support planning in the overall project plan. When transitioning in, these plans and considerations may have been missed by the prior PM. Although there is no "way-back" machine to correct that issue, including tasks to support transition should be part of the revised project plan developed by the incoming PM and delivery team. When reviewing existing project plans and artifacts, check to see if applicable items from these considerations have been included. Also, work with the delivery team and support manager to determine if there have been project changes that require revisiting any of the prior decisions or agreements.

An area that is surprisingly missed on many projects is the use of different tools and processes between the development and support teams. In some cases, the development organization may be transitioning to new methodologies, processes, or tools while the support teams continue to use legacy ones. This is often common as an organization transitions to Agile delivery approaches. Determine which tools were used by the development or project team and/or by the current maintenance team. Questions to consider include:

- Will the ongoing maintenance team use the same tools?
- Do software licenses or tools need to be transferred? If not, ensure adequate time for purchasing new ones.
- Are they the right tools for ongoing maintenance and support?
- Does the support team need training in the use of the tools?
- Are the tools, files, databases, etc., ready to be transferred to the maintenance team?

For IT projects, there may be specific types of tools to consider, including:

- Integrated Development Environment
- Quality Assurance Suite
- Issue/Problem Tracking or Work Ticketing
- Configuration Management
- Build Management
- Change Management Process/Tools
- Requirements Management

Tip: Do not settle for tools that are cheap or free—the downstream costs of poor tools far outweigh any perceived savings.

Tip: *Ensure the participation of all the team leads when evaluating tools—what may work for one team may be unsatisfactory for another.*

Tip: *Changing tools mid-project, or having to port data from one tool to another, is risky, problematic, and inefficient.*

Understanding the business, functional, and non-functional requirements of the application to be maintained is important. An efficient way to do this is to have the Lead BA for the maintenance team participate in the project requirement walk-throughs and reviews. They should be an active participant "listening" for maintenance requirements or issues, and they should follow up with Project BAs if there are questions or concerns. Project tasking and issues take priority at this stage, but note issues requiring follow-up for later action. Agree on how the requirements documentation/data will be transferred to the maintenance team:

- When will this occur?
- Who are the key participants?
- Will there be additional walk-throughs or reviews?
- What are the acceptance criteria for the turnover?
- What tools, files, etc., will be turned over?

With Agile projects, include maintenance personnel in User Story confirmations, so they can directly hear the voice of the Business Owner and ask questions. Participation by maintenance BAs in planning sprint discussion of User Stories and requirement confirmations is another available option.

The maintainability of the end result of the project is a key design consideration. Putting a system onboard a ship that can't be repaired by anyone aboard would not make sense, nor would building a house that required extremely expensive routine maintenance. During the design phase, design reviews should consider maintainability, including a member of the maintenance team, if possible. Their focus should be on the understandability of the design, if issues and errors that occur can be readily identified and resolved, and if handling failures has been considered in the design. For example, a house being built in a hurricane-prone area should be built to withstand high winds and include an electric generator to deal with power outages. For software development projects, there are code analysis tools that can automate looking for design and code issues that impact reliability and maintainability, but their use should still be supplemented with human reviews.

During test planning, the test strategy should address what will carry over to maintenance, not just the immediate needs of the project. While more applicable to software development projects, these considerations can also apply to other projects. For example, how will factory equipment be calibrated and maintained? What test equipment and procedures will be needed to determine the source of a problem with a piece of equipment? Think about which test scenarios or cases will be needed by the maintenance team. Will they need any special equipment, hardware, or software to conduct maintenance and repair?

> **Tip:** Handling this in a planned manner now will speed hand-off later.

As noted earlier, don't leave documentation for the end of the project. Remember to reflect as-built changes into the documentation before turnover (including defect repairs, change requests, etc.). As early in the project as possible, determine if there are documentation standards that must be followed so that documents do not need significant revision near the end of the project. This can be especially important when working with government entities or when specific certifications are required for project acceptance, such as a certificate of occupancy or drug trial approval. A reminder, using

Agile methodologies *does not* mean no documentation, so ensure the necessary documentation is completed and accepted.

Assessing the readiness of the support organization to handle the results of the project should be part of transition planning. The extent and formality of training will vary depending upon a number of factors, including whether it is a totally new development or modifications to an existing product, system, building, etc. The relation of organizations involved also impacts training needs; is the same company/vendor handling support, or is it going to a different team? For example, turning over newly-installed factory equipment to the factory maintenance team will require more effort than if the equipment supplier is going to do all the maintenance. If the extent and quality of existing documentation are poor, more training time is likely to be required. Unfortunately, there are going to be cases where the time available for the hand-off is too short. When this is recognized, seek to provide additional support to the maintenance team, perhaps through checklists and additional support materials or via hotline support for a period of time.

Tip: Agreement on training, documentation, and approvals is critical to identifying "what done looks like."

Tip: Many KA/KT processes and tools for outsourcing also work here; take advantage of them if they are available.

Whether the transition was planned from project initiation or handled as part of the incoming PM and team updating project plans, there should be a formal hand-off to the incoming team. This applies to transitioning the project to another project team as well as to transitioning to maintenance teams, or in the case of house construction, to the homeowners. Ideally, conduct a formal meeting with a published Agenda and Minutes with key members from both teams present. Record attendance in the minutes, along with the agenda and key discussion points (see below for a suggested agenda). Have a formal sign-off by the leaders of both teams that the transition is effective as of X-date—add the meeting minutes to a scanned copy of the signed document in the archives. Many teams have formal transition completion checklists; if available, these should be referenced during this meeting. While this may be a bit too much for some situations and projects, be careful about getting too informal. If issues arise a few weeks or months down the line, there may be allegations that the turnover was not handled properly, information was missing, etc. These recommendations are for the benefit of everyone involved so that there is agreement that the transition has been handled properly and that there are no hidden issues or concerns.

Suggested Hand-Off Meeting Agenda:

- Team Organization and Points of Contact going forward (including vendors and other 3rd parties)
- Documentation List Review (what is being handed over)
- Risk and Issues Log current status— any changes in ownership of specific risks or issues?
- Change Management Log—are all dispositions clear?
- Open Defects—who owns correcting them?
- KA/KT Plan Completion—any remaining issues?
- Current Status—who owns any pending action items?

Tip: Many of the detailed items may have been covered in earlier meetings between the teams. Use **this** meeting to formally note those results.

Following the steps in Chapters 12 and 13 means the project has been completed and handed off to the support team, or the ongoing project has been passed to a new Project Manager. As the PM who took over the ongoing project, perhaps while it was severely challenged, you have worked with the team to get it running smoothly and are headed for a successful conclusion. Sticking with the western analogy,

216

the sheriff has cleaned up the town, and it's time for them to move on. In the next chapter, we'll cover some final wrap-up items and consider the next steps for a successful sheriff (PM). Before we leave transitions behind, some final principles are included in Table 13-4 for your consideration.

Table 13-4: Top 10 Transition Principles

1. Start with a plan, then work your plan—don't wait until the end of the project to plan the transition.
2. Execute the transition plan as the project proceeds.
3. Ensure all teams are informed and involved—ensure good two-way communications, including formal checkpoints, sign-off, and feedback.
4. Ensure the documentation repository is available to both teams.
5. Track transition progress regularly with tools and the right metrics.
6. Ensure "Done" is measurable and agreed upon upfront.
7. Use checklists and joint reviews as the project progresses.
8. Be proactive—ask questions and hold people accountable.
9. Conduct a formal hand-off and acceptance meeting to clearly pass responsibility.
10. Ensure that the maintenance team "owns" the future support of the application.

We're Not Going to Take It!—Results

The Development and Maintenance Teams set up a regular cadence of meetings to address the issues identified in the initial brainstorming session. Additional issues came up, and some problem solutions led to additional tasking for the Development Team, despite their busy schedule getting ready for the production release. The PD and PSM met one-on-one weekly to candidly discuss progress and any concerns. They developed a close professional relationship, as each learned more about the different responsibilities and challenges that they individually faced. Providing opportunities for production team members to shadow their counterparts on the development team as preparations were made for the production release was a key success factor and was well-received by all the members involved. This included having the PSM in all leadership meetings for the production release and in the "War Room" during the 30-day warranty period. Many of the steps and tools described in this chapter were implemented along the way.

The Maintenance Team formally took ownership of the application on the last day of the warranty period in a joint meeting with the Sponsor, Business Owner, and senior management team. During the meeting, the PSM presented letters of appreciation to a number of Development Team members and stated that this was the smoothest transition she had experienced in 25 years.

After the transition was completed, the PSM and PD worked with the PMO and the corporate methodology team to take what had been done during the transition and turn it into a corporate standard. The process, tools, and templates developed were rolled out across the corporation. Subsequent production releases from the original program and from other projects had a successful roadmap to follow. What could have been a political stand-off and major issue had been turned into a win for the entire organization.

CHAPTER 14

RIDING INTO THE SUNSET

> **"A leader is best when people barely know that he exists. ... When his work is done, his aims fulfilled, they will all say, 'We did this ourselves.'"**
>
> —Lao Tzu, philosopher

A key characteristic of movie westerns, projects, and books is that they all have an end. We're at the end of the book but not the end of working together to successfully take over an ongoing project and bring it to a successful conclusion. As we've noted throughout the book, there are additional resources in the form of checklists, guides, templates, and top-ten lists in the Appendices and on our website www.subscribepage.io/24CLmg. Even if your organization has a well-defined methodology and plenty of templates, take some time to review what we've provided. You may find something new or be inspired to create something even better. Most experienced PMs have a toolbox crammed with useful tools and templates they've picked up over the years; I know that I have. Despite having a crowded toolbox, it never hurts to take some time to review other tools. Spend some time checking out what we've provided.

As you went through the book, there were suggested exercises to help you engage and consider how you would handle some of these steps as you assume leadership of a project. You may have skipped these the first time through the book. Don't wait until the next time you are in the process of taking over a project to think about the challenges that were proposed. Take some time to consider the questions and options while thinking back about a project that you took over that went well, or maybe not so well. Would any of the suggestions in this book have aided in avoiding or resolving problems that arose? Are there things that you will do differently next time? One of the reasons that units in the military and first responders practice so much is so that they will have "muscle memory" in a crisis situation. Hopefully, none of us will be faced with similar immediate crises but having thought through some scenarios and how we should best respond to them is a good way to be better prepared if they occur. As noted in the first few chapters, I have never met a PM who has not had to take over a project that was already started. If you have not done so yet, you are very likely to do so in the future, so get ready!

We noted that some of the key benefits of following the processes and steps in this book include:

- Rapidly identifying key issues and problems in an existing project, if there are any
- Identifying leverage points to turn around troubled projects and teams
- Tactics to keep the project team focused and committed despite changing project dynamics

Chapters 2 through 13 covered these topics, and following them has brought us to this point in the project—departing. Whether the project has been successfully completed, terminated, or handed off to another PM, it's time for you to move to the next project. One of the greatest things about being a PM is that no two projects are ever the same. They may be similar but never the same. There are always new opportunities to improve, to do things differently, to work with different people, to use different technologies, and even to change industries. As PMs, we are always learning, evolving, and getting better. The only constant is change. As we move on, just as the sheriff rides off into the sunset to clean up another town, we want to ensure we leave a happy town behind us. The customer and team should also feel that the project was successful and that they have benefitted from the leadership and guidance of the PM. Finally, a successful PM, or sheriff, deserves to be rewarded with the knowledge that they've done the best possible job under the circumstances and that their careers will benefit from the project as well. Let's explore what it takes to wrap up a project with all these happy results.

The Unit is Yours

The U.S. Navy Reserve unit of 50 sailors had been under a cloud ever since a failed command inspection two years previously. A young Lieutenant who had just moved into the area was assigned as the Executive Officer (XO) to help straighten things out, as the Commanding Officer (CO) was simply overwhelmed. In their first meeting, the CO asked the XO if he could create a roadmap to correct the issues thoroughly enough to get them through the follow-up inspection in six months. Knowing that this would be a project with a fixed deadline, the XO confidently said yes, knowing he had the PM experience to make it happen. They pulled the Chief Petty Officers (CPOs) together to build the project plan and gained their buy-in. Each CPO had a specific area to handle, working with the XO to handle the details and set up standard processes and tools to handle it. Training, records administration, transportation, and supply were all areas needing improvement. Progress was irregular, but things started to run more smoothly. The six-month follow-up inspection was graded as "Improving Trend," with another follow-up required in a year. The improvement provided an opportunity for the CO to move up to another assignment, and a new CO joined.

As the change of command reviews were wrapping up, the new CO told the XO to keep things running as they were. There were some policy changes, and the inevitable personnel changes occurred, but the improvement project kept moving

---

forward. At the two-year point, the unit was rated #3 in the Readiness Command out of close to 100 units. It had become a stellar unit with a good reputation, and a number of officers were looking to take over command when the current CO left at the end of his tour. The unit performance had aided the CO being promoted mid-tour, and the word was out—this was a sweet command tour to have.

The CO called the XO up at home one cold January evening to discuss the upcoming change of command. The call took a surprising turn.

"XO, you've done a great job over the past two years, and the unit is running very smoothly. Some of the automated tools and processes you implemented have been passed on to other units, and they are also having good results with them. Your last active-duty tour with our gaining command resulted in a glowing letter of commendation from the command CO about the support you and the unit provided to them over the two-week period. He agrees with me that you have been a key leader in turning this unit around. We recommended that you be given command of the unit instead of a more senior officer from outside the team. I met the Admiral for dinner tonight and made the case. The Admiral agreed, and you will receive orders to take over the unit. You will be the most junior officer commanding a reserve unit in his command. I am confident that you will be an outstanding CO. You've worked hard to make this unit successful; it's time that work was rewarded."

"The unit is yours to command!"

Although the project involved in this story was a long one, reserve units only meet one weekend a month, so think of it as a project that had roughly 24 sprints or work periods. There were many keys to success, but the path closely followed what we've described since Chapter 1. A team that had specific scope to achieve in a set period of time, while complying with specific quality standards with a fixed budget of resources. In other words, a fixed-price project with definite end dates. The project was failing, primarily due to the team being overwhelmed and lacking defined processes that could be handled with the resources available. The XO turned it into a formal project, using project tools and approaches, with the support of the CPOs and eventually the entire unit. The unit CO handled the role of Sponsor, managing the external teams and relationships that were required. As positive results were obtained, morale improved, processes were refined, and the results got even better. The project plan was executed, the project succeeded, and the XO was rewarded by being given a unit command years earlier than was typical. A great ending, but there is more to successfully ending a project than getting a promotion, bonus, or career bump. Let's look at what is involved.

As a leader, the PM has responsibilities to their organization, to their team, and to themselves. Before the PM rides off into the sunset, these each need to be taken care of. We've already covered the organization and project responsibilities in Chapters 12 and 13. Now we'll look at the remaining two aspects.

No PM ever completes projects by themselves. If they did, it would be an individual effort, not a project effort. PMs need to identify those team members ready for increased responsibilities and career growth and assist them along that path. This should occur throughout the project, but there are often projects that are so intense that there may not have been the time or energy available to do so earlier. The end of the project is the time to correct this. Build up team members for new opportunities. This can be done via evaluation inputs to their member managers, project departure evaluations, promotion recommendations, discussions with the members themselves, and through working the informal network within the organization. They contributed to your success; you need to contribute to their success. This is another leadership opportunity for the PM to demonstrate that they understand what it means to lead and to take care of their people.

There may be some team members who struggled mightily on the project. Discuss their challenges with them, and help map out a path forward with them. Perhaps additional training, working with a mentor, moving to different responsibilities, and seeking an opportunity with additional support are all options that should be considered. Sometimes it means a change in focus. A weak developer might become a great Quality Analyst. A Business Analyst may be better suited as a user interface designer or an Organizational Change Management consultant. Help them understand their strengths and weaknesses and seek out opportunities where they can be successful on their next project.

Now take a similar look at yourself. Get ready for your next opportunity. What went well, and what did not go well? Should the next assignment help you reinforce specific skill areas? Would a stretch assignment, perhaps with a coach, lead to more professional growth? If things are getting too routine, is there a specific challenge that would re-energize you? Were you exposed to something that you want to explore in more detail? Perhaps another project using a specific methodology or technology? Maybe an opportunity to refine some tools and templates that you developed or improved to make them even better? Or if the project was especially intense and draining, maybe one that is less challenging so you can recover your energy and reconnect with your friends and family. As the project wraps up, take some time to think things through and be proactive about your next opportunity. Remember, there are no problems, just opportunities to excel!

Take time to celebrate project completion with the team. Sometimes picking the right time to do so may be difficult. In many situations, part of the team stays for a warranty or transition period while the other members head to new assignments. Try to celebrate with the entire team before this happens, and conduct the final lessons learned for the overall project. You can always do a retrospective for the warranty period later and combine them into one report. Celebrate the milestone of crossing the finish line together as a team. Recognize the top performers, share some project stories, hand out mementos, etc. After the Florida insurance project, everyone received a custom T-shirt with a picture of a parrot and the logo "It's 5 O'clock Somewhere … But We're Still Working." They were an instant hit with the team, and many were pinned to cubicle walls as word of the dedication and responsiveness of the team spread through the organization. Small gestures can have big results on team morale and reputation, so take the time to recognize and celebrate the success of your team.

What should YOU take away from this experience? As we noted in the preface, PMs who can take over an ongoing project and bring it to a successful conclusion are respected and desired. Note what worked for you and the team and what didn't. Think about the knowledge, skills, and experience you've gained. How will you put that to use in the future? What should you record for future reference and use? What did YOU learn? Are there things you won't do again? Are there things you should learn more about? If so, what is the path to gaining that knowledge? How will you get it?

What should YOU get from this experience? Were there any specific rewards, bonuses, endorsements, etc., promised? Be sure to follow up with management as part of briefing them on the successful completion of the project. Discussing the approaches that you used, the lessons learned, and new tools that may help the organization are important ways to show that the successful result didn't just happen randomly. You demonstrated your contributions to the project and organization, so communicating them in a factual manner isn't bragging; it is a way to help the organization improve. Offer to help the methodology team, the PMO, or similar organization with what came out of the project so that other projects and PMs can benefit from it as well.

Finally, reward YOURSELF! Taking over an ongoing project is stressful and usually requires a lot of extra work. Long hours, difficult decisions, and challenging issues all take a toll. Try to get a break— perhaps some time off, a family vacation, or just a week or so to document the project, processes, and tools so the organization can benefit in the future. Move the artifacts to the archives, wrap up the contract, close things out, and tie the project up with a bow. Dot the final I's and cross the final T's.

Take a deep breath, and look around the town. The streets are quiet; the townspeople are safe; there is no panic. The project is over, and the town is cleaned up. Climb into the saddle and turn towards the sunset. Ride on, knowing that you've completed a difficult job and you've done it well.

Another opportunity lies ahead.

APPENDIX A

GLOSSARY

Acceptance Criteria – a set of conditions that must be met before a deliverable, artifact, task, or project are approved by the customer.

Activity – a distinct portion of work performed during a project.

Assumption – a factor considered to be true or certain to happen without proof of it actually occurring.

Baseline – the approved version of a work product that can be changed using formal change control procedures and is used as the basis for comparison to actual results (from the PMI Lexicon).

Bill of Material (BoM) – the comprehensive listing of all raw materials, subassemblies, assemblies, parts, and components required to build a product. This can include less tangible items such as firmware and software.

Budget – the allocated funds for the project, usually consisting of work package cost estimates, contingency reserve, and management reserve.

Business Analyst (BA) – team members responsible for bridging the gap between IT and business to assess business processes, determine requirements, and ensure that stakeholder needs are known. The BA team leader is usually referred to as the Lead BA (LBA).

Business Continuity Plan (BCP) – plan established to prevent, mitigate, and recover from events that disrupt the project, program, or portfolio. Also established to support the normal operations of organizations, business processes, or applications.

Business Owner – the individual that holds the rights and responsibilities for a business process, application, or defined entity.

Business Process Reengineering (BPR) – business improvement approach focusing on the analysis and radical redesign of workflows and business processes within an organization, supported by new or improved information technology to significantly improve performance and competitiveness.

Change Control – a process whereby modifications to documents, deliverables, or baselines associated with the project are identified, documented, approved, or rejected by the responsible authority (usually a Change Control Board)

Change Control Board (CCB) – the formal group responsible for reviewing, evaluating, approving, delaying, or rejecting changes requested within the project and documenting and communicating their decisions.

Change Order (CO) – an approved Change Request that modifies the existing project objectives and constraints and that will be implemented by the project team.

Change Request (CR) – a formal proposal to modify a document, deliverable, or baseline (from PMI Lexicon).

Charter – a document that formally authorizes the project and establishes the goals and constraints of the project.

Commercial Off the Shelf (COTS) – items that are produced commercially that are used with little or no modification. Usually referring to the use of commercial components in government or military applications or systems.

Constraint – a factor that limits the options for managing a project, program, portfolio, or process (from the PMI Lexicon).

Contingency Plan – a document describing actions to be taken if certain conditions occur (e.g., bad weather delaying an outdoor event).

Crashing – a schedule compression technique used to shorten the remaining schedule of a project.

Critical Path – the sequence of activities that represents the longest path through a project, which determines the shortest possible duration (from the PMI Lexicon).

Data Item Description (DID) – U.S. Government terminology for the formal description of a deliverable or artifact required under a contract, usually designated by number from a standardized collection of deliverable requirements.

Deliverable – any unique and verifiable product, result, or capability to perform a service that is produced to complete a process, phase, or project (from the PMI Lexicon).

Disaster Recovery Plan (DR Plan) – a documented and structured approach that describes how an organization will respond to unplanned incidents and resume normal operations.

Earned Value Management (EVM) – a methodology that combines scope, schedule, and resource measurements to assess project performance and progress (from the PMI Lexicon).

Executive Steering Committee (ESC) – a group governing a project composed of key executive stakeholders, including the sponsor and business owner.

Gantt Chart – a bar chart of schedule information where activities are listed on the vertical axis, dates are shown on the horizontal axis, and activity durations are shown as horizontal bars placed according to start and finish dates (from the PMI Lexicon).

Governance – the management organization and practices established to ensure that stakeholder objectives are achieved by monitoring performance and compliance against agreed-on direction and prioritization, including providing direction and setting priorities as needed during the project or program.

Issue – a risk that has occurred, creating a problem or opportunity for the project or program and requiring a response from the project team.

Knowledge Acquisition (KA) – the process of members learning, practicing, and remembering new information and skills so they can perform in specific roles and execute specific tasks.

Knowledge, Skills, and Attributes (KSA) – the specific characteristics and abilities required to perform successfully in a designated role. Sometimes Attitudes is used instead of Attributes.

Knowledge Transfer (KT) – the organized plan and activities to share and disseminate knowledge from one part of an organization or team to another. KT seeks to uncover, create, capture, organize, and distribute knowledge and ensure its availability for future use. This can be challenging due to the desired knowledge usually being tacit rather than explicit or documented.

Lessons Learned – the formal collection of knowledge gained during a project, or portion of a project, presented in a manner to improve performance under similar circumstances in the future.

Matrix Organization – an organizational structure where members report to more than one manager (e.g., a functional manager for their professional skills and development and a project manager for tasking on a specific project).

Metric – a quantifiable entity that allows the measurement of the achievement of a goal.

Milestone – a significant point or event within a project or program.

Objective – the formal statement of a desired outcome.

Operation and Maintenance (O&M) – the ongoing support of an application or system while in regular use (in "production"). This includes maintenance, repair of defects or issues, and minor enhancements to the system by an assigned team.

Organizational Change Management (OCM) – applying a framework for managing the rollout of new or changed business processes, changes in organizational structure, or cultural changes within an enterprise, focusing on the people side of change management.

Principal Investigator (PI) – the leading scientist on an R&D project, often having all the responsibilities of a project manager.

Production Support Manager (PSM) – the individual responsible for the operation and maintenance of applications and systems that are in regular use (in "production").

Program – related projects, subsidiary programs, and program activities managed in a coordinated manner to obtain benefits not available from managing them individually (from the PMI Lexicon).

Program Management Office (PMO) – an organization tasked with standardizing program and project management and delivery practices within a larger organization. Sometimes referred to as a Project Management Office. PMOs may also handle management of methodologies, consolidated reporting to senior management, and other support functions for project and program managers.

Project Director (PD) – the manager of one or more project managers, managing multiple projects, sometimes referred to as a Program Director; or a project manager for a large and complex project.

Project Management Body of Knowledge (PMBOK) – information on managing projects collected and organized by the Project Management Institute (PMI) and used for their internationally recognized project manager certification—Project Management Professional (PMP)

Project Management Institute (PMI) – an internationally recognized organization focused on project and program management.

Project Management Professional (PMP) – an internationally recognized certification for project managers, reflecting practical experience managing projects, successful completion of a standardized test on project management principles and practices, along with continuing education in the field.

Project Manager (PM) – the person assigned to lead the team responsible for successful completion of the project and achieving project objectives.

Project Portfolio Management (PPM) – oversight and control over a number of projects, programs, and tasks to achieve the objectives of an organization in the most economical and efficient manner.

Quality – being fit for purpose.

Quality Analyst (QA) – an individual trained in quality assurance and testing principles and practices tasked with verifying the quality of software or other deliverables within a project. Also known as Quality Engineers.

Quality Assurance (QA) - systematic efforts taken to ensure that the deliverables provided to customers meet the agreed performance, design, reliability, and maintainability expectations. Quality Assurance seeks to prevent mistakes and defects from occurring instead of discovering them after the fact.

Risk – an uncertain event or condition that, if it occurs, has a positive or negative effect on one or more project objectives (from the PMI Lexicon).

Scope – the specified and approved features, functions, and capabilities that are required to be provided to the designated stakeholders at the completion of the project. Project scope should be defined in a formal document such as a project charter or requirements document.

Scope Creep – expansion of project scope without going through the change management process, resulting in unplanned changes to the time, cost, and/or resources needed to complete the project.

Skill – the learned ability to achieve specific desired results.

Sponsor – an individual or a group that provides resources and support for the project, program, or portfolio and is accountable for enabling success (from the PMI Lexicon).

Stakeholder – an individual, group, or organization that may affect, or be affected by, or perceive itself to be affected by, a decision, activity, or outcome of a project, program, or portfolio (from the PMI Lexicon).

Statement of Work (SOW) – contractual definition of the objectives of a project, including the triple constraints between the benefitting organization (customer) and the performing organization (vendor or contractor).

Subject Matter Expert (SME) – professionals who have advanced knowledge in a specific field, area, or topic. They can benefit a team by providing guidance and strategy to the team and by mentoring less experienced team members.

What's In It For Me (WIIFM) – colloquial expression used to reinforce the need to communicate the benefits to a member of policies, changes, or decisions that are being implemented to try to gain their support

Work Breakdown Structure (WBS) – a hierarchical decomposition of the total scope of work to be carried out by the project team and supporting organizations to accomplish the project objectives and scope, including creating the required deliverables.

Work Package – the work defined to the lowest level of the work breakdown structure for which cost, resources, and duration are estimated and managed.

APPENDIX B

ADDITIONAL RESOURCES

These materials have informed my project management journey to this point. Although not directly used in the preparation of this book, they provide useful additional information for Project Managers. Note that some of these books have more recent editions.

Management and Systems Thinking

Covey, Stephen R., *The 7 Habits of Highly Effective People*, Free Press, New York, 2003.

Cummings, Thomas G. and Worley, Christopher G., *Organization Development and Change 5th ed.*, West Publishing Company, New York, 1993.

Deresky, Helen, *International Management: Managing Across Borders and Cultures*, Prentice Hall, Saddle River, NJ, 2011.

Haines, Stephen G., *The Manager's Pocket Guide to Systems Thinking & Learning*, HRD Press, Amherst, MA, 1998.

Hellriegel, Don and Slocum, John W. Jr., *Organizational Behavior*, 11th ed., Thomson-Southwestern, Mason, OH, 2007.

Paul Hersey, Kenneth Blanchard, and Dewey Johnson, *Management of Organizational Behavior*, 10th ed., Pearson, New York, 2012.

Howell, Jon P. and Costley, Dan L., *Understanding Behaviors for Effective Leadership*, Prentice Hall, Upper Saddle River, NJ, 2006.

Kotter, John P., *Leading Change*, Harvard Business School Press, Boston, MA, 1996.

Robbins, Stephen P. and Coulter, Mary, *Management*, 11th ed., Pearson, New York, 2012.

Robbins, Stephen P. and Judge, Timothy A., *Organizational Behavior*, 15th ed., Pearson, New York, 2013.

Schermerhorn, John, *Management*, 11th ed., John Wiley and Sons, Hoboken, NJ, 2010.

Vandeveer, Rodney C. and Menefee, Michael L., *Human Behavior in Organizations*, Pearson-Prentice Hall, Upper Saddle River, NJ, 2006.

Weisbord, Marvin R., *Productive Workplaces: Organizing and Managing for Dignity, Meaning, and Community*, Jossey-Bass Publishers, San Francisco, 1987.

Situational Leadership II (Participant Workbook), Ken Blanchard Training and Development, Escondido, CA, 1994.

Methodologies

Davenport, Thomas H., *Process Innovation: Reengineering Work through Information Technology*, Harvard Business School Press, Boston, MA, 1993.

Evans, James R. and Lindsay, William M., *An Introduction to Six Sigma & Process Improvement,* South-Western, Mason, OH, 2005.

Goldratt, Eliyahu M., *Critical Chain*, The North River Press, Great Barrington, MA, 1997.

Poppendieck, Mary and Poppenieck, Tom, *Lean Software Development: An Agile Toolkit*, Addison-Wesley, New York, 2003.

Poppendieck, Mary and Poppenieck, Tom, *Implementing Lean Software Development: From Concept to Cash*, Addison-Wesley, New York, 2007.

Project and Program Management

Brooks, Frederick P. Jr., *The Mythical Man-Month: Essays on Software Engineering*, Addison-Wesley, Reading, MA, 1979.

Horine, Gregory M, *Absolute Beginner's Guide to Project Management*, Que Publishing, Indianapolis, IN, 2005.

Kapur, Gopal K., *Project Management for Information, Technology, Business, and Certification*, Pearson Education, Upper Saddle River, NJ, 2005.

Kerzner, Harold, *Project Management: A System's Approach to Planning, Scheduling, and Controlling, 9th ed.*, John Wiley & Sons, Hoboken, NJ, 2006.

Milosevic, Martinelli, and Waddell, *Program Management for Improved Business Results,* John Wiley & Sons, Hoboken, NJ, 2007.

Pressman, Roger S., *Software Engineering: A Practitioner's Approach, 4th ed.*, McGraw-Hill, New York, 1997.

Project Management Institute Publications

These practices, standards, and guides are published by the Project Management Institute (PMI), Newtown Square, PA, and are available directly from PMI. They are a good starting point for each subject area.

A Guide to the Project Management Body of Knowledge (PMBOK) – Seventh Edition and The Standard for Project Management (2021)

Agile Practice Guide (2017)

Business Analysis for Practitioners: A Practice Guide (2015)

Benefits Realization Management: A Practice Guide (2019)

Choose Your WoW! A Disciplined Agile Approach to Optimizing Your Way of Working (2nd ed.) (2022)

Governance of Portfolios, Programs, and Projects: A Practice Guide (2016)

Managing Change in Organizations: A Practice Guide (2013)

Navigating Complexity: A Practice Guide (2014)

PMI Lexicon of Project Management Terms (2017)

The PMI Guide to Business Analysis (2017)

Practice Standard for Project Configuration Management (2007)

Practice Standard for Project Estimating (2nd ed.) (2019)
Practice Standard for Work Breakdown Structures (3rd ed.) (2019)
Requirements Management: A Practice Guide (2016)
The Standard for Earned Value Management (2019)
The Standard for Portfolio Management (4th ed.) (2017)
The Standard for Program Management (4th ed.) (2017)
The Standard for Organizational Project Management (OPM) (2018)
The Standard for Risk Management in Portfolios, Programs, and Projects (2019)

Quality

Golze, Sarbiewski, Zahm, *Optimize Quality for Business Outcomes: A Practical Approach to Software Testing*, Wiley Publishing, Hoboken, NJ, 2008.

Jarvis, Alka and Crandall, Vern, *Inroads to Software Quality*, Prentice Hall PTR, Upper Saddle River, NJ, 1997.

Paulk, Weber, Curtis, Chrissis (editors), *The Capability Maturity Model: Guidelines for Improving the Software Process*, Addison-Wesley, Reading, MA, 1994.

Budgeting and Estimating

Gulledge, Hutzler, and Lovelace (editors), *Cost Estimating and Analysis*, Springer-Verlag, New York, 1992.

Ward, John, and Daniel, Elizabeth, *Benefits Management: Delivering Value from IS & IT Investments,* John Wiley & Sons, West Sussex, England, 2006.

Metrics and Status Reporting

Axson, David A.J., *Best Practices in Planning and Management Reporting*, John Wiley & Sons, Hoboken, NJ, 2003.

Boehm, Barry W., *Software Engineering Economics*, Prentice-Hall, Englewood Cliffs, NY, 1981.

McWhirter, Kurt and Gaughan, Ted, *The Definitive Guide to IT Service Metrics*, IT Governance Publishing, Cambridgeshire, UK, 2012.

Parmenter, David, *Key Performance Indicators*, John Wiley & Sons, Hoboken, NJ, 2010.

Putnam, Lawrence H. and Myers, Ware, *Five Core Metrics: The Intelligence Behind Successful Software Management*, Dorset House Publishing, New York, 2003.

Putnam, Lawrence H. and Myers, Ware, *Measures for Excellence, Reliable Software on Time, within Budget*, Yourdon Press, Upper Saddle River, NJ, 1992.

Tufte, Edward R., *The Visual Display of Quantitative Information*, Graphics Press, Cheshire, CT, 2007.

APPENDIX C

SUPPORTING TOOLS AND TEMPLATES

Tools for Chapter 2 Challenges With Taking Over an Ongoing Project

The chapter discussed reasons why taking over an ongoing project is different than starting a new project from scratch. Table 2-1 listed some of the challenges and issues related to taking over ongoing projects. While PMs often take over projects that are going well, in many cases there are ongoing challenges contributing to the decision to bring in a new PM, or to have an experienced PM review an ongoing project. Here are some of the most common reasons that projects have trouble and signs that more trouble is likely to occur.

A. **10 Reasons Projects Go Astray**

1. Insufficient support from project sponsor
2. Unclear/poor requirements or target
3. Poor scope and change management
4. Poor project planning or estimating
5. Poor communication
6. Lack of formal PM practices

7. Unclear roles and responsibilities
8. Lack of resources
9. Technical challenges
10. Inexperienced team members (availability is not a skill set)

B. **10 Signs of Project Trouble**

1. Team members working overtime – all the time
2. Customer refuses to accept deliverables
3. Executive Sponsor/Customer seems apathetic
4. Cover Your A** (CYA) e-mail trail has started
5. PM not sure of real status
6. Intermediate progress points being missed, but assurances given that milestones will still be met
7. Missing or out of date planning documents
8. Team relationships are problematic
9. Resources assigned without proper skillsets, or resources are abruptly changed
10. Reports seem suspicious e.g. same completion percentage for multiple periods, or lack objective progress measures

Tools for Chapter 3 Getting the Call to Action

The focus of this chapter is on why a new project manager is being brought in and providing the incoming PM a sense of the current status of the project from the executive viewpoint.

11 Questions to Ask Before Taking Over a Project

1. Why are we changing the PM now?
2. What does success look like?
3. What is the current status of the project?
4. If it is not on track, what caused it to go off track?
5. Why was I selected for this project?
6. What do you need from me to help this project succeed?

7. Do you intend for me to stay as PM through the end of the project? If not, what is the desired project status to trigger my transition out?
8. What authority will I have over the project team?
9. What authority will I have over external teams or resources that we need to succeed?
10. What will you do to help this project succeed?
11. Do I have the option to turn down this assignment?

Tools for Chapter 5 Determine the Current Status— Lay of the Land

The goal of this phase is to determine the actual status of the project and identify any critical situations or issues that may need immediate action. While there will be materials to review, at this stage most of the PM's time will be spent meeting with key stakeholders and project team members. In addition to learning more about the project these meetings provide opportunities to learn more about the other people involved with the project, and to start building a relationship with them. Information gathering interviews usually go more smoothly with some advance preparation, including having a list of questions for the people involved. We have provided some standard questions to ask typical project stakeholders that you can tailor for the specifics of your project and organization.

STAKEHOLDERS TO INTERVIEW

The key stakeholders are listed in preferred order. If this approach can be followed, it will provide a top-down view of the project while respecting the management hierarchy. Be careful to note any political or interpersonal issues that may impact the project or project team as well. While it is important to trust the people being interviewed, keep their potential biases in mind, and remember that reviewing project reports, deliverables, and other materials may be necessary to verify the true facts. Be careful not to make any promises or commitments at this point since you are still learning about the true status of the project and the capabilities of the project team.

- Sponsor
- Business Owner
- Manager Owning Project Delivery
- Project Management Office (PMO) liaison for the project
- Steering/Executive Committee Members
- Agile/Scrum Coach (if applicable)
- Current PM (if available, even if they have moved to another project or organization)
- Scrum Master (if applicable)
- Finance/Budget Manager
- Customer/Client Team Managers (if applicable), including Contract or Procurement Manager for the project
- Project Team Members, starting with team leads
- Customer/Client Team Members on the Project Team (if applicable)

TYPICAL QUESTIONS FOR EACH STAKEHOLDER

Tailor these standard question lists as needed for the specifics of the project being reviewed.

A. Sponsor

1. What is the current status of the project?
2. What does success look like? (Has this changed since the project started?)
3. Why is it important that this project be successful?
4. If it is not on track, what caused it to go off track?
5. When did the project start to go off track (if it is not Green now)?
6. What were the problem indicators that came to the attention of the ESC?
7. What should be done to keep it on track or get it back on track? (the Silver Bullet question)

8. Are there financial challenges? If so, is a joint approach possible (when dealing with a contract)?
9. Is there someone we should get for the team to improve our chance of success?
10. What can you do to help this project succeed?
11. What do you need from me to help this project succeed?
12. Do you have any other concerns about this project?
13. Will you work with me to help this project succeed?
14. Do you have any questions for me?

B. Business Owner

1. What is the current status of the project?
2. What does success look like? (Has this changed since the project started?)
3. Why is it important that this project be successful?
4. If it is not on track, what caused it to go off track?
5. When did the project start to go off track (if it is not Green now)?
6. What were the problem indicators that came to your attention?
7. What should be done to keep it on track or get it back on track? (The Silver Bullet question.)
8. What actions have already been taken to try to get the project back on track?
9. Are there financial challenges? If so, is a joint approach possible (when dealing with a contract)?
10. What is each executive stakeholder willing to commit to make the project successful?
11. Does the project have the resources needed to be successful?
12. What is the right mix of resources to get back on track?
13. Is there someone we should get for the team to improve our chance of success?
14. What can you do to help this project succeed?
15. What do you need from me to help this project succeed?
16. Do you have any other concerns about this project?

17. Will you work with me to help this project succeed?
18. Do you have any questions for me?

C. Manager Owning Project Delivery

1. What is the current status of the project?
2. What does success look like? (Has this changed since the project started?)
3. Why is it important that this project be successful?
4. What is the project complexity? What makes it more or less complex?
5. If it is not on track, what caused it to go off track?
6. When did the project start to go off track (if it is not Green now)?
7. What were the problem indicators that came to your attention?
8. What should be done to keep it on track or get it back on track? (The Silver Bullet question)
9. What actions have already been taken to try to get the project back on track?
10. Are there financial challenges? If so, is a joint approach possible (when dealing with a contract)?
11. If there are financial challenges, will the customer and/or supplier commit to share the cost of items in dispute?
12. Will all parties put financial and/or resource "skin in the game"?
13. What is each executive stakeholder willing to commit to ensure that the project is successful?
14. Does the project have the resources needed?
15. What is the right mix of resources to get back on track?
16. What do team turnover statistics look like? Do you have any concerns over member turnover?
17. Is there someone we should get for the team to improve our chance of success?
18. What can you do to help this project succeed?
19. What do you need from me to help this project succeed?

20. Do you have any other concerns about this project?
21. Will you work with me to help this project succeed?
22. Do you have any questions for me?

D. Project Management Office (PMO) liaison for the project

1. What is the current status of the project?
2. What does success look like? (Has this changed since the project started?)
3. Why is it important that this project be successful?
4. What is the project complexity? What makes it more or less complex?
5. If it is not on track, what caused it to go off track?
6. When did the project start to go off track (if it is not Green now)?
7. What were the problem indicators that came to the attention of the PMO?
8. What should be done to keep it on track or get it back on track? (The Silver Bullet question)
9. What actions have already been taken to try to get the project back on track?
10. Does the project have the resources needed to be successful?
11. What is the right mix of resources to get it back on track?
12. Is there someone we should get for the team to improve our chance of success?
13. What do team turnover statistics look like? Do you have any concerns over member turnover?
14. Are there financial challenges? If so, is a joint approach possible (When dealing with a contract)?
15. Is there a specific financial problem? E.g. accounts receivable growing, invoices being refused or delayed, unfunded changes
16. Will the customer and/or supplier commit to share the cost of changes in dispute?
17. Will all parties put financial and/or resource "skin in the game" to make the project successful?

18. What can you do to help this project succeed?
19. What do you need from me to help this project succeed?
20. Do you have any other concerns about this project?
21. Will you work with me to help this project succeed?
22. Do you have any questions for me?

E. Steering/Executive Committee Members

1. What is the current status of the project?
2. What does success look like? (Has this changed since the project started?)
3. Why is it important that this project be successful?
4. If it is not on track, what caused it to go off track?
5. What were the problem indicators that came to the attention of the ESC?
6. What should be done to keep it on track or get it back on track? (The Silver Bullet question)
7. What can you do to help this project succeed?
8. What do you need from me to help this project succeed?
9. Do you have any other concerns about this project?
10. Will you work with me to help this project succeed?
11. Do you have any questions for me?

F. Agile/Scrum Coach (if applicable)

1. What is the current status of the project?
2. What does success look like? (Has this changed since the project started?)
3. Why is it important that this project be successful?
4. What is the project complexity? What makes it more or less complex?
5. If it is not on track, what caused it to go off track?
6. When did the project start to go off track (if it is not Green now)?
7. What were the problem indicators that came to your attention?

8. What should be done to keep it on track or get it back on track? (The Silver Bullet question)
9. What actions have already been taken to try to get the project back on track?
10. Does the project have the resources needed to be successful?
11. What is the right mix of resources to get back on track?
12. Is there someone we should get for the team to improve our chance of success?
13. What do team turnover statistics look like? Do you have any concerns over member turnover?
14. What can you do to help this project succeed?
15. What do you need from me to help this project succeed?
16. Do you have any other concerns about this project?
17. Will you work with me to help this project succeed?
18. Do you have any questions for me?

G. Current PM (if available, even if they have moved to another project or organization)

1. What is the current status of the project?
2. What does success look like? (Has this changed since the project started?)
3. Why is it important that this project be successful?
4. What is the project complexity? What makes it more or less complex?
5. If it is not on track, what caused it to go off track?
6. When did the project start to go off track (if it is not Green now)?
7. What were the problem indicators that came to your attention?
8. What should be done to keep it on track or get it back on track? (The Silver Bullet question)
9. What actions have already been taken to try to get the project back on track?
10. Are there any critical upcoming milestones or events that must be handled?

11. Were there any resource issues?
12. What is the right mix of resources to get back on track?
13. Is there someone we should get for the team to improve our chance of success?
14. What do team turnover statistics look like? Do you have any concerns over member turnover?
15. Are there financial challenges? If so, is a joint approach possible (when dealing with a contract)?
16. Will the customer and/or supplier commit to share the cost of changes in dispute?
17. Do you have any advice for me on what is needed for the project to be delivered successfully?
18. Will you be available to answer questions or help with issues in the future, if there are any?

H. Scrum Master (if applicable)

1. What is the current status of the project?
2. What does success look like? (Has this changed since the project started?)
3. Why is it important that this project be successful?
4. If it is not on track, what caused it to go off track?
5. What were the problem indicators that came to your attention?
6. When did the project start to go off track (if it is not Green now)?
7. What should be done to keep it on track or get it back on track? (The Silver Bullet question)
8. What actions have already been taken to try to get the project back on track?
9. Does the Scrum Team have the resources needed to be successful?
10. What is the right mix of resources to get back on track?
11. Is there someone we should get for the team to improve our chance of success?
12. What can you do to help this project succeed?

13. What do you need from me to help this project succeed?
14. Do you have any other concerns about this project?
15. Will you work with me to help this project succeed?
16. Do you have any questions for me?

I. Finance/Budget Manager

1. What is the current status of the project?
2. What does success look like? (Has this changed since the project started?)
3. Why is it important that this project be successful?
4. If it is not on track, what caused it to go off track?
5. What were the problem indicators that came to your attention?
6. What should be done to keep it on track or get it back on track? (The Silver Bullet question)
7. What can you do to help this project succeed?
8. Do you have any other concerns about this project?
9. Are there financial challenges? If so, is a joint approach possible (when dealing with a contract)?
10. Are there specific financial problems? E.g. accounts receivable, invoices being refused or delayed, unfunded changes, etc.
11. Will the customer and/or supplier commit to share the cost of changes in dispute?
12. Will all parties put financial "skin in the game" to reach a successful conclusion?
13. Will you work with me to help this project succeed?
14. Do you have any questions for me?

J. Customer/Client Team Managers (if applicable), including Contract or Procurement Manager for the project

1. What is the current status of the project?
2. What does success look like? (Has this changed since the project started?)

3. Why is it important that this project be successful?
4. If it is not on track, what caused it to go off track?
5. When did the project start to go off track (if it is not Green now)?
6. What were the problem indicators that came to your attention?
7. What should be done to keep it on track or get it back on track? (The Silver Bullet question)
8. What actions have already been taken to try to get the project back on track?
9. Does the project have the resources needed to be successful?
10. What is the right mix of resources to get back on track?
11. Is there someone we should get for the team to improve our chance of success?
12. What do team turnover statistics look like? Do you have any concerns over member turnover?
13. Are there financial challenges? If so, is a joint approach possible (when dealing with a contract)?
14. What can you do to help this project succeed?
15. What do you need from me to help this project succeed?
16. Do you have any other concerns about this project?
17. Will you work with me to help this project succeed?
18. Do you have any questions for me?

K. Project Team Members, starting with team leads

1. What is the current status of the project?
2. What does success look like? (Has this changed since the project started?)
3. Why is it important that this project be successful?
4. If it is not on track, what caused it to go off track?
5. What should be done to keep it on track or get it back on track? (The Silver Bullet question)
6. Does the team have the resources needed to be successful?
7. What is the right mix of resources to get back on track?

8. Is there someone we should get for the team to improve our chance of success?
9. What can you do to help this project succeed?
10. What do you need from me to help this project succeed?
11. Do you have any other concerns about this project?
12. Will you work with me to help this project succeed?
13. Do you have any questions for me?

L. Customer/Client Team Members on the Project Team (if applicable)

1. What is the current status of the project?
2. What does success look like? (Has this changed since the project started?)
3. Why is it important that this project be successful?
4. If it is not on track, what caused it to go off track?
5. What should be done to keep it on track or get it back on track? (The Silver Bullet question)
6. Does the team have the resources needed to be successful?
7. What is the right mix of resources to get back on track?
8. Is there someone we should get for the team to improve our chance of success?
9. What can you do to help this project succeed?
10. What do you need from me to help this project succeed?
11. Do you have any other concerns about this project?
12. Will you work with me to help this project succeed?
13. Do you have any questions for me?

GENERIC QUESTIONS TO ASK WHILE ASSESSING CURRENT PROJECT SITUATION

1. What is the current status of the project?
2. What does success look like? (Has this changed since the project started?)
3. Why is it important that this project be successful?

4. What is the project complexity? What makes it more or less complex?
5. If it is not on track, what caused it to go off track?
6. When did the project start to go off track (if it is not Green now)?
7. What were the problem indicators that came to your attention?
8. What should be done to keep it on track or get it back on track? (the Silver Bullet question)
9. What actions have already been taken to try to get the project back on track?
10. Do you have the resources you need?
11. What is the right mix of resources to get back on track?
12. Is there someone we should get for the team to improve our chance of success?
13. What do team turnover statistics look like? Do you have any concerns over member turnover?
14. What can you do to help this project succeed?
15. What do you need from me to help this project succeed?
16. Do you have any other concerns about this project?
17. Will you work with me to help this project succeed?
18. Do you have any questions for me?

Financial Situation (discuss with members handling finances)

1. Are there financial challenges? If so, is a joint approach possible (when dealing with a contract)?
2. Is there a problem? E.g. accounts receivable, invoices being refused or delayed, unfunded changes
3. Will the customer and/or supplier commit to share the cost of changes in dispute?
4. Will all parties put "skin in the game"?
5. What is each executive stakeholder willing to commit to fix the project?

Chapter 6 – Learn the Territory

As noted within Chapter 6 this is not a quick 'one and done' exercise. It is unlikely that there will be sufficient time to examine all of the materials in detail before needing to revise plans and keep the project moving forward. It will be important to compile as complete a list as possible at the start of this effort and update it as progress is made. Add other materials to be reviewed to the list as the investigation progresses, including relevant materials from related projects. For example, progress reports from a software application that must interface with the software being developed in the project being taken over.

Chapter 6 is particularly relevant for members of the Project Management Office (PMO) or similar organization that are conducting an independent review of a project. The lists below should be used to develop a review plan and document list adjusted for the industry, technology, and methodology of interest. The lists provided below are generic but provide a foundation to work from.

Key Documents to Examine

1. Project Charter
2. Project Requirements/Specifications
3. Design Documents
4. Latest Schedule, Resources and Budget
5. Status Reports
6. Risks and Issues Log
7. Change Log
8. PMO reports
9. Stakeholder expectations (if written)
10. Critical Dependency Lists
11. Test Strategy, Test Plans, and Test Reports

Key Questions to Answer for Each Artifact

1. Are all of the artifacts that should be available at this stage of the project actually available?
2. Are the artifacts complete? Are there a lot of to-be-determined statuses (TBDs)?
3. Are the artifacts approved?
4. Have approved changes been incorporated in the documents?
5. Is the document change history accurate and up to date?
6. Do the artifacts show that the delivery team is following the methodology and templates applicable to this project? If not, why not?
7. If there were deviations from the methodology, were these deviations approved by the correct stakeholders?
8. Do the artifacts provide evidence that the delivery team understands the methodology and associated artifacts that they are using?
9. Are the artifacts accurate?
10. Do the artifacts properly reflect the objectives and requirements of the project?
11. Do they appear to be internally consistent? For example, are there conflicting requirements within the Business Requirements document?
12. Are they consistent with other artifacts? For example, do the Functional Requirements tie back to the Business Requirements? Can each functional requirement be easily traced back to a Business Requirement? Do the User Stories support the Epics? Are there test cases for the Epics and User Stories that support the Definition of Done?
13. Are the artifacts realistic? Do future projections reflect experience to date?
14. Do reports reflect the real status of the project? Are any trends shown? Do any of the trends require action?
15. Are the artifacts being used properly by the right members, both internal and external to the project team?

16 Will the artifacts need to be updated to get the project completed with the current or revised plan?

17 If artifacts need to be updated, has the time and effort to do so been included in the schedule?

18 If time has not been allocated for artifacts that need to be updated, what is a reasonable estimate of the time and effort needed to make the updates? Can that time and effort be worked into the schedule and budget?

Are there any artifact issues that require slowing or stopping work within the project to get them corrected?

SAMPLE RISK AND ISSUE LOG

Last Reviewed: 04/16/2022

Next #   9

Last Updt	Date Started	Risk Num	Risk (If)	Impact (Then)	Assumptions	Potential Impact (5) High (4) Med-High (3) Medium (2) Med-Low (1) Low	Probability (6) High (4) Med-High (3) Medium (2) Med-Low (1) Low	Risk Factor	Actions	Assigned to	Date Due	Status / Comments
									Risk Mitigation Actions (Should be specific and actionable)			
4/16/22	3/6/22	1	DOI does not approve AACME Insurance filing on time	Delays policy, effective dates, conversion, and BPO Team start	DOI is motivated to push approvals through on time	4	2	8	Monitor progress with AACME Insurance	Garry Schwab		4/16 received DIR consent for AACME Insurance to operate in state
4/16/22	3/6/22	2	Telecom company fails to install new lines and numbers by due date	Delays installing support for claims, new policies, etc	Telecom companies are frequently late	5	1	5	Place orders immediately, closely monitor progress and escalate if delayed	Alan Schmitzen		Orders placed, no issues foreseen
4/16/22	3/6/22	3	Printing set up is delayed, possibly due to late approval of forms	Delays ability to send renewal/conversion packets to customers, potentially other required communications	Printing services need to be implemented and ready with all forms on go-live date	4	2	8	Establish and publish printing readiness plan, monitor closely	Susan DiLeo		No special requirements; stock acquired, forms requirements have been reviewed by DMS, no concerns
4/16/22	3/6/22	4	Conversion of incoming files is delayed	Delays acceptance of policies for processing and support, delaying consultant revenue	DOI is motivated to move policies to AACME ASAP	3	1	3	Ensure conversion capabilities are available and tested as early as possible. Work with AACME Insurance to track DOI identification and transfer of policies	Terry Yonkers (conversion), Matt Fields (admin)		Obtained sample files but need to translate to Excel format and compare mapping to existing conversion program
4/16/22	3/10/22	5	Compressed schedule leads to omitted or partial requirements	Large number of defects or change requests at production release, potentially delaying production release	Requirements elicitation needs to be thorough, and properly reviewed and approved	3	3	9	Ensure elicitation strategy is done, complete, and properly IDs all SMEs and hidden users	Pam Griffin		BRD in good shape, though behind schedule. Full participation in walkthrough will ensure good results
								0				

Last Reviewed: 04/16/22

Last Updt	Issue Num	Issue	Impact	Assumptions	Impact Rating (5) High (4) Med-High (3) Medium (2) Med-Low (1) Low	Actions	Assigned to	Date Due	Status / Comments
						Issue Resolution Actions (Should be specific and actionable)			
04/16/22	6	Takeout of XYZ Policies means Claims BPO and functionality within application required prior to rest of application	Claims functionality may be required to support claims adjudication	1. Claims personnel will have access to policy info in XYZ system until renewed as AACME Insurance policies 2. Functionality required to support claims adjudication can be identified and delivered first, if req'd	4	1. Confirm that we will have access to XYZ system for claims 2. Identify application capabilities required to support claims 3. Schedule claims required items as early as possible on the schedule	Susheel Khartik	02/19/22	Will provide claims entry, capability, and Policy view as Day 1 (6/10) requirements. On track to do so

ACME Insurance   Closed Issues

Last Updt	Issue Num	Issue	Impact	Assumptions	Impact Rating (5) High (4) Med-High (3) Medium (2) Med-Low (1) Low	Issue Resolution Actions (should be specific and actionable) Actions	Assigned to	Date Closed	Status / Comments
Issues Closed									
03/08/22	7	Print Suppression will be required in the initial system	Include print suppression in DEV system setup, include throughout project	Print Suppression O/R for I/O addresses AACME Insurance requirements (need to confirm this)	2	Confirm AACME Insurance print suppression requirements. Include print suppression in all requirements, plans, etc.	Terry Y	03/18/22	Print suppression code included with initial setup of DEV & TEST. It is required/included in test matrix.
03/18/22	6	Need to include ISO Reporting, GUASR Reporting, state Cat Fund Reporting, and Premium Tax Reporting with initial system	Include these changes to the base system in the initial delivery. Increases development and test efforts	These have been defined for another state client, so requirements should be available now	2	Confirm these are required, locate requirements, include effort in all estimates	Terry Y	03/18/22	These are required, will be included in Day 2/3 delivery. Some reports have been planned but not put into production previously. Some are in production.

259

SAMPLE PROJECT REVIEW/AUDIT REPORT

Project: PROJECT REVIEW   Report Date:

ID	PROJECT REVIEW - CHECKLIST	FOUND?	QUALITY RATING	FINDINGS
	Note: The Rating is a qualitative assessment (1 - 5) by the reviewer of the degree of artifact compliance with the selected methodology and the potential impact of this factor on the overall success of the project. Low scores indicate a negative impact on project success.			
2	PROJECT GOVERNANCE			
A1	Is the position of this project within the governance structure of the overall organization clearly defined and appropriate?	Yes	5	Project established and aligned appropriately
A2	Are the project reporting relationships clearly defined and being followed? E.g. reporting via a PMO	Yes	5	Standard reporting via the PMO is being done
A3	Is there an Executive Steering Committee (ESC) in place?	Yes	4	ESC formed, membership is not complete
A4	Is the membership of the ESC appropriate for this project?	No	2	Business stakeholders not included in ESC
A5	Does the ESC meet regularly, with all required members in attendance?	No	1	ESC has only met once, some members missing
A6	Are the results of the ESC documented and communicated appropriately?			
A7	Are appropriate actions taken when actual results deviate from the project plan?			
A8	Are external project reviews held at intervals appropriate for the complexity, size, and risks of the project?			
A9	Was a project kick-off meeting conducted and the results documented and distributed to stakeholders?			
3	PROJECT PLANNING			
B1	Does the project have an approved project charter?			
B2	Is there a formal Project Plan?			
B3	Is the Project Plan clear and complete?			
B4	Has the Project Plan received formal approval?			
B5	Have project management standards and practices been established and documented?			
B6	Was a structured approach used to break work effort into manageable components? E.g. was a Work Breakdown Structure (WBS) used?			
B7	Were team members involved in the development of activities, tasks, and estimates for the Project Plan?			

Quality Rating: 1- Not Acceptable 2- Poor 3- Average 4- Good 5- Excellent

PROJECT REVIEW

Project: Report Date

B8	Are multiple estimation methods being used to estimate costs and schedules?	
B9	Are project estimates subject to independent review by members with the correct expertise?	
B10	Was data from previous projects of a similar nature compared to estimates and plans for this project?	
B11	Is the project being tracked by Earned Value Analysis (EVA) or similar methods?	
B12	Do the EVA results indicate that the project will complete on time, on budget, on scope, with the desired quality?	
1	**PROJECT SCOPE**	
C1	Is the project currently considered to be meeting its defined scope?	
C2	Is there an approved charter that clearly defines the scope of the project (definition of done)?	
C3	Is the current scope of the project substantially different than what was originally defined and approved?	
C4	Has the scope document been kept up to date with approved change requests?	
C5	Are the business requirements well structured, complete, testable, and approved?	
C6	Are the user requirements well structured, complete, testable, and approved?	
C7	Are the project requirements stable?	
C8	Does the project team believe the requirements are achievable within the budget and schedule?	
C9	Are any assumptions and constraints identified and documented?	
3	**PROJECT CHANGE MANAGEMENT**	
D1	Is there an approved Change Management Plan (this may be included in the Project Plan for smaller projects)?	
D2	Are the processes in the Change Management Plan being followed?	

Quality Rating: 1 Not Acceptable 2 Poor 3 Average 4 Good 5 Excellent

D3	Does the Change Control Board (CCB) meet regularly to consider change requests?	
D4	Are all impacted parties provided an opportunity to contribute to change decisions?	
D5	Is there a Change Log being maintained that accurately reflects the current status of pending, approved, and disapproved change requests?	
3	**PROJECT SCHEDULE**	
E1	Is the project currently considered to be on schedule?	
E2	Does the project have a Project Schedule showing task durations and dependencies (CPM or PERT)?	
E3	Does the Project Schedule go to the appropriate level of detail?	
E4	Has the Project Schedule been approved and published?	
E5	Are all the required activities included in the Project Schedule? (refer to the WBS)	
E6	Have critical milestones, gates, and reviews been included in the Project Schedule?	
E7	Does the Project Schedule include any contingency time?	
E8	Do the activities in the Project Schedule coordinate with the resource assignments in the Resource Plan?	
E9	Does the Project Schedule show progress to date and revised completion dates based upon productivity to date?	
E10	Is a critical path defined for the overall project? Are team members aware of the tasks on the critical path?	
E11	Is the Project Schedule reviewed regularly with team members to identify potential issues or changes?	
E12	Is the Project Schedule realistic?	
E13	Is the Project Schedule updated as Change Requests are approved?	
E14	Are any dependencies on external projects shown in the Project Schedule?	
E15	Is the progress of other teams on the external projects being used to updated the Project Schedule?	

Quality Rating: 1- Not Acceptable 2- Poor 3- Average 4- Good 5- Excellent

Project: **PROJECT REVIEW**   Report Date:

	PROJECT BUDGET			
3				
F1	Is the project currently considered to be within its approved budget?			
F2	Does the project have an approved budget?			
F3	Is the budget sufficiently detailed for a project of this size and complexity?			
F4	Do the current project estimates fall within the approved budget?			
F5	Is the project budget adjusted for approved change requests?			
F6	Are project costs being tracked on a regular basis?			
F7	Are actual costs being used to project future costs and compared against the project budget?			
F8	Are there potential issues with the budget due to future risks or issues?			
F9	Is the budget adequate for the scope, schedule, and resources for this project?			
F10	Is the project properly set up in the timekeeping and accounting systems?			

	PROJECT QUALITY			
3				
G1	Does overall project quality appear appropriate in relation to the scope, schedule, budget, and charter?			
G2	Is there an approved Quality Plan? (note: this may be included in the overall Project Plan for small projects)			
G3	Is there a clear relationship between project goals (definition of done) and the test and quality requirements?			
G4	Are there approved Test Strategies, Test Plans, and associated test planning materials, following the project delivery methodology and organization standards?			
G5	Have appropriate quality metrics been established in coordination with key stakeholders and the project team?			
G6	Are the agreed upon metrics being collected, analyzed, and reported on a regular basis?			

Quality Rating: 1- Not Acceptable 2- Poor 3- Average 4- Good 5- Excellent

G7	Are there established quality gates suitable for the nature of this project and the delivery methodology being used?
G8	Are quality issues being documented, tracked, and resolved on a regular basis?
G9	Is there adequate time allowed for defect repair and retesting?
G10	Are the resources assigned to quality roles adequate for a project of this type?
G11	Do all team members have a 'quality mindset'?
G12	Are there established design standards i.e. coding standards?
G13	Are the established design standards being followed?
3	PROJECT METHODOLOGY/TECHNOLOGY
H1	What delivery methodology is being used?
H2	Is the delivery methodology suitable given the charter and constraints of the project?
H3	Is the delivery team familiar with the delivery methodology being used?
H4	Does the delivery team have the tools that are needed for this project, considering the methodology and technology being used?
H5	Is the delivery team comfortable with the tools and processes being used?
H6	Are there any issues related to the delivery methodology being used?
H7	Are there any special technology issues with this project?
H8	Is the delivery team familiar with and comfortable using the technology for this project?
H9	Are there any concerns or issues with the methodology or technology that should be noted?
H10	Is there a project repository for all key documents that team members have access too? Is it well organized?
H11	Are project metrics being collected and tracked regularly, and used to revise plans, schedules, and budgets?

Quality Rating: 1- Not Acceptable 2- Poor 3- Average 4- Good 5- Excellent

Project: Report Date:

PROJECT REVIEW

H12	If there are Service Level Agreements (SLA) or similar target metrics with the customer, are these clear, communicated, and being tracked?	
3	**PROJECT ORGANIZATION & STAFFING**	
I1	Has the project organization been formally defined and published?	
I2	Is the project organization suitable for a project of this scope and complexity?	
I3	Is the project organization suitable for the delivery methodology being followed?	
I4	Are the funding and staffing estimates sufficiently detailed for a project of this scope and complexity?	
I5	Is the project fully staffed?	
I6	Are there any staffing needs or gaps?	
I7	Are there any skill gaps within the current team?	
I8	Are there any other staffing issues?	
I9	Is this a new organization that may not have experience with the delivery methodology, industry, or technology?	
I10	Does the Project Manager have experience with this organization, industry, business process, and methodology?	
3	**PROJECT RISK MANAGEMENT**	
J1	Do there appear to be any unusual risks or issues with this project?	
J2	Is there an approved Risk Management Plan in place? (note: this may be included in the overall Project Plan for smaller projects)	
J3	Was a risk assessment completed and documented at the start of the project?	
J4	Is there a process in place to monitor risks, and is it being followed?	
J5	Are all risks and issues documented in a risk log, with members assigned to each one?	

Quality Rating: 1- Not Acceptable 2- Poor 3- Average 4- Good 5- Excellent

PROJECT REVIEW

Project: Report Date:

J6	Are risks and issues tracked to completion, with closed risks and issues noted as such?	
J7	Is the level of risk management appropriate for a project of this scope, complexity, and type?	
3	**PROJECT COMMUNICATIONS**	
K1	Is there an approved Project Communications Plan? (for smaller projects this may be contained in the overall Project Plan)	
K2	Is project status reported on a regular basis to the required stakeholders?	
K3	Do project status reports accurately describe the current status of the project?	
K4	Is project status reviewed at appropriate management levels on a regular basis (including the PMO)?	
K5	Are internal project status meetings held at reasonable intervals?	
K6	Are the results of project status meetings documented and communicated shortly after meeting completion?	
K7	Do project team members regularly report their activities, status, and progress (no less than bi-weekly)?	
K8	Are remote team members kept fully informed and involved in the project? Are they included in project meetings?	
K9	Are meeting results documented and distributed appropriately to keep all team members informed?	
3	**PROJECT STAKEHOLDER MANAGEMENT**	
L1	Have all stakeholders been identified?	
L2	Is there an approved Stakeholder Management Plan (or Organizational Change Management Plan) in place? (Note: for smaller projects, this may be included in the overall Project Plan)	
L3	Does the Stakeholder Management Plan include communication requirements and methods for key stakeholders?	

Quality Rating: 1- Not Acceptable 2- Poor 3- Average 4- Good 5- Excellent

PROJECT REVIEW

Project: Report Date:

L4	Are all stakeholder requirement tasks included in the Project Schedule?		
L5	Do there appear to be any missing, or 'hidden' stakeholders?		
L6	Is the Stakeholder Management Plan being executed?		
3	VENDOR MANAGEMENT		
M1	Are there formal vendor management procedures? (these can be at the organization or the project level)		
M2	Are the formal vendor management procedures being followed?		
M3	Is the vendor scope of work clearly identified and formally approved with the required contractual documents?		
M4	Are the vendor organization and responsibilities clearly identified in the Project Plan, organization charts, communication plan, etc.?		
M5	Are all vendor tasks and deliverables appropriately included in the project schedule?		
M6	Is the vendor using the same methodology and technology as the remainder of the project team?		
7	Are vendor representatives included in project status and review meetings?		
M8	Are there any issues with vendor performance?		
M9	If there are issues with the current vendor, can the vendor be easily replaced?		
3	ASSOCIATED PROJECTS		
N1	Does this project depend on any external projects for successful completion? If so, list those projects.		
N2	Are there procedures in place for coordination with these projects, and are those procedures being followed?		
N3	Are there any concerns about the status of these external projects?		
N4	If there are concerns about any external projects, is action being taken to address them?		

Quality Rating: 1- Not Acceptable 2- Poor 3- Average 4- Good 5- Excellent

Tools for Chapter 7 – Take Required Immediate Actions

At this point there is probably a growing list of tasks that need to be done. The PM needs to conduct triage and determine what needs to be done immediately, what can wait a bit, and what can be put off a bit longer. It is critical to remember that the PM has a team to work with, and that everything does not need to be done by the PM. Include appropriate members of the team, and get help from outside the team when needed. Based on the results of the interviews, document reviews, and information gathered to date, some or all of the tasks below should move to the top of the priority list.

Specific Tasks to Do ASAP

1 Update the Communication Plan – ensure frequent steering committee and team meetings are planned and conducted to keep everyone informed and aligned.

2 Update the list of Risks and Issues based on the current reality – communicate them to the team and key stakeholders and prioritize prevention and mitigation actions to align with the timing, likelihood of occurrence, and potential impact of identified risks. Address current issues with support from the team.

3 Work with the team and reschedule the project as needed – identify resource needs, potential scope changes, etc. to stay within the triple constraints as much as possible, get formal approval when the constraints need to be modified.

4 Work with sponsor and adjust scope if required.

5 Identify ways people outside the team can help – ask for it and get it – especially if there are key external dependencies.

6 Get formal agreement from the customer to promptly review and approve deliverables – prevent backsliding on receiving timely reviews and approvals.

7 Determine if any preceding work needs to be redone – i.e., fixing requirements – you may have to live with what you

have, but record the issues that were found so they may be addressed in the future.

8   Identify any opportunities to do things better, or differently and work with the team to make adjustments to processes, tools, etc.

These should be started while meeting with the team and stakeholders, but may not be completed until those meetings are done.

Tools for Chapter 8 – Revise the Plan

Stakeholder Management Plan

As noted in the chapter, it is very important to ensure that all the project stakeholders are identified, along with a plan on how to keep them informed and supporting the project. There are many materials available on identifying and classifying stakeholders, primarily from the Organizational Change Management (OCM) community. Here is just a brief overview of some key information to be considered in communications planning when assuming management of an ongoing project.

Key information that should be covered in a stakeholder analysis and management plan includes:

1.   The identity (name and title), role, and contact information of each stakeholder.
2.   The degree of interest and commitment this stakeholder has in the success of the project.
3.   What does this stakeholder need from the project during development and after delivery?
4.   What expectations does this stakeholder have for the project during development and after delivery?
5.   What is this stakeholder's greatest concern about the project?
6.   What does the project need from this stakeholder?
7.   What is the risk if this stakeholder is not engaged and supportive?

8. Should we monitor this stakeholder, keep informed, keep satisfied, or manage closely?
9. Describe the communication strategy for this stakeholder. Include the channels, methods, timing, and frequency in the communications plan.
10. What information should be provided to this stakeholder and what concerns should be addressed? (Include this information in the communications plan.)
11. Describe the engagement approach for key stakeholders, including actions that may go beyond what is in the communication plan.
12. Is engagement by this stakeholder needed in any specific project phases?
13. Which team member(s) is responsible for engaging with this stakeholder?

For larger projects, the Stakeholder Management Plan may be a separate document, developed as a sub-task within the project. For smaller projects, it may be included as a section in the Project Management Plan, and result from a few sessions with the Sponsor and team. Some organizations may have separate OCM or training teams that handle this effort, but the incoming PM should review the existing plans with the assigned members and identify if any issues need further action. The plan should identify project stakeholders, identify their level of engagement and impact on the project, how they will be managed, and the approaches taken to manage stakeholders. The information noted above should be in the Stakeholder Management Plan and/or the Communication Plan, since they are closely aligned. The plans do not need to be overly wordy or complicated, here is a simple example of the results of a stakeholder analysis, contained in a Stakeholder Management Plan.

Sample Stakeholder Management Grid

Stakeholder	Organization	Location	Impact on Project	Impacted by Project	Change Readiness Now	Desired Change Readiness	Power	Interest	Notes
Underwriters	Personal Lines	Home Office	L	H	R	S	H	H	Emphasize WIIFM, benefits to company and Agents
Customer Service Representatives	Personal Lines	Home Office	L	H	U	S	H	L	Must be trained and see benefits of new rules
Agents	Various	IL, IN, WI	L	H	U	S	L	H	Provide training and WIIFM
Agent Training Team	Personal Lines	Various	M	M	N	L	L	H	Include in requirements reviews, training development, and testing

Impact Levels – High (H), Medium (M), or Low (L)

271

Change Readiness

Unaware (U) – have no information about the project or likely impacts on them

Resistant (R) – aware of the project and resistant to the changes and potential impacts of the project

Neutral (N) – aware of the project and potential impacts of the project, but not supportive or resistant at this time

Supportive (S) – aware of the project and potential project impacts and is supportive

Leading (L) – aware of the project and potential project impacts and is actively engaged to ensure the project's success

Power Levels

High (H) – has significant formal or informal authority to impact the project

Low (L) – unlikely to have formal or informal authority to significantly impact the project

Interest Levels

High (H) – interested in the progress, outcomes, and impacts of the project

Low (L) – little interest in the progress, outcomes, and impacts of the project

Typical Power/Interest Combinations and Approaches

High Power/High Interest – Manage Closely

High Power/Low Interest – Keep Satisfied

Low Power/High Interest – Keep Informed

Low Power/Low Interest – Monitor (minimize effort, but do not ignore)

TOOLS FOR CHAPTER 10 Move to the Finish Line Together

Pro-active and successful Project Managers usually demonstrate Courageous Project Management, which is different than Heroic Project Management. Some of the key differences in the approaches are listed below.

Courageous PMs

- Are proactive - recognizing early signs that trouble is brewing and taking action before issues arise
- Make the tough and often unpopular decisions early to keep the project on track, regardless of personal risk
- Understand hard choices may need to be made early in projects to prevent big problems later
- Recognize that sometimes heroic measures by the PM and team are required, but as a last resort

"Mary's projects are always successful, but she tends to bring up lots of issues"

Heroic PMs tend to be:

- Reactive - overcoming obstacles and challenges that arise during a project to complete the project – no matter the cost
- Leading (pushing?) a team to meet deadlines and achieve difficult goals
- The go-to PM for impossible project deadlines because the project goals <u>always</u> come first

"That project would not have gotten done without Joe as the PM"

Some of the steps that should be followed by Courageous PMs throughout assuming responsibility for an ongoing project and successfully delivering it include:

- Set the conditions for success
- Set and enforce clear acceptance criteria and quality gates from the start
- Set quality standards – educate the team, assign responsibilities, and enforce meeting the quality standards that have been set
- Actively manage scope, schedule, quality, and risk targets among all stakeholders
- Be proactive – demonstrate a bias towards action as things change
- Forecast and compare expected versus actual results
- Adjust assignments, processes, and solutions to improve results along the way
- Follow the situational leadership approach and adjust as circumstances change
- Assess and act when issues arise
- Enforce quality gates and standards at each phase of the project
- Do not sacrifice quality for budget, scope, and schedule
- Address root causes of defects (people, process, tools)
- Measure and act on individual performance as well as at the overall project level
- Change leadership styles if needed
- Sometimes circumstances change and planned approaches are no longer valid – be flexible
- Some challenges may require heroic efforts from you and the team – lead and support the team through these periods
- Return to a standard pace when realistic and practical

Colin Powell's 18 Leadership Tips

1. Being responsible means pissing people off.
2. The day soldiers stop bringing you their problems is the day you have stopped leading them. They have either lost

confidence that you can help them or concluded that you do not care. Either case is a failure of leadership.

3. Don't be buffaloed by experts and elites. Experts often possess more data than judgment. Elites can become so inbred that they produce hemophiliacs who bleed to death as soon as they are nicked by the real world.

4. Don't be afraid to challenge the pros, even in their own backyard.

5. Never neglect details. When everyone's mind is dulled or distracted the leader must be doubly vigilant.

6. You don't know what you can get away with until you try.

7. Keep looking below surface appearances. Don't shrink from doing so just because you might not like what you find.

8. Organization doesn't really accomplish anything. Plans don't accomplish anything either. Theories of management don't much matter. Endeavors succeed or fail because of the people involved. Only by attracting the best people will you accomplish great deeds.

9. Organization charts and fancy titles count for next to nothing.

10. Never let your ego get so close to your position that when your position goes, your ego goes with it.

11. Fit no stereotypes. Don't chase the latest management fads. The situation dictates which approach best accomplishes the team's mission.

12. Perpetual optimism is a force multiplier.

13. Powell's Rules for Picking People: Look for intelligence and judgment and, most critically, a capacity to anticipate, to see around corners. Also look for loyalty, integrity, a high energy drive, a balanced ego and the drive to get things done.

14. Great leaders are almost always great simplifiers, who can cut through argument, debate, and doubt, to offer a solution that everybody can understand.

15. Part I: Use the formula $P = 40$ to 70, in which P stands for the probability of success and the numbers indicate

the percentage of information acquired. Part II: Once the information is in the 40-70 range, go with your gut.

16. The commander in the field is always right and the rear echelon is wrong, unless proven otherwise

17. Have fun in your command. Don't always run at a breakneck pace. Take leave when you've earned it. Spend time with your families.
    - Corollary: Surround yourself with people who take their work seriously, but not themselves, those who work hard and play hard.

18. Command is lonely.

5 Leadership Lessons From Fleet Admiral Halsey

1. **Leaders Plan Ahead** – plan for eventualities, so quick decisions and balanced risks can be taken when events go differently than foreseen. Planning is the key that unlocks successful risk taking.

2. **Leaders Never Stop Learning** – push to learn new skills and continue to study the evolution of your field, industry, and profession.

3. **Leaders Build Teams that Win Without Them** – No one is indispensable. Leaders must ensure they are developing their junior personnel at all times, to be ready to cover if a key member is not available.

4. **Leaders Endure Failure** – no one wins all the time, acknowledge the failure, learn the lessons from failure, and move on. Learning to overcome setbacks and defeat is part of developing as a leader. Persevere until the next victory.

5. **Leaders Know that People Matter Most** – it takes the contributions of more than one person for all but the most trivial tasks to be completed successfully. Recognize the need to apply a diverse team, each member bringing their own strengths to contribute to the team. Share the glory of the success with that team, looking for ways to promote and reward those ready for additional responsibility.

Adapted from "Hit Hard, Hit Fast, Hit Often!" by Commander Robert McFarlin, USN, USNI Proceedings, July 2021, pp 74-76

Tools for Chapter 11 – Ride Herd and Avoid a Relapse

Project metrics vary widely across industries, project types, and methodologies. This section provides some generic guidelines for selecting appropriate metrics for your project, along with some universal project metrics and some that are more closely related to software development projects. There should be similar metrics available for the type of project and methodology being used. Start with the key questions for determining which metrics are needed and work from there. Keep in mind that every metric being collected and each report being made have a cost in time and effort, so eliminate those metrics that do not provide clear value to the PM, project team, or key stakeholders.

Key Questions to Determine Which Metrics to Use

- Ask these key questions when designing metrics
  - Who is the intended audience?
  - What decisions do they need to make?
  - What information is needed to make these decisions?
  - Is trend information needed to make any of these decisions?
  - When is the information needed to make these decisions?
  - What is the best form to provide the required information?
    - Table
    - Graph
    - Indicators (i.e. stoplight)
  - What supporting information is needed (and where should it go?)

- o Where does the required information come from? Does it need to be transformed?

- Key questions for implementing metrics
  - o Can the data collection be automated?
    - ▫ E.g. direct feed of hours from time tracking system, costs from accounting system
  - o Can the data transformation be automated?
    - ▫ E.g. six-week moving average used to project future results
  - o Can the decision criteria be automated?

    - ▫ E.g. if actual completion date more than 5 days late, print in red

Earned Value Metrics

Using Earned Value (EV) metrics is a time-tested way to track project progress and costs, including the overall impact of trends. For example, if the Estimate at Completion (EAC) for costs increases with each report, it is clear that project costs are not under control. Further research into what the cost issues are, and how they can be corrected is required.

Acronym	Term	Description
PV	Planned Value	PV is the authorized budget assigned to the scheduled work to be accomplished for a scheduled activity or work breakdown structure component.
EV	Earned Value	EV is the value of completed work expressed in terms of the approved budget assigned to that work for a scheduled activity or work breakdown structure component. The cumulative EV is the sum of the approved budgets for activities completed during a given period.
AC	Actual Cost	AC is the total costs incurred and recorded in accomplishing work performed during a given time period for a scheduled activity or work breakdown structure component. Actual cost can sometimes be direct labor hours alone; direct costs alone; or all costs, including indirect costs
BAC	Budget at Completion	BAC is the total amount of funds to be spent at the completion of the task.
EAC	Estimate at Completion	EAC is used by project managers to give their best estimate of the total costs of projects based on actual costs to date. The most frequently used formula for EAC is AC plus ETC; this formula is typically used when previous assumptions regarding costs are wrong.
ETC	Estimate to Complete	ETC is the expected cost needed to complete all the remaining work for a scheduled activity, a group of activities, or the project. ETC helps project managers predict what the final cost of the project will be upon completion.
VAC	Variance at Completion	VAC forecasts the difference between the Budget-at-Completion and the expected total costs to be accrued over the life of the project based on current trends.

Acronym	Term	Formula	Description
CV	Cost Variance	CV = EV – AC	CV provides the cost performance of the project to help determine whether the project is proceeding as planned. Subtracting AC from EV calculates the cost variance.
SV	Schedule Variance	SV = EV – PV	SV indicates the project's schedule performance. This value can indicate whether the project work is proceeding as planned. Calculate the SV by subtracting the PV from the EV.
CPI	Cost Performance Index	CPI = EV / AC	For the CPI of individual budgets, divide EV by AC. For a cumulative CPI, divide the sum of all EV budgets by the sum of all ACs. A CPI of less than one indicates that the project is over budget, and a CPI of over one indicates that the project is coming in under the estimated budget.
SPI	Schedule Performance Index	SPI = EV / PV	Project managers can use the SPI to help predict when their projects will be completed. To calculate the SPI, divide EV by PV. An SPI of one indicates the project is on schedule; greater than one indicates it is ahead of schedule; and less than one indicates it is behind schedule.
EAC	Estimate at Completion	EAC = BAC / CPI EAC = AC + ETC EAC = AC + (BAC - EV)	EAC is used by project managers to give their best estimate of the total costs of projects based on actual costs to date. The most frequently used formula for EAC is AC plus ETC; this formula is typically used when previous assumptions regarding costs are wrong.

Acronym	Term	Formula	Description
ETC	Estimate to Complete	ETC = EAC – AC	ETC is the expected cost needed to complete all the remaining work for a scheduled activity, a group of activities, or the project. ETC helps project managers predict what the final cost of the project will be upon completion.
VAC	Variance at Completion	VAC = BAC – EAC	VAC forecasts the difference between the Budget-at-Completion and the expected total costs to be accrued over the life of the project based on current trends.
CPI^c	Cumulative Cost Performance Index	CPI = ΣEV/ΣAC	Cumulative CPI Method forecasts the total amount to be spent by adding costs incurred to date to the remaining work to be earned, which has been weighted against the current CPI performance value. Usually not beneficial until the project has reached the 20 percent completion point. At that point project performance trends should have been established.

Common Agile Methodology Metrics

Burn Up Chart - Provides clear way to measure progress, and indicate where scope has been added - although usually used for Agile Projects, it can be used with other methodologies

Development Metrics

- Effort Variance
- Schedule Variance
- Peer Review Productivity
- Code Productivity
- Defect Density by Phase
- Defect Removal Efficiency
- Requirements Volatility Index

Agile - Sprint Level Metrics

- Velocity = $\sum$story points completed/number of sprints completed This provides the anticipated number of story points a team can handle per sprint
- Story Points Remaining/Velocity = estimated number of sprints required to complete the product backlog
- % of scope creep = percentage of effort spent during the sprint on tasks those were not part of sprint backlog
- % of rework = percentage of effort spent in correcting review or test defects per sprint
- % of test coverage = percentage of test cases that are executed
- Post sprint defect density = number of defects detected after sprint release against the output of the sprint e.g. defects/1,000 Source Lines of Code (SLOC)

Agile - Project Level Metrics

- Effort variance = Planned effort – Actual effort
- Schedule variance = Planned period – Actual period (number of days)
- Post release defect density = number of defects detected after final project release against the output of the project e.g. defects/1,000 Source Lines of Code (SLOC) Note: some approaches relate number of defects to expended effort, but this approach should be used with caution e.g. defects found/100 hours of labor

Burn Down Chart

- Commonly used in Agile projects, it shows what is left to be completed in terms of fully tested and integrated code, measured in terms meaningful to the end user.
- Changes in scope (additional user stories or re-estimation of story points) are shown as negative numbers in this format.

Typical Software Quality Metrics

- Defect Density (usually number of defects/1,000 SLOC)
- Mean Time Between Failures (MTBF)
- Defect Removal Efficiency (DRE)
- First Time Right
- Defect Rates by:
    - Module / Subsystem
    - Team
    - Root Cause
    - SDLC Phase (including Peer Review defects)

Test Coverage Metrics

- Can be defined by planned test coverage (test cases by component, feature, use case, etc.)
- Usually tracked by completed test cases against planned by unit/component
- If the software is instrumented, may measure which functions, objects, lines, have been exercised during testing
- Often used as a confidence builder, but by itself it does not establish if all the desired test scenarios have been run

Tools for Chapter 12 – Finish Successfully

Tips for Conducting Lessons Learned

As noted in Chapter 12, do not wait until the end of the project to conduct lessons learned sessions. They can be very beneficial at key milestones or gates throughout the project and at the end of each sprint if following an Agile methodology. The goal is to get team members to assess their own and team performance, processes, tools, and results so that improvements can be made. Remember that lessons can be positive (keep doing this) as well as negative (don't do this again). Here are some very basic tips for conducting lessons learned sessions with your team.

Preparing for a Lessons Learned Meeting

- Determine who should participate
- Invite the desired participants to the working session(s) (break large teams into smaller groups when required, divide sessions by project phase or type of activity, or into other groupings to ensure thorough reviews.)
- Ask those planning to attend to review the project or phase goals, reflect upon what went smoothly and what was challenging, and to consider suggestions for improvement. Note that the session is not meant to be a complaint session. Based on the experience of the current team with lessons learned sessions of this type, it may be useful to provide sample outputs from other sessions or teams
- Create an agenda considering the things to be discuss and the group size, as the number of participants may affect the order of events or the time allotted for the meeting. Generally, meetings should last no more than an hour, but make sure to allow ample time for each agenda item. Include time for a brief introduction, feedback and discussion, and to highlight next steps.
- Prepare the room with the tools to be used. Provide writing utensils and sticky notes and other materials that participants will use. Designate a note-taker and/or secure whiteboards or wall space so everyone can see the comments. Provide comfortable seating for all attendees, and consider providing snacks and light refreshments for the meeting as well. Be sure to include remote attendees and set up a virtual room along with the physical one.
- Consider using a facilitator. Using a neutral facilitator from outside the delivery team may help smooth the flow of conversation for a team that is not comfortable sharing opinions openly. Pick a facilitator who is familiar with the project and the team, but not directly involved — perhaps another project manager or someone who has led a similar project in the past.

How to Structure a Lessons Learned Meeting

Meetings should include a brief introduction, time to gather and discuss feedback, and a plan for next steps. Here's a breakdown of those steps:

- **Introduction:** Make introductions and share the agenda. Establish ground rules by letting everyone know why they are here and what is expected from them. Note that members are not to criticize other members for bringing up topics or ideas, this is a 'safe space' for objective discussion.
- **Gather Feedback:** Facilitate discussion and participation from team members. Encourage everyone to provide input. Note that we want to know what went right and wrong in the project so we can all learn from the experience. Emphasize that the meeting is not meant to resolve issues or problems that come up, but to document them for additional investigation as needed. Have the designated note-taker document the feedback. Use some questions to get the discussion going, or to organize the discussion into manageable chunks.
  - o What did we do well?
  - o What processes need improvement?
  - o How well was your role on this project defined?
  - o How effective was teamwork and leadership?

- **Lead Discussion and Encourage Team Input:** Allow and encourage everyone to give feedback ensuring that everyone has a chance to speak. Organize feedback notes into sections or categories that relate to the process or the project. The facilitator shouldaim to keep the conversation neutral and avoid finger-pointing or shifting blame. Depending on the size of your group, it might be beneficial to split into smaller groups to facilitate the conversation and amplify the voices of people less willing to share in a large group setting.

- **Evaluation:** Discuss the feedback and use it as a basis for critically examining the lessons learned. Organize observations into lists or categories and begin to brainstorm answers to problems. Depending upon the size of the team, number of items raised, and the complexity of the items raised, developing solutions to them may be done is separate meetings with smaller groups of people. If there are a large number of items, consider having the group vote on which topics they feel are the most important to prioritize the follow on activities.

- **Conclusion:** Review the most critical discussion items and their actionable solutions. Ensure that everyone responsible for a solution or action item knows when to follow up. Ask for any last-minute questions or comments, and thank everyone for their participation.

- **Follow-Up:** Organize the results of the meetings in a format that provides a means of easily identifying open issues and action items, and provide it to the attendees. The final report should be in a format that other teams can benefit from. This means it must be easy to search for specific problems or solutions, by project phase or type, and indicating both the impacted and action groups. If there are any open action items, make sure that they are completed within the agreed upon time.

Advance Survey for Lessons Learned Meetings

Depending upon the circumstances of the project, it may be beneficial to gather some feedback prior to the lessons learned meeting. The following three questions have proven useful in the past for the author, but feel free to generate your own.

1. Name three things you feel are going well.
2. Name three things you feel are not going well.
3. Name three processes you would change to address your answers to the previous question.

Lessons Learned Meeting Goals

At the end of a lessons learned meeting the participants should feel good about the whole process. There are benefits for the team members, the delivery organization, and stakeholders from well-run lessons learned sessions. These include:

- **Team Members Should Feel They Were Heard:** Everyone should have the opportunity to provide feedback, both positive and negative, without fear of reprisal. Clarify that there are no repercussions for sharing to help foster growth and unity within the team.
- **Questions Should Be Answered:** The team should feel free to voice their questions and concerns, and receive answers when possible.
- **Acknowledge the Success of a Team:** Even if the project as a whole was unsuccessful, it is important to praise the things the team did well.
- **Identify Potential Changes to Processes:** Use the delivery team to identify changes to processes that are not working well. Ask them how things can be done better and use their input for this and future projects. Be sure to identify processes, or process changes, that worked well and should be continued.
- **Establish Easily Measured Follow-Up Actions:** Assign tasks to team members and follow up with them later. Ensure they have the tools they need to complete these actions on time.
- **Generate Feedback for Lessons Learned Repositories:** One of the most important benefits from any lessons learned meeting is the report generated from the input gathered. Make sure that it supports the lessons learned repository data structure, so the lessons developed can be easily located and acted upon by this project team, and other project teams, in the future.

Lessons Learned Meeting Follow Up

Send post-meeting reports out to meeting participants within a few days. Label and store these reports somewhere for future reference, like a shared drive or cloud storage. For best results, the organization should have a formal lessons learned database that is accessible by all members. The database should be easy to use, especially when searching for tips for specific teams, use of tools and methodologies, any by phase of the project.

Tips for Facilitating Large Lessons Learned Meetings

Large groups require additional planning. You may decide to use a survey prior to the meeting to gather feedback to save time, or even split a large meeting into smaller groups.

Meeting Size	Techniques	Meeting Time
≤ 8 participants	Round robin discussion, sticky notes on large notepad, or write on a whiteboard. Brainstorm as a single group	60 minutes
9-15 participants	Consider a pre-session survey, come prepared with visual aids such as project metrics or trend reports, break into smaller discussion groups if needed and share findings with the entire group	90 minutes
≥ 15 participants	Consider breaking into smaller meeting groups. Strongly consider a pre-session survey, or similar device to gather inputs for each meeting. After the small group meetings have been held, conduct a joint meeting with a representative from each group to create consolidated lessons learned report. For example, the developers, business analysts, testers, and infrastructure teams my hold their own sessions before the consolidated session.	60-90 minutes per meeting

Tips for Facilitating Lessons Learned for Unsuccessful Projects

Not every project is successful. When that happens conducting lessons learned can be very difficult, but it is even more important to do so than for successful projects. Members may be reluctant to be honest about how things went, and there may be a tendency to assign blame to other parties or groups. Members may also be afraid of retaliation if they are too candid and honest. These concerns may be reduced by ensuring anonymity, and noting that no one individual or group is responsible for the failure.

- **Anonymous Surveys:** Strongly consider collecting feedback anonymously before the session, via online or written surveys. Ensure it stays anonymous. Organize anonymous input and present it to the group for discussion and brainstorming without any identifying information.
- **Utilize a Third-Party Facilitator:** Using an outside facilitator, potentially an outside consultant hired just for this effort, is a good way to convince members that they can provide honest feedback without fear of retaliation. They should be experienced with conducting lessons learned activities and fully understand the desired output. In some cases, it maybe necessary for the facilitator to gather information with each member individually, then follow-up with a group session where the inputs are presented without any identifying information
- **Do Not Place Blame:** Emphasize that the intent is not to place blame, and that any issues raised are collective issues at the project level. This can help smooth things over without highlighting mistakes by any one team or member.

Tips for Facilitating Remote Lessons Learned Meetings

Remote lessons learned meetings present additional challenges, especially with a multi-cultural team. Remote meetings should strive to maintain focus, encourage participation, and adhere to a schedule. Especially in the post-Covid world, these meetings are likely to be conducted via video conference.

- **Everyone must turn on their video camera**: Be presentable, professional, and meet your fellow participants eye to eye. It is important to see body language in order to know if they agree, don't agree, or if the meeting is getting out of control
- **Review expectations for the session**: Do this at the beginning of the meeting, and summarize them at the end to ensure they were met.
- **Document minutes:** This should include action items and their owners. Share the minutes and any other reports and outputs of the session where everyone knows how to find them and has access.
- **Mute Your Line When Not Talking:** Remind participants to mute their lines when they are not talking.
- **No Multi-tasking!** Everyone needs to totally focused on the meeting, listening to others, and sharing their observations and opinions. Other than the note taker, there should be no one click-clacking on their keyboard. No checking e-mail, smartphones, etc. during the meeting.
- **Share a Screen while Documenting Input:** Just like using a whiteboard in person, write down notes in real-time where everyone can see them. To ensure participants focus on the member talking, input may be documented in a separate screen that participants can view, or in the chat. Work out the best approach available with the technology being used in advance, and let the participants know how it will be done.

- **Use Surveys and Other Online Tools to Encourage Engagement:** Send out a survey prior to the meeting to gather input and prepare charts and visual aids to keep attendees engaged.
- **Keep to Your Agenda:** Most people only stay engaged in a meeting for the first 30-45 minutes. Make sure that the meeting stays informative, but does not go too long. If needed, break into smaller discussion groups periodically, have formal breaks every 45 minutes or so, or break the meeting into several shorter sessions.
- **Remember Time Zones:** When dealing with remote teams, there are likely to be a number of different time zones involved. Be careful about scheduling meetings outside of members' regular work hours. Members' energy levels are likely to vary at different times of the day, impacting their participation. For example, it may be morning for some team members and late afternoon or evening for others. Try to establish a meeting time that places all participants on an even footing.

APPENDIX D

INDEX

ABOUT THE AUTHOR

Martin J. Fenelon III, Sc.D. is a certified Project Management Professional (PMP) who has successfully managed projects for more than 40 years across a variety of industries, often with global companies, leading both local and global delivery teams. His experience managing projects in diverse industries such as defense systems, retail, manufacturing, government, insurance, and financial services provides the practical knowledge and experience incorporated in this book. Research and academic experience from his MBA in Operations Management and Doctor of Science (Sc.D.) in Management Systems, and teaching experience as an Adjunct Professor of Management provide the structure, systems, and training aspects of his practical approach to project management.

Urgent Plea

Thank you for reading my book!

I really appreciate all your feedback, and I love hearing what you say.

I need your input to make the next version of
this book and my future books better.

Please take two minutes now to leave a helpful review on
Amazon letting me know what you thought of the book.

Thank you very much!

Marty Fenelon